AF614847

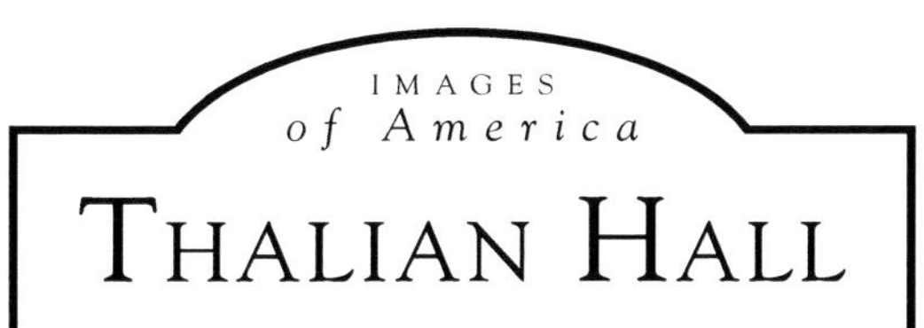
IMAGES
of America
THALIAN HALL

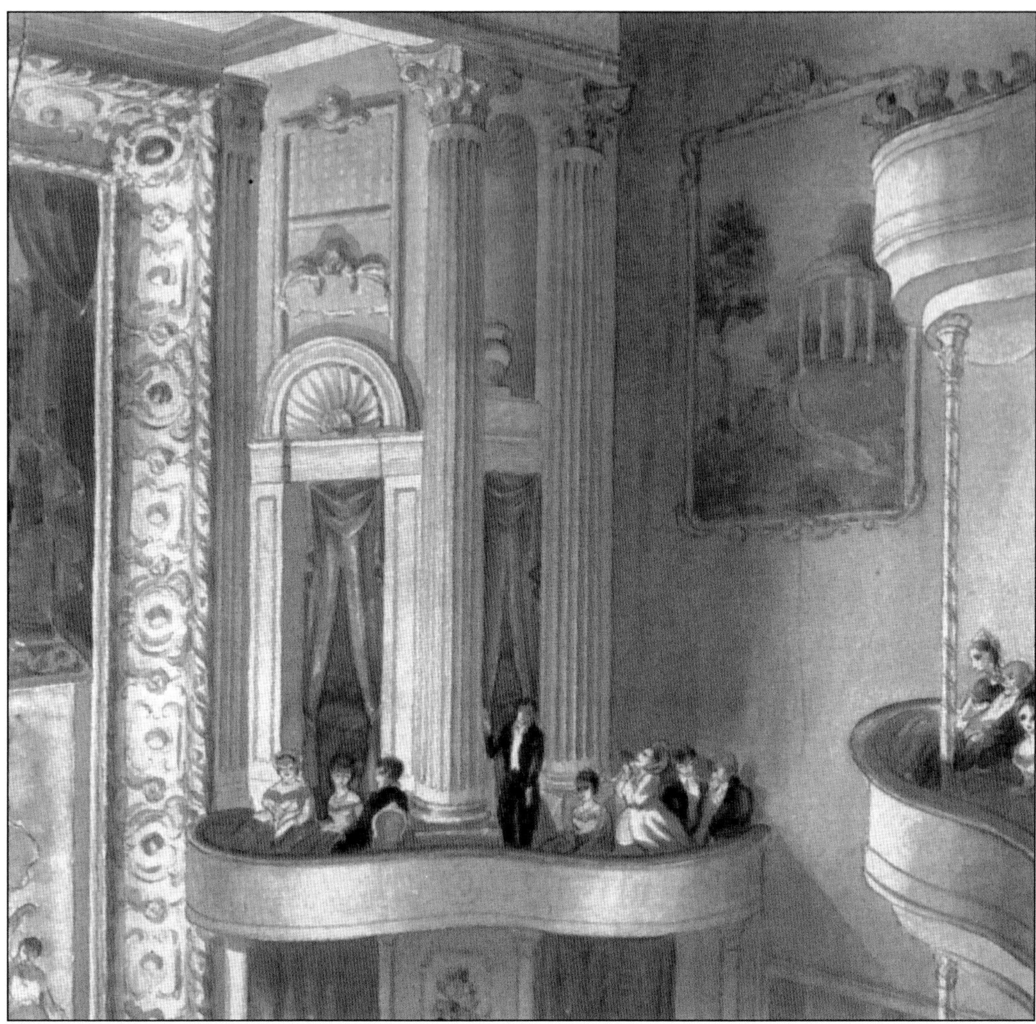

This 1938 watercolor was painted by Henry MacMillan to create interest in the preservation of Thalian Hall. In 1937, he spent the summer at the Colorado Springs Fine Arts Center. While in Colorado, he attended a dramatic festival at the restored Opera House in Central City. Inspired by this experience, MacMillan became a principal spokesperson for the preservation of Thalian Hall in the 1930s. (Historical Society of the Lower Cape Fear.)

On the Cover: This photograph was taken in 1934 by Louis T. Moore, head of the chamber of commerce, which was located across the street from Wilmington City Hall. Several city employees stand beside their vehicles in front of Thalian Hall. The sign above the entrance announces the film *Judge Priest*, starring Will Rogers. Howard Amusement Co. held the lease on Thalian Hall and would screen films there when its other movie theatres were closed for repairs. The company also leased the theatre for live events. (Louis T. Moore Collection, New Hanover County Library.)

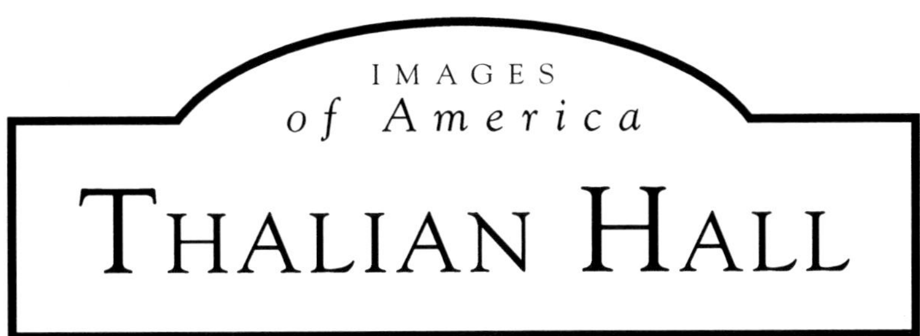

D. Anthony Rivenbark

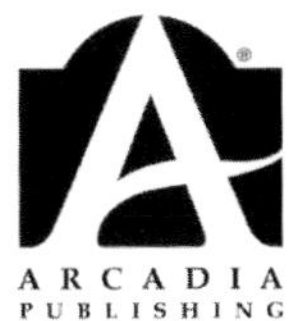

ISBN 978-1-4671-2122-4

Published by Arcadia Publishing
Charleston, South Carolina

Printed in the United States of America

Library of Congress Control Number: 2013946736

For all general information, please contact Arcadia Publishing:
Telephone 843-853-2070
Fax 843-853-0044
E-mail sales@arcadiapublishing.com
For customer service and orders:
Toll-Free 1-888-313-2665

Visit us on the Internet at www.arcadiapublishing.com

Dedicated to Doug W. Swink: actor, director, teacher, designer, playwright, historian, and the theatrical father of hundreds of thespians.

Contents

Acknowledgments

The completion of this book would have not been possible without the extraordinary help of Angela Rowe and the wonderful support of Ronna Zimmer and Mike Jones. Thanks to Shane Fernando for his preservation of Doug Swink's Wilmington College theatre photographs. A thank-you also goes to Isabel M. Williams for writing a history of Thalian Hall and for the monumental research that went into its compilation.

This book benefited from the assistance of Beverly Tetterton, Thom Clemmons, Frank P. Hall, Lee Crouch, Susan Block, John Debnam, Dorothy Pastis, Sam Garner, Steve E. Cooper, Paul Wilson, Virginia Callaway, Beth Hawthorne, Beth Fineberg, Curt Hursey, Gary Tucker, Musette Morgan, Annie Gray Johnston, Nancy Horton, Joseph Sheppard, Walter Pancoe, the Wilmington Ministering Circle, Frank McNeil, Jennifer Daugherty, Calie Voorhis, and Ruth Jordan. Thanks also go to the staff of the Thalian Hall Center for the Performing Arts, Inc.

The images in this volume appear courtesy of Thalian Hall Center for the Performing Arts Archive Collection (THCPA), New Hanover County Public Library (NHCPL), Cape Fear Museum of History and Science (CFM), and the Historical Society of the Lower Cape Fear (HSLCF), as well as from families and organizations otherwise noted.

Introduction

Since its construction in 1855–1858, the City Hall/Thalian Hall building has had the unusual distinction of serving as both the area's political and cultural center. Listed in the National Register of Historic Places, Thalian Hall is the only surviving theatre designed by John Montague Trimble, one of America's foremost 19th-century theatre architects. It was built at a time when Wilmington, then the largest city in the state, was experiencing unparalleled growth and prosperity.

The new edifice was built by the Town of Wilmington in cooperation with the Wilmington Thalian Association, a gentlemen's acting society. The new building housed the town government and the library, as well as the "opera house." The seating capacity of 1,000 people represented 10 percent of the 1858 population of the city. Wilmington had been a center of theatrical activity since the end of the 18th century, hosting professional touring companies as well as amateur theatre. With the building of its new opera house, Wilmington became a major stop on the Southern theatrical circuit.

The official opening took place on October 12, 1858, with a production by the G.F. Marchant Stock Company from Charleston, South Carolina. The group remained in residence for the first two seasons, presenting a wide variety of popular melodramas and plays by Shakespeare. The opening play was *The Honey Moon*, a romantic drama in blank verse. One of the highlights of the evening was the unrolling of a painted stage curtain by Russell Smith of Philadelphia. It is currently on display in the old lobby. Though performances by the resident company and the few amateur groups were well attended, the net income received was not sufficient to cover the debts and the rent. In June 1860, the Thalian Association surrendered all interest in the theatre to the town. From 1860 until 1936, private entrepreneurs leased the theatre, booking road shows and star attractions, and the organization ceased to function as a corporate entity.

Originally, the auditorium had a flat floor with movable seating, which accommodated large-scale events. The stage was only a few feet above the main floor, and a forestage jutted into the seating area. The first balcony joined the stage in a U-shaped arrangement. The tall, arched windows were glazed with large panes of glass, allowing a great deal of light on the white and gold interior. In the evenings, light was provided by 188 gas burners.

During the Civil War, Thalian Hall was in almost constant use as a place of amusement, as hundreds of performances were held during the war years. Following the Civil War, the most famous lessee of the theatre was John T. Ford, formerly of Ford's Theatre in Washington, DC. He leased Thalian Hall from 1867 to 1871, and under his management the theatre was advertised as the Wilmington Opera House.

Some of the artists who appeared in the hall in the 19th and early 20th centuries included Lillian Russell, Buffalo Bill Cody, John Phillip Sousa, Joseph Jefferson, and Maurice Barrymore. Oscar Wilde, William Jennings Bryan, and Booker T. Washington gave important lectures. Between engagements, the theatre was rented for local events, including community concerts, amateur dramatics, recitals, meetings, graduations, and exhibitions.

The great heyday of touring theatre occurred during the first two decades of the 20th century. At this time, the theatre came under the control of Simeon A. Schloss. His theatre circuit operated a number of venues in North and South Carolina, and his offices were located in Wilmington. Under his management, the hall's name was changed to the Academy of Music. Using the services of Wilmington architect Henry Bonitz, Schloss made major renovations to the auditorium and installed the ornate proscenium arch. The theatre was redecorated in a red, green, and gold color scheme, with decorative stenciling on the balconies, boxes, and above the proscenium. The current restoration is based on the theatre's appearance during this period.

The hall continued to host touring events and repertory companies until the middle of the 1930s, when the great days of touring theatre came to an end. Though the theatre was used less frequently by touring shows, it remained in use for locally sponsored events, including classical concerts and sporting events. A new civic theatre group called the Thalian Association was established in 1929, taking the name of its 19th-century counterpart. The association began an annual series of theatrical productions, and it has been joined by other companies, like Opera House Theatre Company, that regularly present theatre on the historic stage.

In 1932, the venue's name was changed to Thalian Hall. George Bailey, of Howard & Wells Amusements, relinquished his lease in 1936 so that the theatre could be used as a civic auditorium. The building's survival came into question in 1939 with the collapse of the north wall of Wilmington City Hall. In 1946, the theatre was closed because of structural issues with the balconies. In each case, the community and the city took the necessary steps to insure its preservation.

In 1963, the Thalian Hall Commission, Inc., now known as the Thalian Hall Center for the Performing Arts, Inc., was chartered to restore the theatre. Following a small but damaging fire in the auditorium in 1973, the theatre was restored to its turn-of-the-century appearance. After reopening in 1975, Thalian Hall witnessed a dramatic increase in use by professional artists and community groups. In 1983, the commission developed a master plan for the expansion of the theatre and renovation of the stage house.

Citizens of Wilmington overwhelmingly approved the plan, and in 1985 a $1.7 million bond issue passed. In addition, the North Carolina State Legislature, the City of Wilmington, and the private sector generated $3 million for the project. Under the direction of the city and Thalian Hall Center for the Performing Arts, construction began in 1988. The expanded Thalian Hall/City Hall complex reopened on March 2, 1990. Another extensive restoration of the theatre's historic interior was completed in May 2010, including new floors in the auditorium, new theatre seats, the reapplication of decorative painting, installation of a grand period chandelier, and upgrading of all technical systems.

Today, Thalian Hall serves more than 30 area arts groups, civic organizations, and educational institutions. These groups provide a wide array of performances in music, theatre, and dance by local and regional artists. The Thalian Hall Center for the Performing Arts regularly presents the Main Attractions concert series featuring international artists, as well as the Cinematique series, which screens first-release films from around the world. The complex is owned by the City of Wilmington. City hall continues to serve as the principal office of the municipal government. Thalian Hall operates year-round, with over 400 events and 85,000 people entering its doors. To learn more about Thalian Hall and its many programs, visit www.ThalianHall.org.

One

Setting the Stage 1759–1850

Wilmington will always have a unique place in American theatre history. In 1759, Thomas Godfrey sent his play *The Prince of Parthia* from Wilmington to David Douglass, the most prolific theatre manager in America. It was produced at Philadelphia's Southwark Theatre four years later, making it the first play written by an American and produced on the American stage.

Also in 1759, Col. James Innes created a will at his Castle Hayne plantation, north of Wilmington, prior to leaving for the French and Indian War. It stipulated that his estate was to be used for the "establishment of a school for the benefit of the youth of North Carolina." This bequest was not implemented until the end of the American Revolution in 1783, which was the same year the ban on theatre performances was lifted.

In 1787, The American Company, managed by Lewis Hallam Jr., played Edenton and Wilmington. According to a letter written to James Iredell, these performers inspired the young men of Edenton to organize amateur performances. The following year, the Kenna Family played Wilmington. These actors had the same effect on the gentlemen of Wilmington. Stephen Weeks, in his 1896 history of literature in North Carolina, stated, "It was due, no doubt to the influence of these players, that the Thalian Association of Wilmington was organized about this time."

Unfortunately, there are very few records of performances. But it is known that, by 1800, a number of groups had been established, including the Fayetteville Thalian Association and the New Bern Thespian Society; however, none of these groups would achieve the vitality and influence of the Wilmington Thalians. In 1803, the Trustees of the Innes Academy purchased the three lots where Thalian Hall now stands for the construction of a "house suitable for an Academy and Theatre." Similar theatres were designed for New Bern and Fayetteville, indicating a strong connection between the theatre and the community.

The Innes Academy stood for 50 years, and its theatre was the primary venue for many professional acting troupes. It also served the gentlemen of the Thalian Association, whose amateur productions were sometimes augmented by professional actors and actresses.

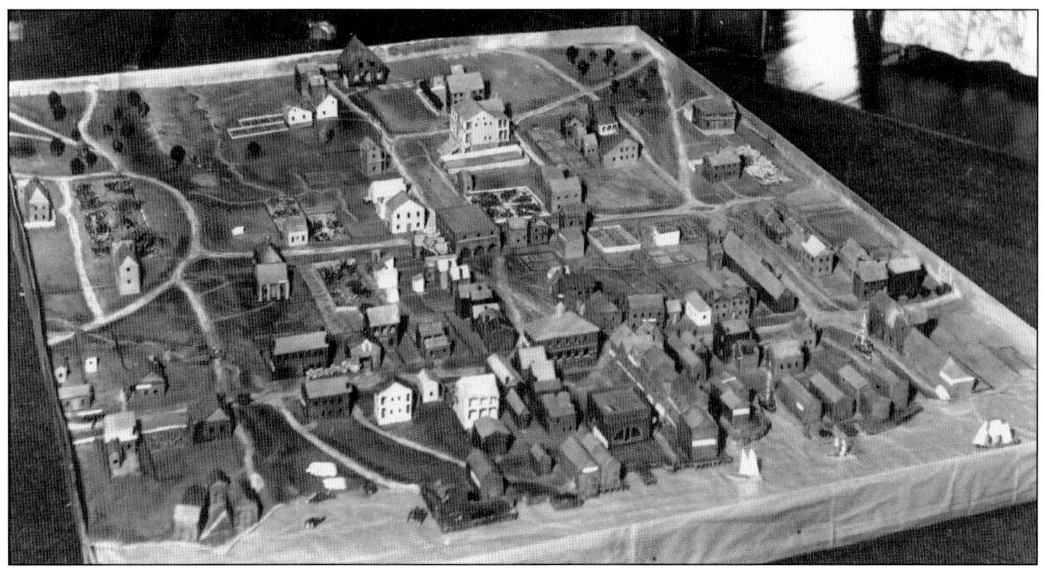

There are no extant images of the town of Wilmington as it appeared in the 18th century. In the 1940s, historian Elizabeth McKoy created this model based on historical records. The diorama presents a bird's-eye view of what Wilmington may have looked like when it was the second-largest city in the colony of North Carolina. (CFM.)

By Authority.

NEVER PERFORMED BEFORE.

By the AMERICAN COMPANY,

At the NEW THEATRE, in *Southwark*,

On *FRIDAY*, the *Twenty-Fourth* of *April*, will be preſented, A TRAGEDY written by the late ingenious Mr. *Thomas Godfrey*, of this city, called the

PRINCE *of* PARTHIA.

The PRINCIPAL CHARACTERS by Mr. HALLAM, Mr. DOUGLASS, Mr. WALL, Mr. MORRIS, Mr. ALLYN, Mr. TOMLINSON, Mr. BROAD-BELT, Mr. GREVILLE, Mrs. DOUGLASS, Mrs. MORRIS, Miſs WAINWRIGHT, and Miſs CHEER.

To which will be added, A *Ballad Opera* called

The CONTRIVANCES.

To begin exactly at *Seven* o'Clock.--*Vivant Rex & Regina.*

This 1767 handbill advertises Thomas Godfrey's play, presented by the American Company in Philadelphia. In 1759, this young Wilmington merchant and poet completed his play and sent it to David Douglass at the Southwark Theatre. Godfrey died at the age of 27 in 1763, and he is buried in St. James Church Churchyard, one block from Thalian Hall. (THCPA.)

In 1962, Doug Swink of the Wilmington College drama department staged one of the only recorded productions of Thomas Godfrey's *The Prince of Parthia*. In this production photograph, Ray Oxendine, as a Parthian prince, confronts Pat Beasley, in the role of Evanthe. In the first production, in 1767, the lead role was played by Lewis Hallam Jr. He formed the New American Company of Comedians after the American Revolution. (THCPA.)

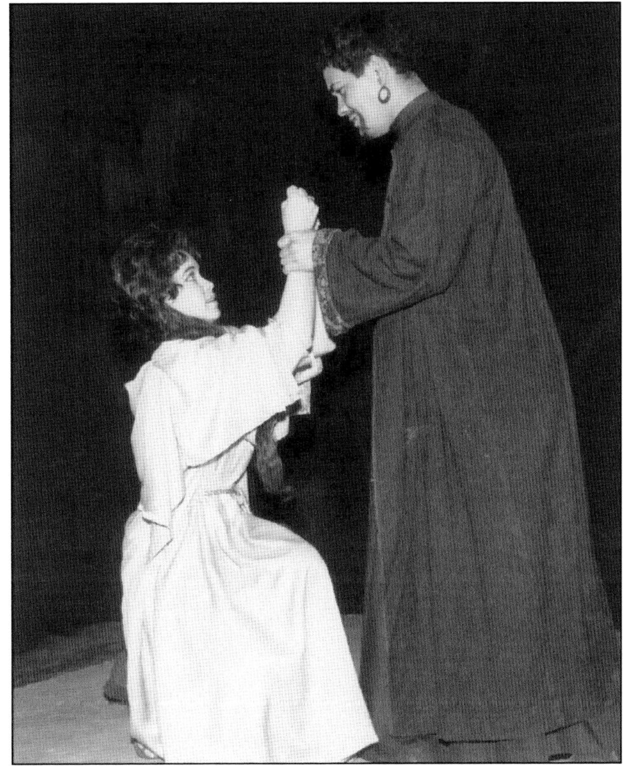

THE ſubſcribers being appointed to contract for building a Houſe in the town of Wilmington ſuitable for an Academy & Theatre—give notice that they or any one of them, will receive propoſals for building by contract a Brick-Houſe, ſeventy feet long, forty feet wide, and thirty feet high, including the foundation. The perſons contracting to find all the labour neceſſary to complete the brick work, and to cover the roof with ſlate or tile.

They will alſo contract for the purchaſe of two hundred & twenty thouſand bricks, and about four thouſand buſhels of lime, to be delivered at Wilmington in the courſe of the enſuing ſummer.

JOSHUA G. WRIGHT,
NATHANIEL HILL,
J. W. WALKER,
S. R. JOCELYN,
A. J. DE ROSSETT.
Wilmington, April 21.

In 1803, the Trustees of the Wilmington Academy solicited proposals for a building suitable for an academy and theatre. The planned structure was to be 70 feet long, 40 feet wide, and 30 feet high. (NHCPL.)

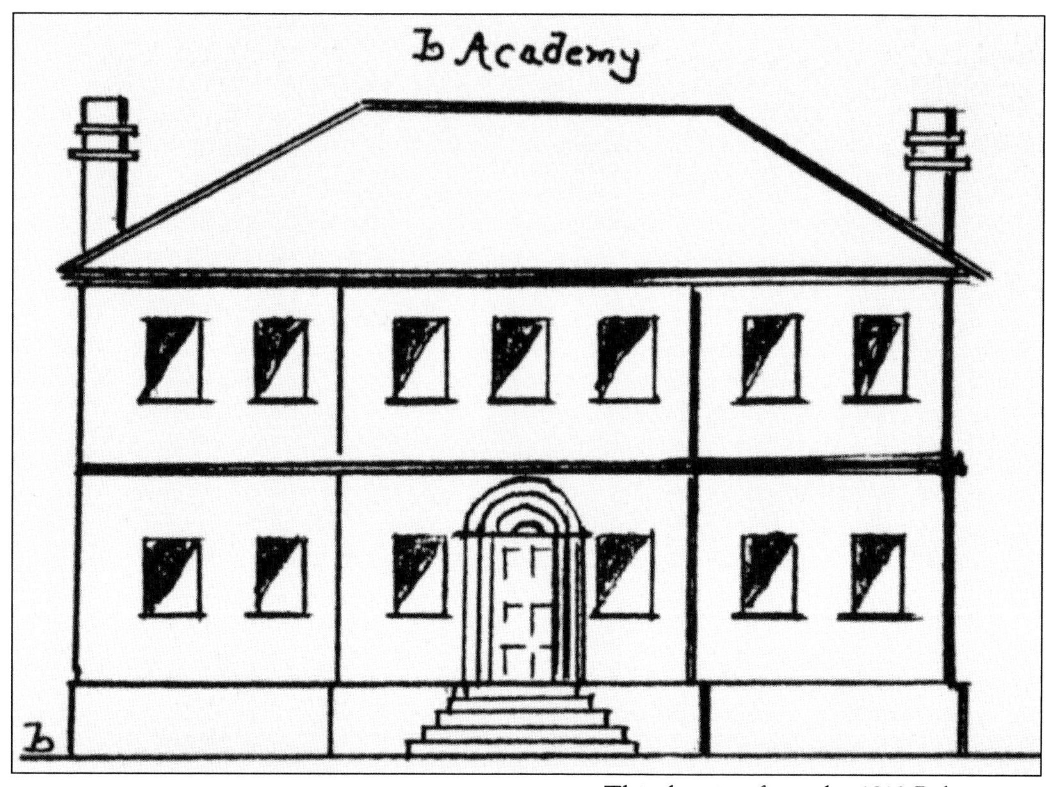

This drawing from the 1810 Belanger map shows the Innes Academy, which stood on the site of present-day Thalian Hall. The school was on the top floor, and the theatre was below. The stage took up approximately one third of the first floor and was equipped with stage machinery, a front curtain, and an orchestra pit. The venue seated about 200. The population of Wilmington at this time was around 2,500 people. (New Hanover County Register of Deeds.)

THEATRE.

On Thursday evening the 11th inst.

Will be performed,

By the THALIAN ASSOCIATION,

Mrs. Inchbald's Translation of Kotzebue's justly celebrated Comedy in 5 Acts, called

LOVERS' VOWS.

To which will be added Garrick's much admired Farce in 2 Acts, of

NECK OR NOTHING.

Tickets may be had of the Treasurer, of Lloyd and Anderson and of H. Pelham, at One Dollar each, Children 50 Cents.

Doors open at 6 and curtain rise precisely at 7 o'clock.

The public are informed that this Association have been to a very considerable expence in fitting up the house engaged for Exhibition, and in obtaining scenery, &c. It is therefore hoped that they will give that encouragement which the Association justly merits, when it is understood that our object is to assist the completion of the Academy, &c.

Wilmington, Dec. 9.

This 1806 advertisement in the *Wilmington Gazette* notes the first documented performance by the Thalian Association and the first performance on the Thalian Hall site. The play, *Lovers' Vows,* about moral ambiguity, had a cast of six men and four women. Most likely, all the parts were played by men, as it was considered improper for a "lady" to appear on the stage. (NHCPL.)

On April 30, 1847, the *Wilmington Journal* reported, "A number of our young men have formed a thalian company in this place. They made their 1st appearance on Tuesday night last, when they performed Bulwer's celebrated, The Lady of Lyons." According to James Burr, the group's historian, the membership was made up of 70 gentlemen, and it was the largest of the antebellum Thalian Associations. The members of this group were instrumental in the building of Thalian Hall. (THCPA.)

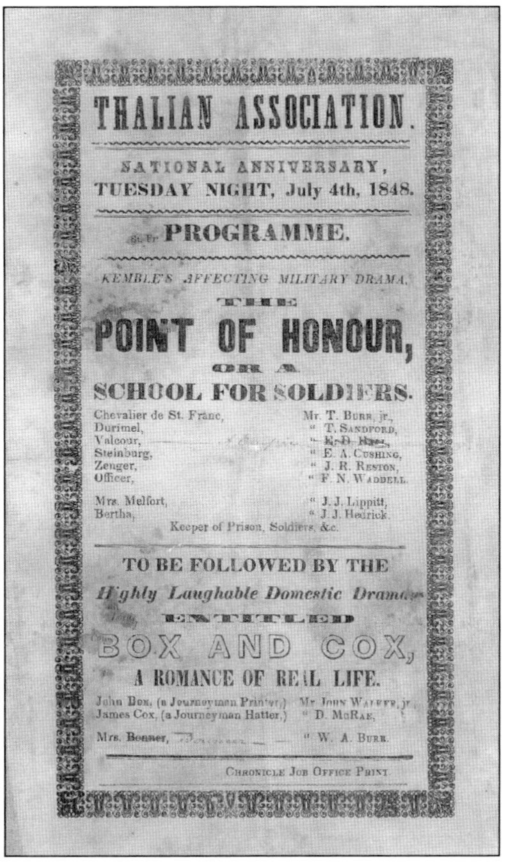

THALIAN ASSOCIATION.

NATIONAL ANNIVERSARY,
TUESDAY NIGHT, July 4th, 1848.

PROGRAMME.

KEMBLE'S AFFECTING MILITARY DRAMA,

THE

POINT OF HONOUR,

OR A

SCHOOL FOR SOLDIERS.

Chevalier de St. Franc,	Mr. T. Burr, jr.,
Durimel,	" T. Sandford,
Valcour,	" ~~E. D. Hall~~,
Steinburg,	" E. A. Cushing,
Zenger,	" J. R. Reston,
Officer,	" F. N. Waddell.
Mrs. Melfort,	" J. J. Lippitt,
Bertha,	" J. J. Hedrick.

Keeper of Prison, Soldiers, &c.

TO BE FOLLOWED BY THE

Highly Laughable Domestic Drama,

ENTITLED

BOX AND COX,

A ROMANCE OF REAL LIFE.

John Box, (a Journeyman Printer,)	Mr. John Walker, jr.
James Cox, (a Journeyman Hatter,)	" D. McRae,
Mrs. Bonner,	" W. A. Burr.

Chronicle Job Office Print

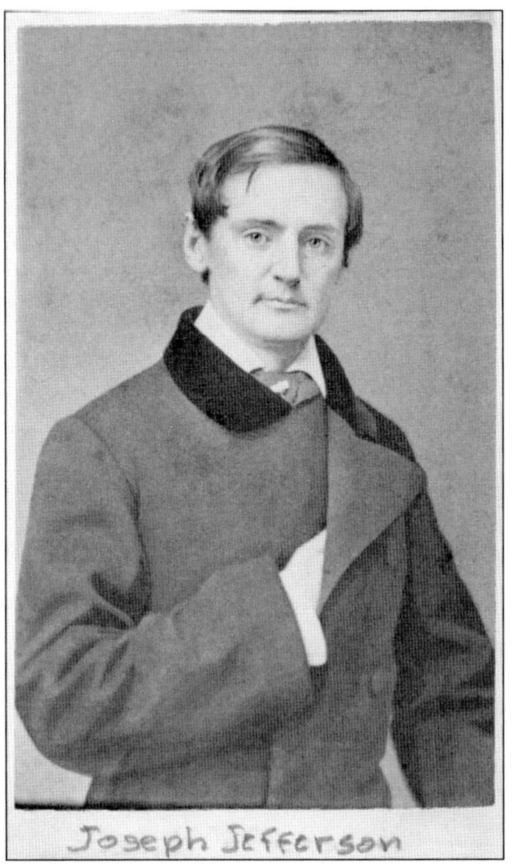

The young Joseph Jefferson arrived with his company in 1850 and played to Wilmington audiences for an extended period. They presented a nightly bill of popular comedies and plays by Shakespeare. By this time, the academy was in disrepair; Jefferson later referred to it as "the dusty rat trap of a theatre." Jefferson never forgot his Wilmington experience and always expressed affection for those early days in his curtain speeches for return engagements. (American Antiquarian Society.)

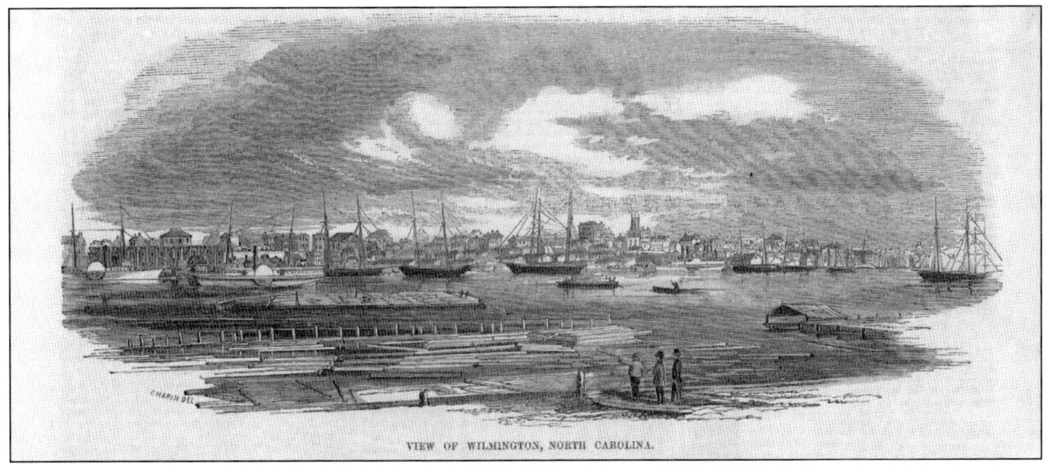

By the 1850s, Wilmington had become a major railroad center and the largest town in the state. This 1853 view of Wilmington shows the Innes Academy to the right of the ship at center. During this period, the academy theatre hosted many touring companies. (CFM.)

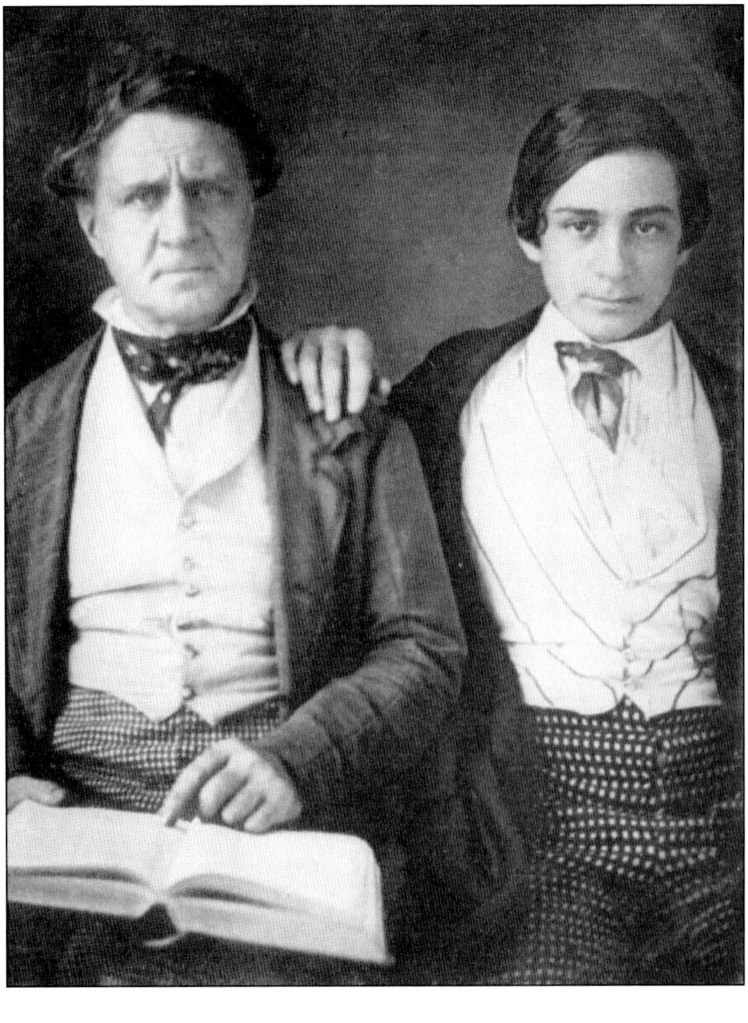

In 1850, the famous Junious Brutus Booth (left) and his company gave a number of plays in the academy. Acting with Booth for the first time was his 16-year-old son Edwin (right), who would become America's most acclaimed tragic actor. Also in the company were Mr. and Mrs. Henry Preston. Henry had served as the stage manager, and his wife was the lead actress for the Thalians in the 1830s. This group has been referred to by historians as the Third Thalian Association. (American Antiquarian Society.)

Two

A New Town Hall and Theatre 1850–1870

In 1853, the Wilmington town commissioners appointed a committee to seek a suitable site for the building of a town hall. The obvious site appeared to be the academy building, which was no longer a school, and its theatre was antiquated. The newspapers had mentioned the need for a new theatre for several years, and it seems that the determination to build a proper theatre was a major factor in the choice of a noted New York theatre architect, John Trimble, to design the new hall.

The land was acquired by a complicated negotiation involving the University of North Carolina, the Thalian Association, and the Odd Fellows. By 1854, permission had been given by the state legislature for the town to issue bonds in the amount of $50,000. The following year, the academy was demolished, and construction began on the town hall. By the spring of 1856, the town and Thalians reached a final agreement, which called for an annual rent of seven percent of the cost of the theatre and land, and construction began on the theatre.

For the opening on October 12, 1858, Marchant's Stock Company of Charleston, South Carolina, provided the bill. G.F. Marchant, a prominent theatrical figure, booked the theatre for the first two seasons, and most of the performances presented were given by companies he managed. For the first two years, there were over 85 performances each season. The financial arrangement between Marchant and the Thalians is not known, but by the end of the second season the Thalian Association had not been able to recoup sufficient funds to pay the rent. In 1860, the amount had grown to $3,000. The cost of the interior, the outlay in expense for wardrobe and scenery, and the age of the members were all factors in the decision to surrender their interest in the theatre.

For the next 76 years, the theatre was leased to private entrepreneurs, who managed the theatre. During the Civil War, the Wilmington Theatre, as it was known then, was a popular place for entertainment. The town was a hub of commercial activity as a result of wartime blockade-runners.

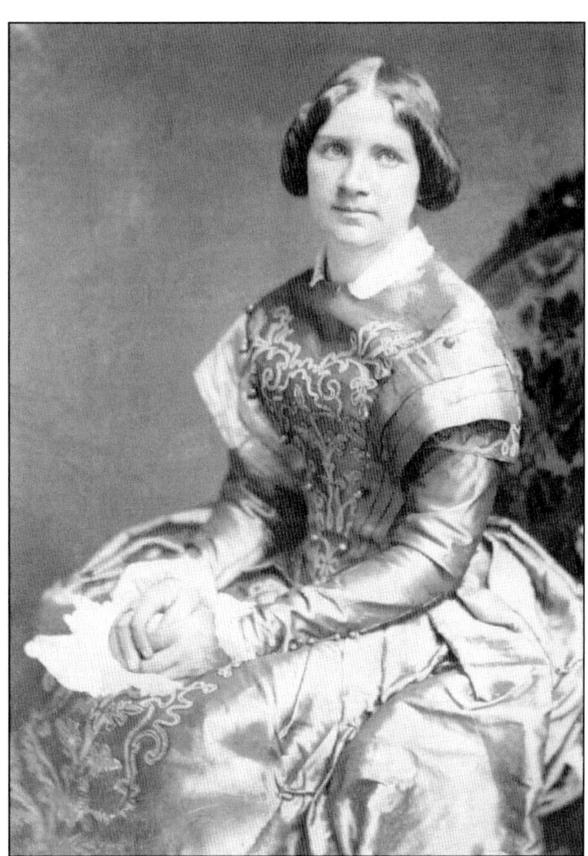

Historian James Sprunt gives an 1850 account of a visit by Jenny Lind, the famous "Swedish Nightingale," who stopped in Wilmington on her way to Charleston, South Carolina. At the train station, she was greeted by a group of fans wishing her to perform. When informed of the seating capacity of the academy, her manager, P.T. Barnum, responded, "Gentlemen, my orchestra would fill a large part of that space." Many of Wilmington's citizens felt that it could support a larger theatre. (Library of Congress.)

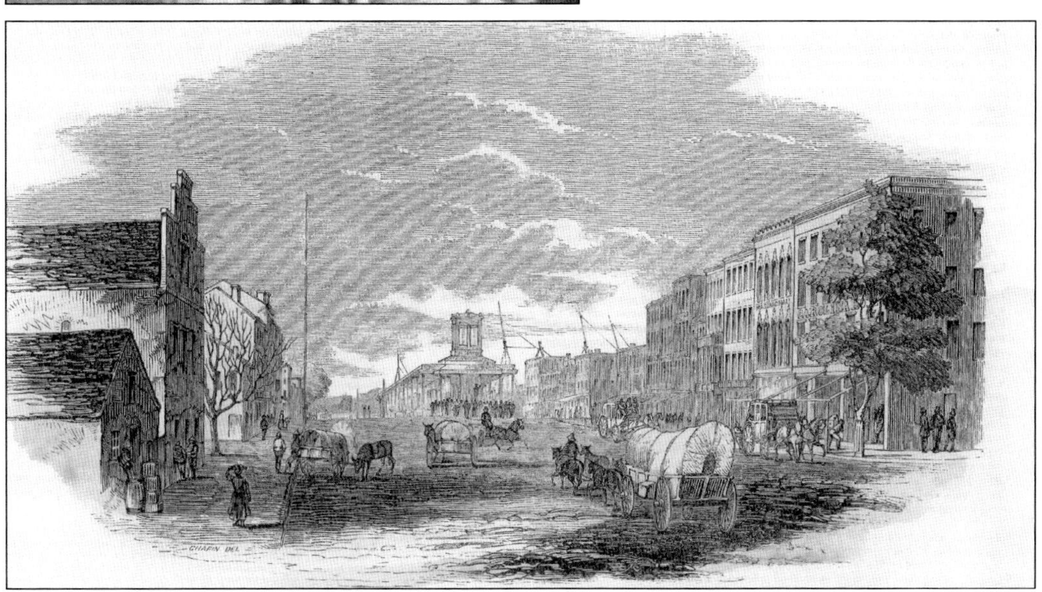

This view looks toward the City Market and the river in 1853. Being the terminus of three railroads, home to a thriving port, and with a rapidly growing population, Wilmington had become a center of commerce in the South. In 1853, the town commissioners were meeting in a rented hall and looking for a permanent home. (THCPA.)

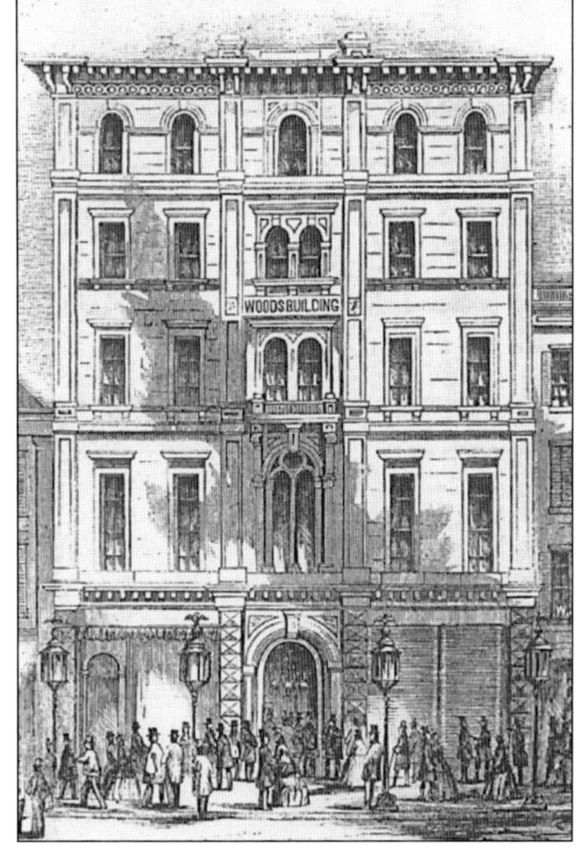

Wood's Marble Hall in New York City was one of the 40 theatres and concert halls designed by John M. Trimble, one of the most noted theatre architects of the 19th century. (Harvard Theatre Collection.)

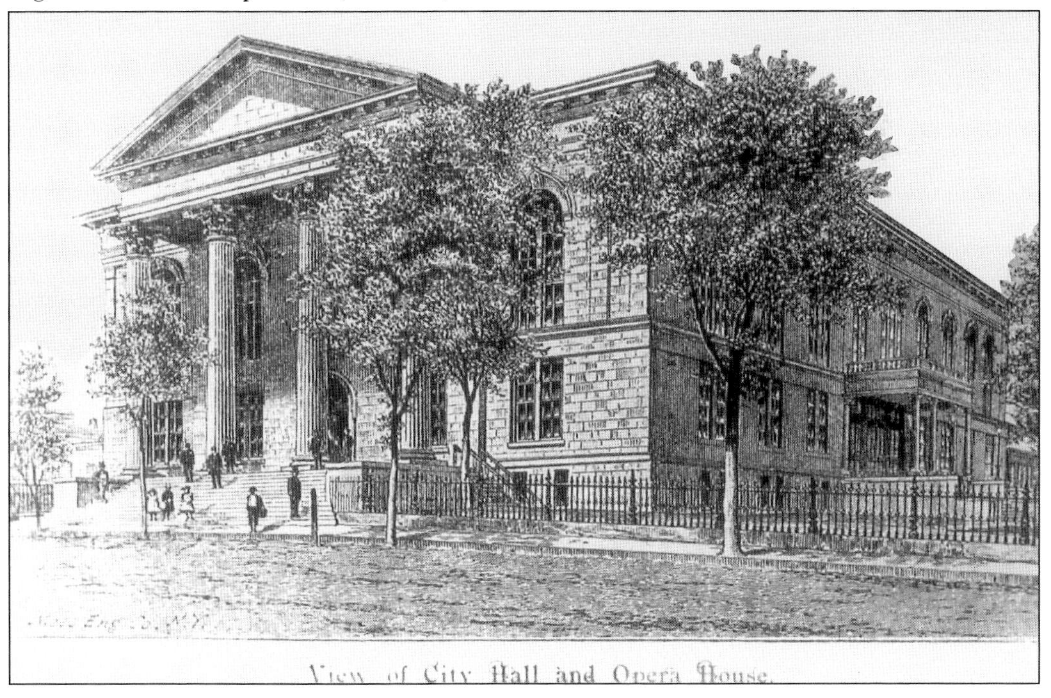

In 1855, a contract was let for the construction of the new building for $35,786. The old academy was pulled down, and enough of the foundation had been laid to permit the cornerstone ceremonies on December 27. The Thalians wanted to extend the theatre by 10 feet, which delayed an agreement until spring 1856, when construction began on the theatre portion. (NHCPL.)

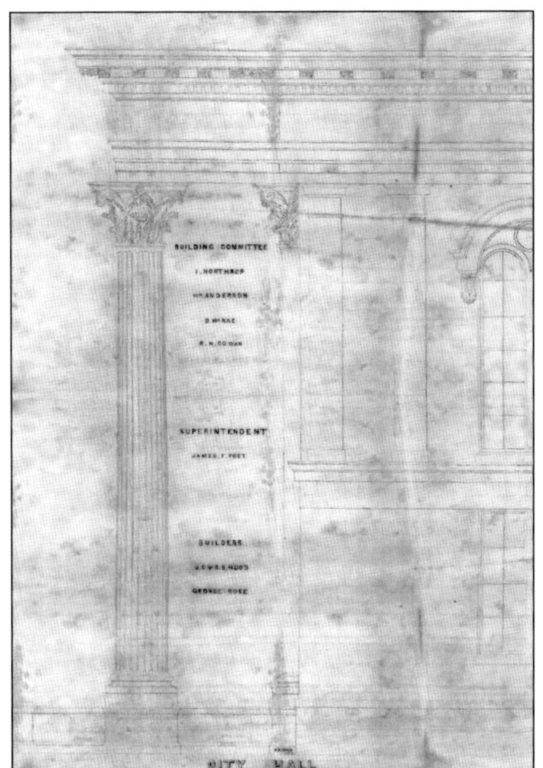

This 1855 drawing on linen was made by Robert Wood. He and his brother John Wood were prominent Wilmington architects. Trimble's original plans called for a one-story porch, similar to the one on the Thalian Hall facade. A major change was made in the design of an impressive two-story portico. The massive pediment, supported by concrete-covered brick columns with ornate, cast-iron capitals, has been the backdrop for community events ever since. (THCPA.)

Robert Wood (pictured) and his brother John were originally brick masons from Nantucket who came to Wilmington to build St. James Episcopal Church. They designed many important buildings in Wilmington. (Dr. Thomas Fanning Wood Family Papers, William Madison Randall Library, University of North Carolina at Wilmington.)

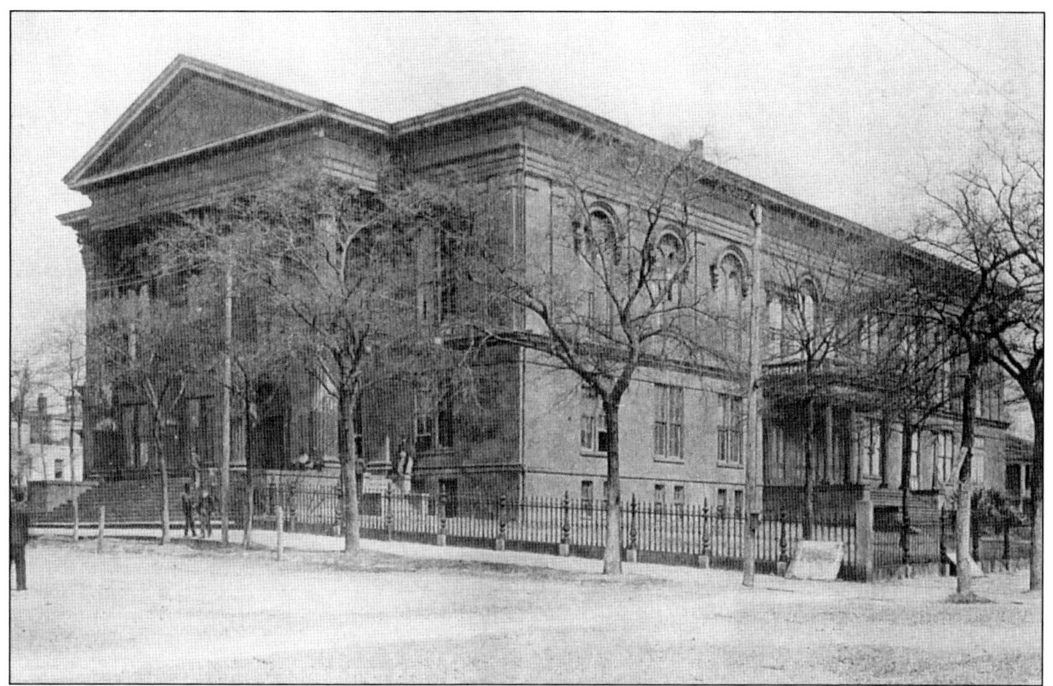

Audiences entered Thalian Hall from Princess Street through a one-story portico beneath a Palladian window. The Italianate design, with its heavy cornices and semicircular arched windows crowned with pediments, became popular simultaneously with the manufacturing developments of sheet glass. This allowed for the installation of large paned windows. (A. Emerson Willard and Martin S. Willard Jr.)

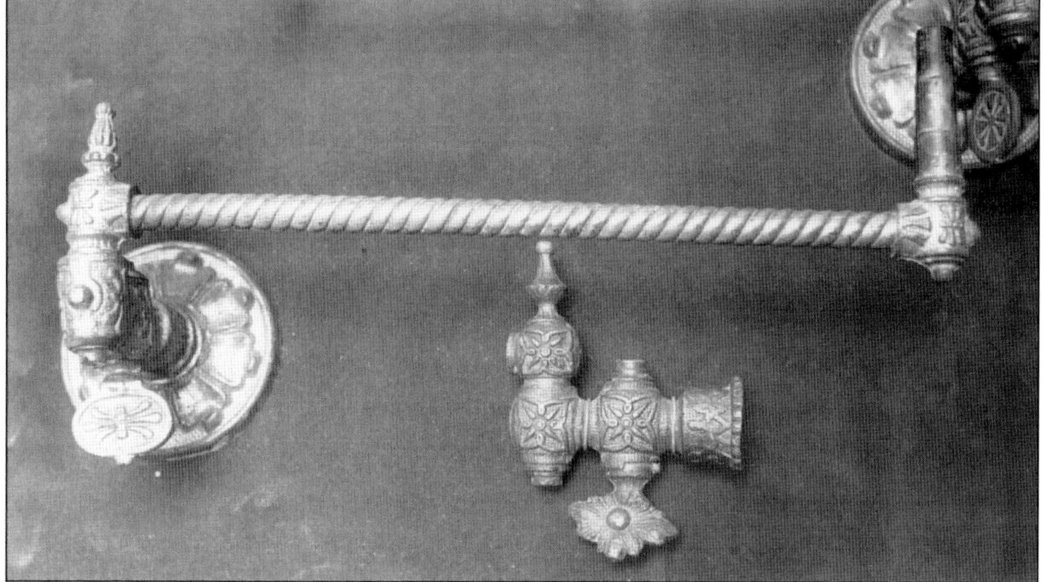

Thalian Hall was the first public building in Wilmington to be illuminated with gas. Originally, there were 188 gas burners throughout the passages, stage, and auditorium. The original fixtures shown here were salvaged by Doug Swink after the 1973 fire. In 1886, an electric light was installed at the entrance; electricity was installed throughout the building in 1898. (THCPA.)

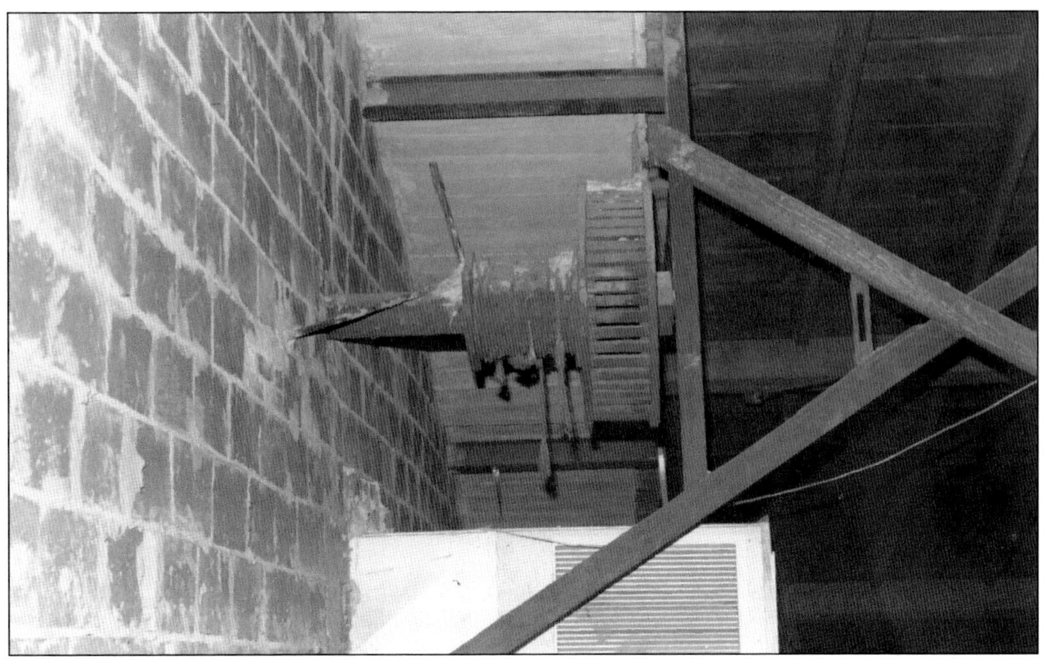

This 1981 photograph shows the hall's original "windless," a piece of stage equipment used for the synchronized changing of scenery through a system of ropes and pulleys. Scene changes were often done *a vista*, meaning "before the eye," and were an important part of the magic of theatre performance for 19th-century audiences. (THCPA.)

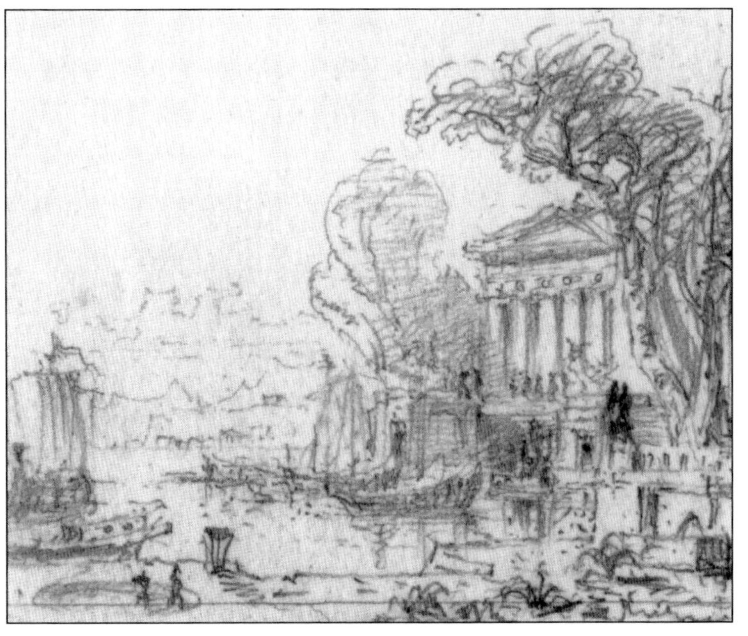

While the theatre equipment was being installed in Wilmington, Russell Smith was working on the creation of a magnificent front curtain at his studio north of Philadelphia. Shown here is the original drawing for the curtain from his sketchbook. Smith, one of the most highly acclaimed painters and scenic artists of the mid-19th century, designed curtains for the Philadelphia Academy of Music. (Old York Road Historical Society.)

Several pieces of original machinery installed in Thalian Hall are still in working order. This wooden cylinder is the rain machine, located in the attic above the original forestage and directly over the present orchestra pit. By the use of ropes, the cylinder is turned, causing loose gravel inside to roll against the sides, creating the sound of rain. Below the rain machine are two wooden troughs that form the "thunder roll." (THCPA.)

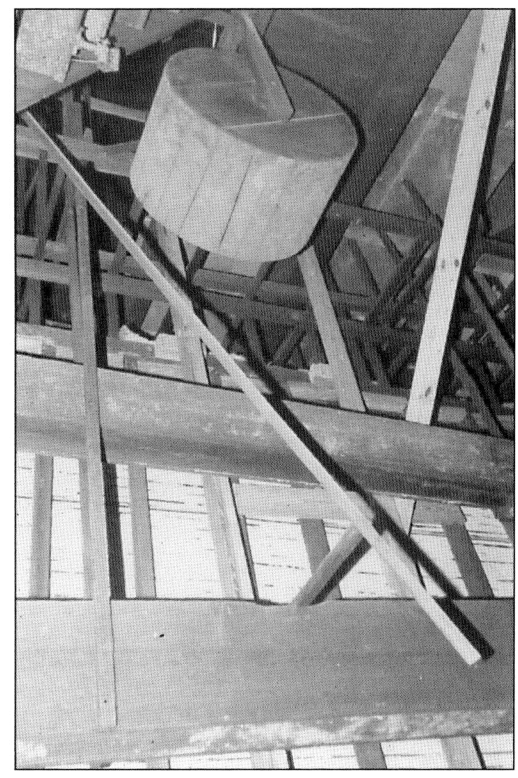

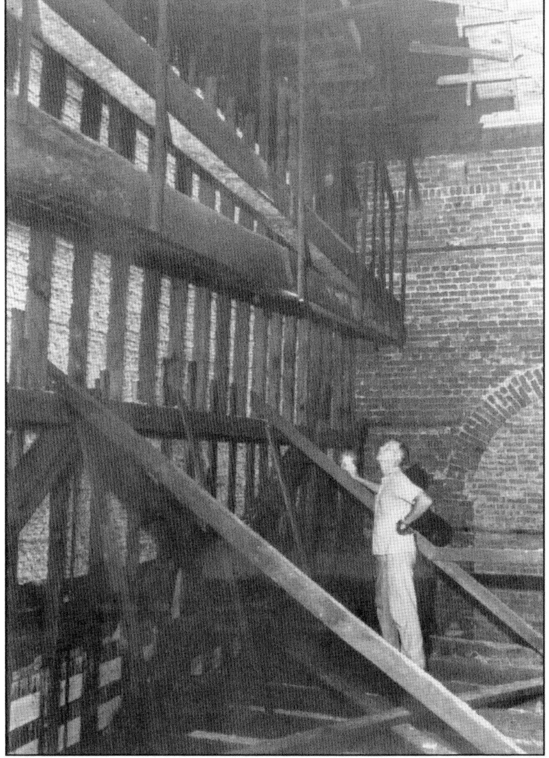

Doug Swink is seen in the Thalian Hall attic around 1965. He is standing on ceiling joists over the proscenium arch looking up at the north end of the thunder roll. The iron cannonballs roll down the top trough, to the south end, and then return by rolling back in the lower trough. This is the only extant thunder roll in the United States. (THCPA.)

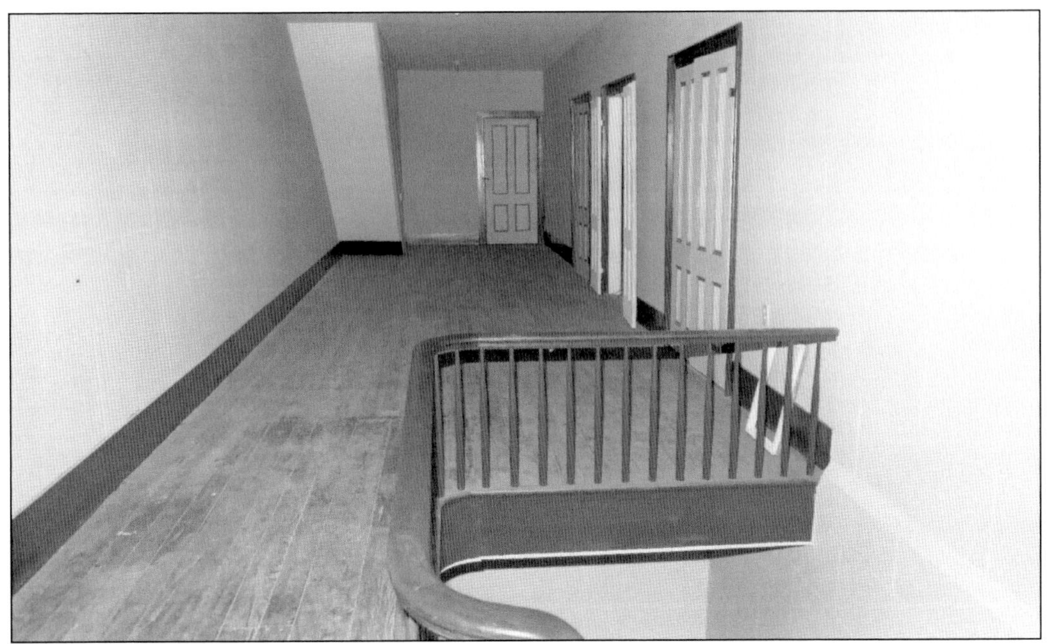

The Gallery Lobby on the fourth floor was unchanged from the original construction until 1990, when the new lighting control room and second exit stairway were added. The doors and hardware are original and still in use. (THCPA.)

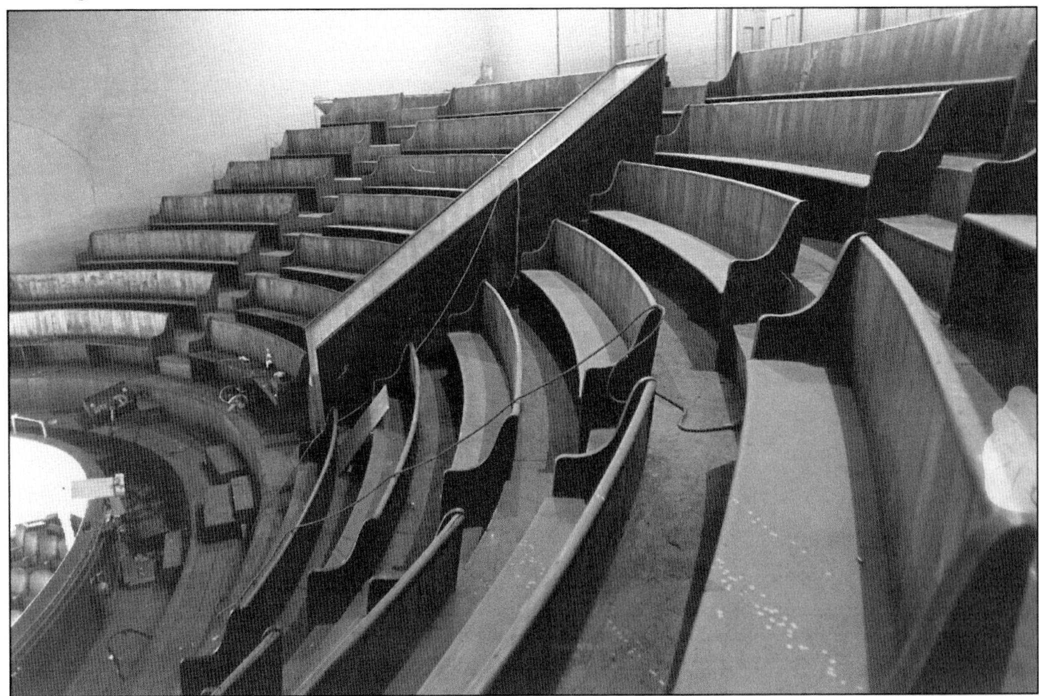

The gallery level occupied the third and fourth floors of the theatre. The wooden benches and platforms seen in this 1981 photograph were essentially unchanged from when the theatre opened in 1858. These benches were copied for the reconstruction of the interior of Ford's Theatre in the 1960s. (THCPA.)

Architect John M. Trimble was noted for his well-ventilated theatres, important in the days before air-conditioning. The five cast-iron grilles in the ceiling are original to the 1858 structure. They served as ventilators and were directly under louvered towers, allowing hot air to escape. (THCPA.)

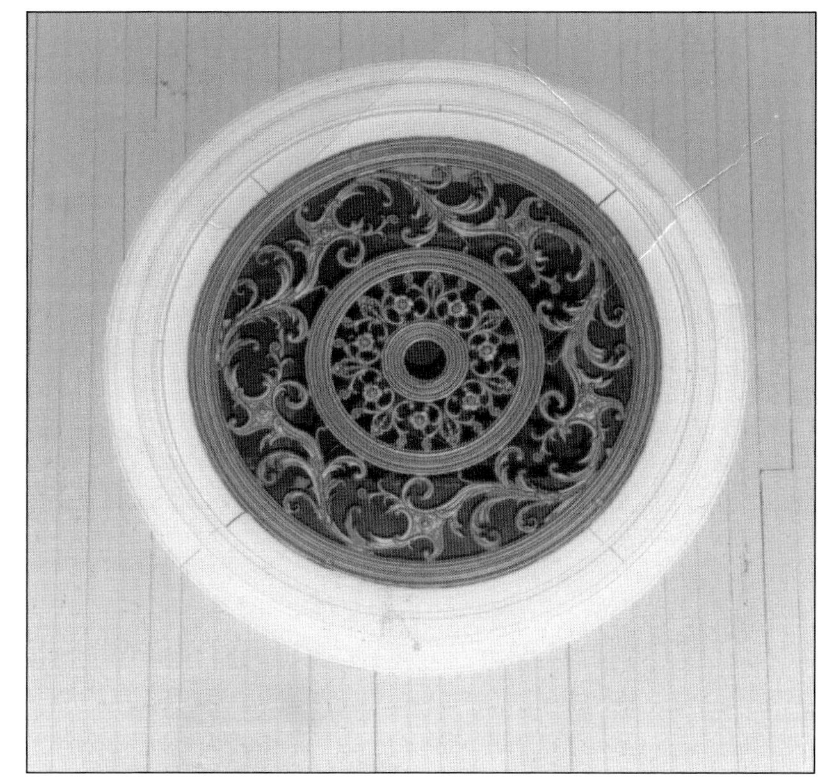

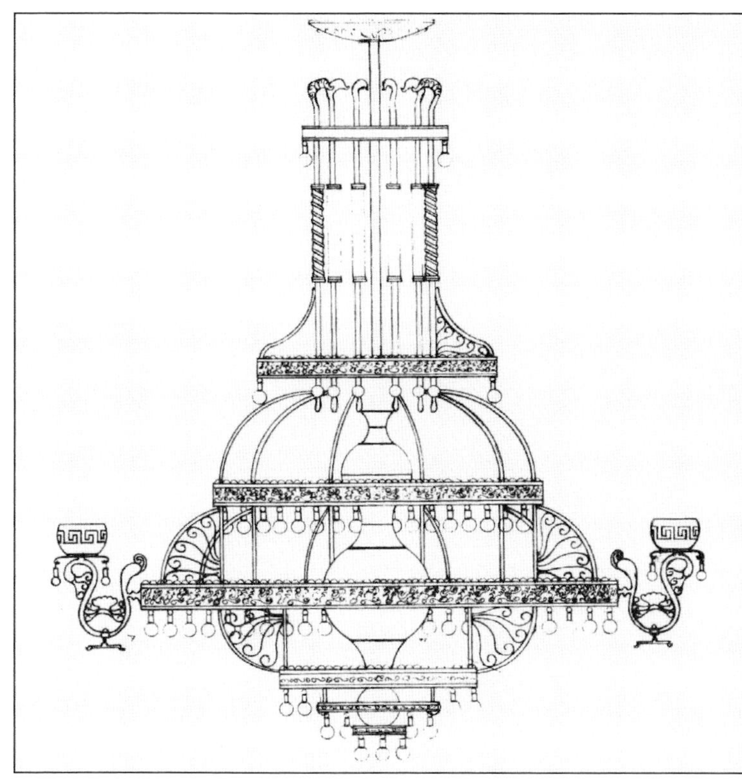

Original plans called for a chandelier to be suspended from the central grille, but it was not until 1871 that a 30-arm gas fixture was installed. It was removed in the 1909 renovation when electrical lighting equipment was installed for the stage. This 1871-style chandelier was designed for the 1990 restoration, but it was not installed until 2010. It is named "Alice." (THCPA.)

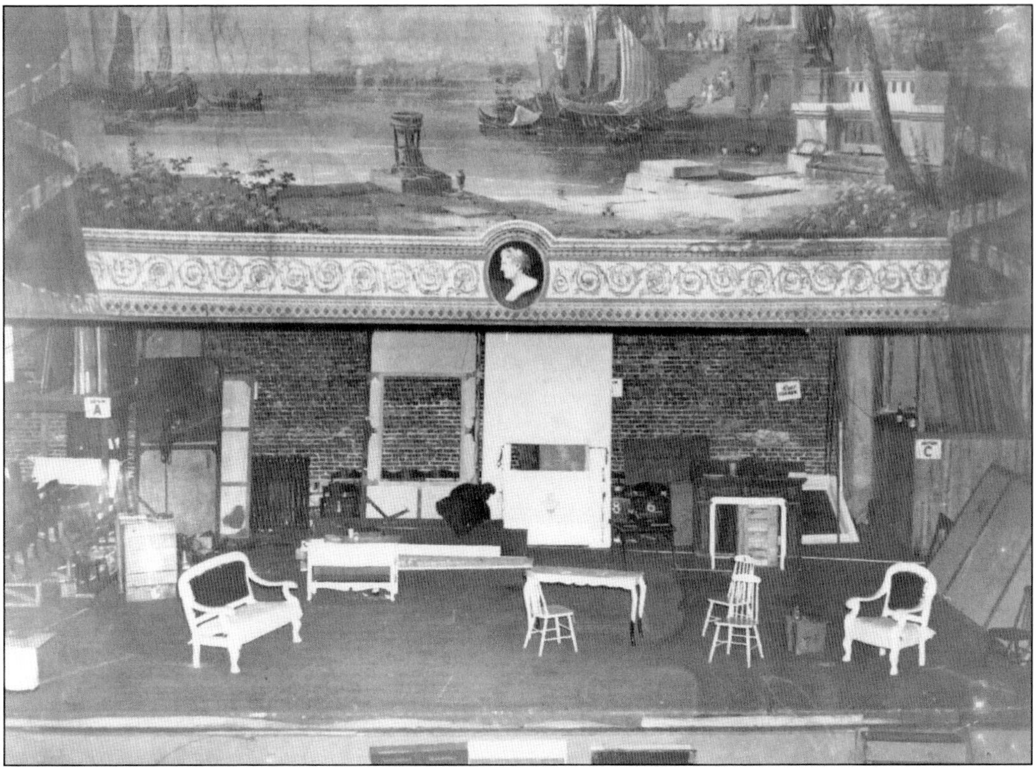

One of the highlights of attending a performance at Thalian Hall after it opened in 1858 was the brilliantly painted front curtain by Russell Smith. The $200 curtain was a gift of Donald McRae, E.D. Hall, O.S. Baldwin, George Myers, and L.A. Hart, all prominent leaders of the community. This photograph of the curtain was taken in 1947 after the top half had been removed. (THCPA.)

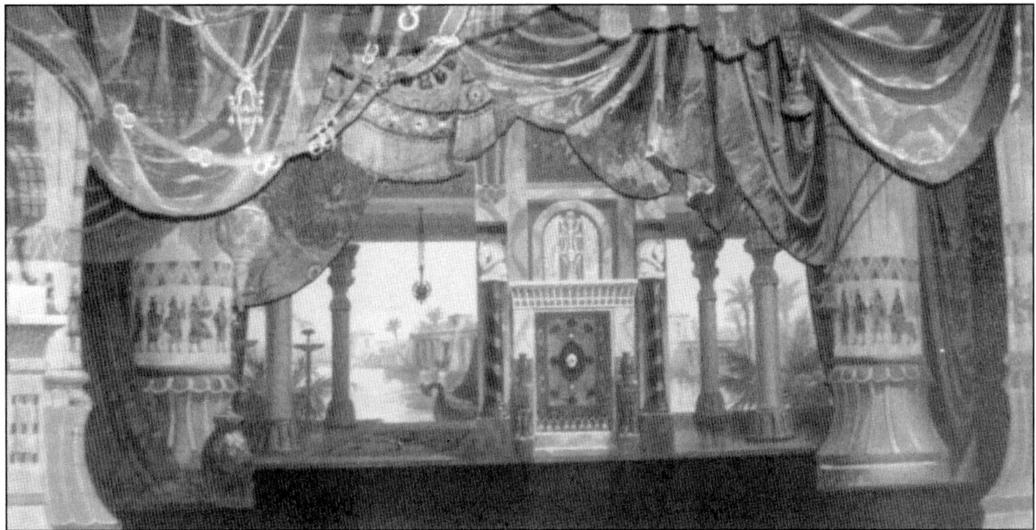

In addition to Smith's front drape, there are accounts of a beautiful street curtain and descriptions of a stage equipped with numerous scenes combining wing-and-drop sets. An example of this type of scenery is seen in this 1989 photograph of one of the wing-and-drop sets in the fifth floor theatre at the Old Masonic Temple building in downtown Wilmington. (THCPA.)

NEW ADVERTISEMENTS.

THALIAN HALL.

LESSEE AND MANAGER.......Mr. G. F. MARCHANT.

MR. MARCHANT BEGS TO INFORM THE PUBLIC of Wilmington, that this elegant place of entertainment will open this Evening, Tuesday, October 12th, 1858.

The entertainment will commence with the comedy in five acts of the

HONEY MOON.

Dance La Espagnola.............MRS. A. REYMOND.

To conclude with the musical Farce of the

"LOAN OF A LOVER."

For particulars, see Programmes.

Oct. 12, 1858. 31-1t

In October, it was announced that the new theatre had been leased to G.F. Marchant, the manager of the Charleston Theatre. His company would open the theatre with John Tobin's *The Honey Moon*, a romantic play in blank verse similar to *The Taming of the Shrew*. Marchant would provide most of the entertainment in the new theatre for the first two seasons. (NHCPL.)

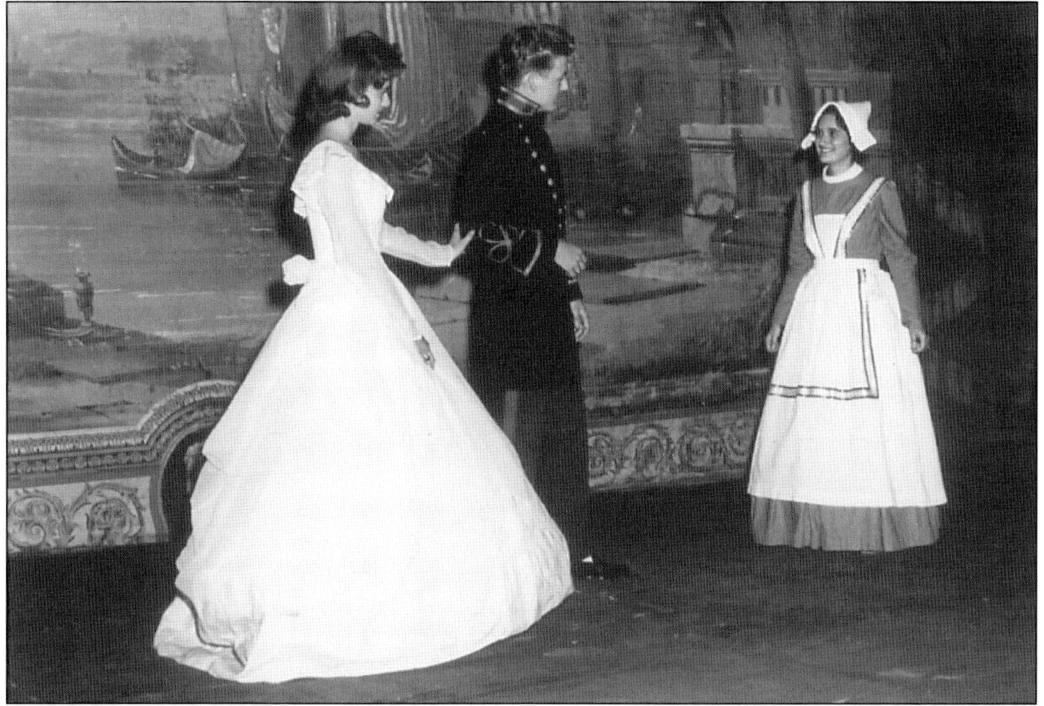

A scene from *The Loan of a Lover* is re-created in this photograph for the centennial celebration, held in 1958. This one-act farce served as the "afterpiece" following the performance on the opening night in 1858. Shown here are Connie Lennon (left), Ray Hansley (center), and Mildred Spivey. (THCPA.)

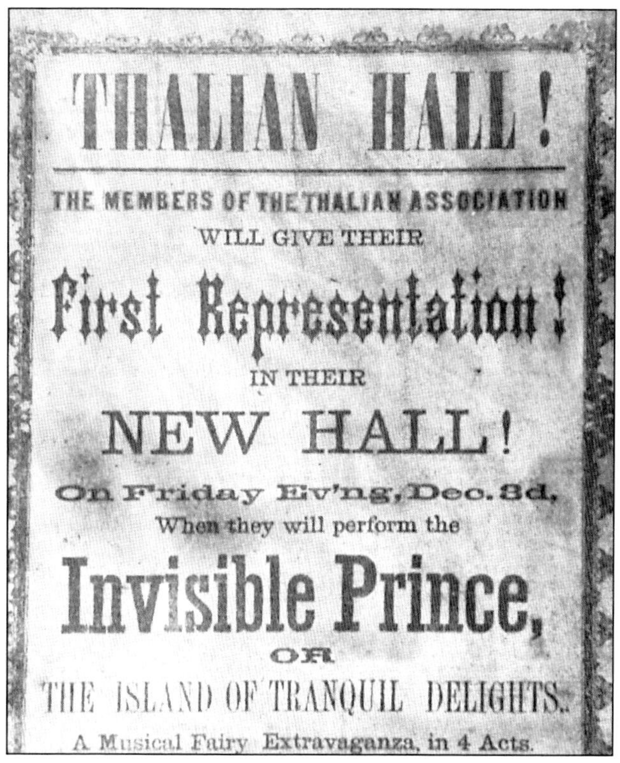

After opening night on October 12, the Marchant's Company arranged for a different play almost nightly until mid-November. Then, the Thalian gentlemen presented the first of three performances during their control of the theatre. This is a facsimile of an original program (now lost) for their first production, when over 20 members appeared in *The Invisible Prince*, a fantasy play in rhyming verse, followed by *Box and Cox*. (THCPA.)

NEW ADVERTISEMENTS.

THALIAN HALL!

ON TO-MORROW EVENING, 16th inst., the WILMINGTON THALIAN ASSOCIATION will perform the sterling old English Comedy of

"THE HEIR AT LAW,"

To be followed by the pleasant affair of

"TWO BONNYCASTLES.

Doors opened at 7½ o'clock; performance to commeece at 8 o'clock.

Admittance 50 Cents; Children and Servants half price

☞Tickets to be had at Pierce's Book Store, and Lippitt's and Meares' Drug Stores, and at the door.

June 15, 1859. 240-2t

The final production by the antebellum Thalians was *Heir at Law*, presented in June 1859. The *Wilmington Herald* stated, "The greatest obstacle in the way of successful representation by amateurs is the great and very natural difficulty in making boys look like girls." The theatre marked the beginning of a new era, but it also signaled the end of the old gentlemen's acting societies, which almost totally disappeared throughout the state by the end of the Civil War. (NHCPL.)

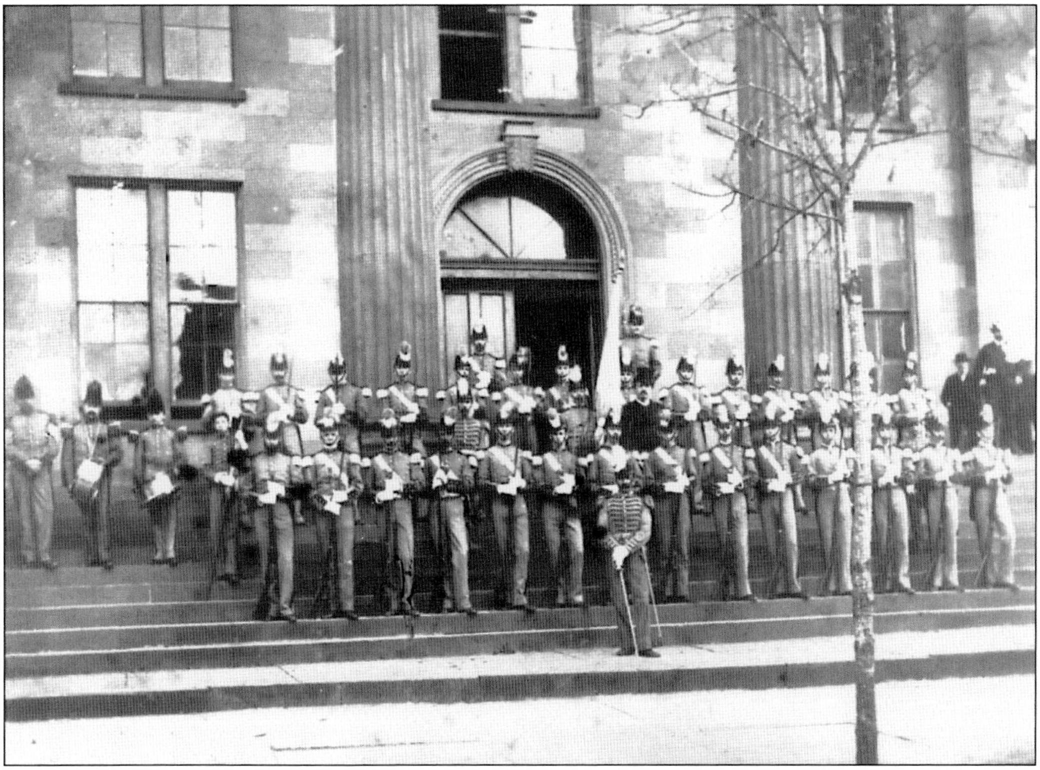

The Wilmington Light Infantry stands on the steps of town hall. The Cape Fear Guards made use of the basement as an armory. The *Wilmington Journal* announced on October 19, 1858, that the performance that evening would be *Romeo and Juliet* and the "Wilmington Light Infantry will attend as a company and in uniform." (CFM.)

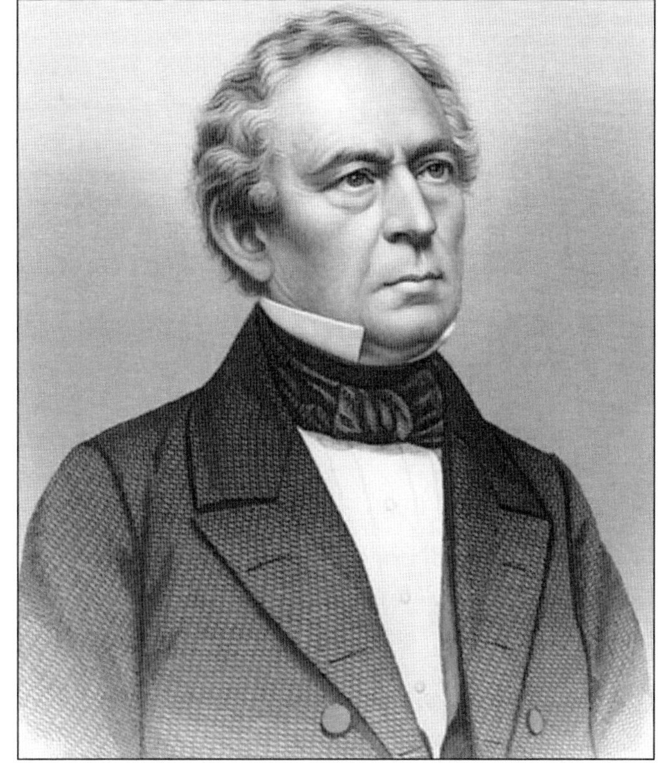

On December 12, 1860, the theatre hosted its largest audience since its construction. Entire families turned out to hear Edward Everett's lecture on George Washington, presented as a benefit for the Mount Vernon Ladies Association. (Library of Congress.)

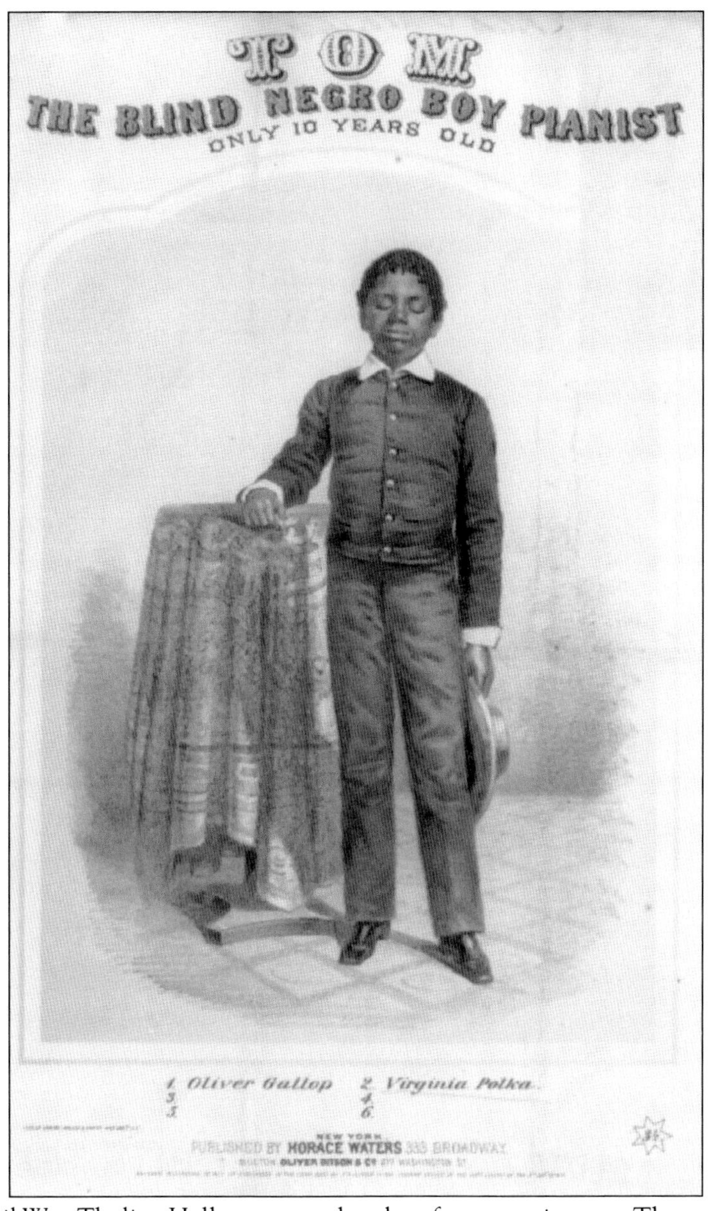

During the Civil War, Thalian Hall was a popular place for entertainment. The town's population swelled due to the commercial activity created by the blockade. For the 1863–1864 season, there were 285 performances. The resident companies presenting plays included Bates and Jenkins, the Bailey Family, and the Katie Estelle Company. Other entertainments included benefits, minstrel shows, and the French Souaves. One of the most popular events was Lee Mallory's Pantechnoptomon of the Battle of Manassas. This was a combination of moving canvas, mechanical figures, and narration, much like a movie newsreel. Theatergoing was so popular, the second floor of Wilmington City Hall was converted for theatre use. Thomas Green Bethune, seen in this poster, was a musical prodigy better known as Blind Tom. He composed music and performed astonishing feats of memory on the piano, first as a slave and then as freeman. His first appearance at Thalian Hall was in May 1862, and he would play Wilmington several times over the next 25 years. He gave his last performance at the Wilmington Opera House (Thalian Hall) in 1901. (Library of Congress.)

During the Civil War, there were as many theatrical performances in Wilmington as in any city in the South; however, this is the only example of a program from a performance at Thalian Hall to survive from that era. The Bailey Family, a professional acting troupe, began performing at Thalian Hall in 1862 and remained in residence through the end of the war. (State Library.)

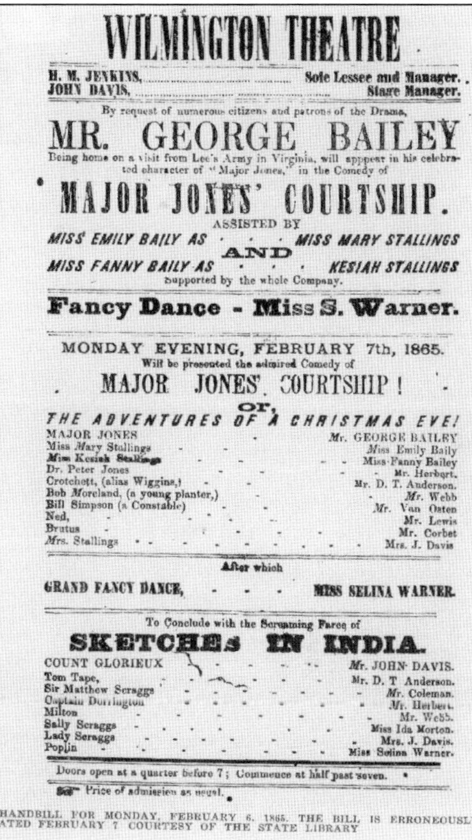

WILMINGTON THEATRE

H. M. JENKINS, ... Sole Lessee and Manager.
JOHN DAVIS, ... Stage Manager.

By request of numerous citizens and patrons of the Drama,

MR. GEORGE BAILEY

Being home on a visit from Lee's Army in Virginia, will apppear in his celebrated character of "Major Jones," in the Comedy of

MAJOR JONES' COURTSHIP.

ASSISTED BY

MISS EMILY BAILY AS . . . MISS MARY STALLINGS
AND
MISS FANNY BAILY AS . . . KESIAH STALLINGS

Supported by the whole Company.

Fancy Dance - Miss S. Warner.

MONDAY EVENING, FEBRUARY 7th, 1865.

Will be presented the admired Comedy of

MAJOR JONES' COURTSHIP!
or,
THE ADVENTURES OF A CHRISTMAS EVE!

MAJOR JONES - Mr. GEORGE BAILEY
Miss Mary Stallings - - Miss Emily Baily
Miss Kesiah Stallings - - - - Miss Fanny Bailey
Dr. Peter Jones - - - - Mr. Herbert.
Crotchett, (alias Wiggins,) - - Mr. D. T. Anderson.
Bob Moreland, (a young planter,) - - Mr. Webb
Bill Simpson (a Constable) - - Mr. Van Osten
Ned, - - - - Mr. Lewis
Brutus - - - - Mr. Corbet
Mrs. Stallings - - - - - - - - - Mrs. J. Davis

After which

GRAND FANCY DANCE, - - - MISS SELINA WARNER.

To Conclude with the Screaming Farce of

SKETCHES IN INDIA.

COUNT GLORIEUX - - - - Mr. JOHN DAVIS.
Tom Tape, - - - - Mr. D. T Anderson.
Sir Matthew Scraggs - - - - - - Mr. Coleman.
Captain Dorrington - - - - - - Mr. Herbert.
Milton - - - - - - - Mr. Webb.
Sally Scraggs - - - - - - Miss Ida Morton.
Lady Scraggs - - - - - - - Mrs. J. Davis.
Poplin - - - - - - - Miss Selina Warner.

Doors open at a quarter before 7; Commence at half past seven.

Price of admission as usual.

HANDBILL FOR MONDAY, FEBRUARY 6, 1865. THE BILL IS ERRONEOUSLY DATED FEBRUARY 7 COURTESY OF THE STATE LIBRARY

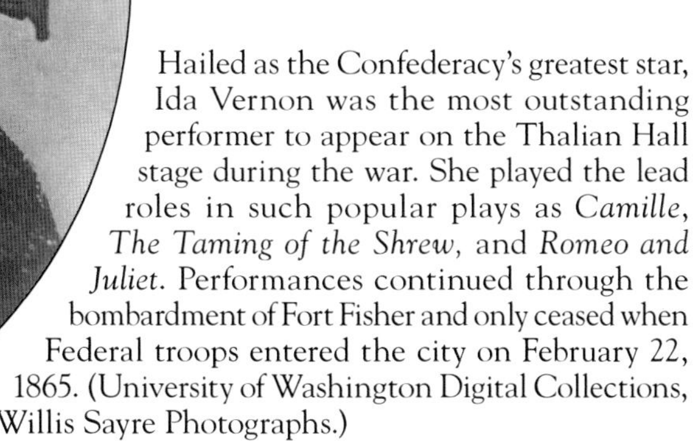

Hailed as the Confederacy's greatest star, Ida Vernon was the most outstanding performer to appear on the Thalian Hall stage during the war. She played the lead roles in such popular plays as *Camille*, *The Taming of the Shrew*, and *Romeo and Juliet*. Performances continued through the bombardment of Fort Fisher and only ceased when Federal troops entered the city on February 22, 1865. (University of Washington Digital Collections, J. Willis Sayre Photographs.)

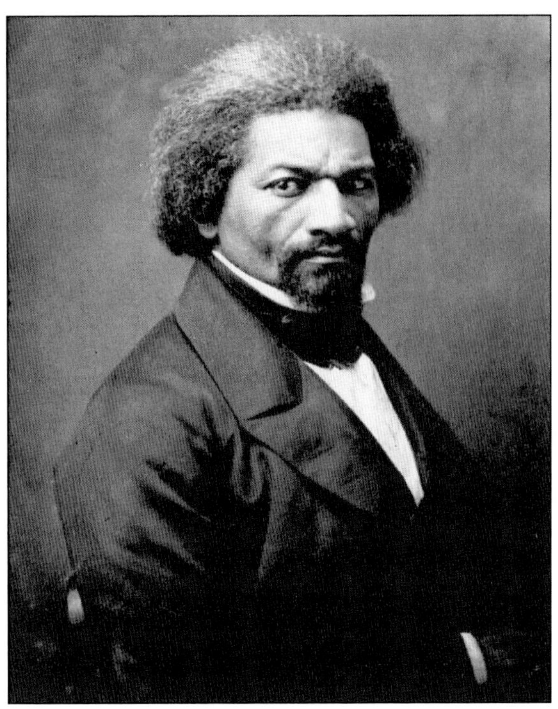

Throughout Thalian Hall's history, numerous speakers, road shows, concerts, and special events were sponsored by local African American organizations. Frederick Douglass (pictured), the abolitionist, author, and women's rights advocate, gave an eloquent speech in the Lecture Room occupying the second floor of Wilmington City Hall on August 1, 1872. He spoke about his own history and of the changed relations between the races. (Collection of the New York Historical Society.)

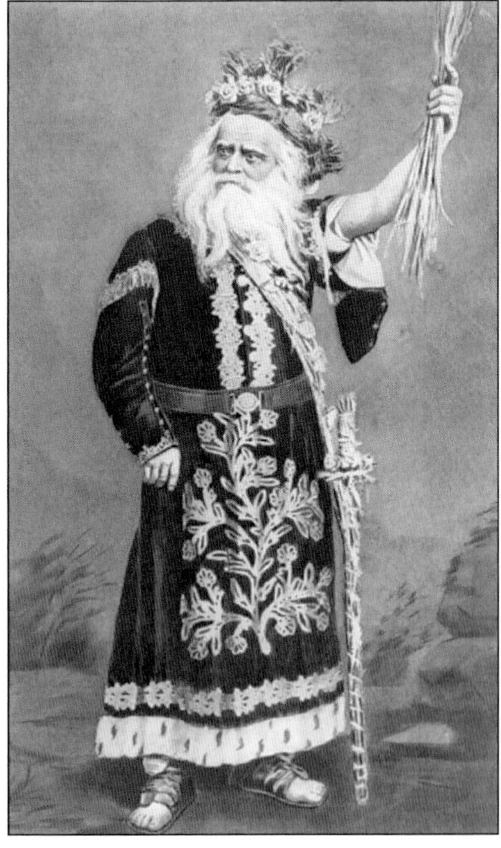

Star performers appearing at the Opera House frequently acted in the plays of Shakespeare. Edwin Forrest was the first American actor to achieve fame in the United States and abroad. On his last tour, Forrest appeared in three productions at Thalian Hall in 1870, including *King Lear.* (Photogravure by Gebbie & Husson Co., Ltd.)

Three

The Opera House 1870–1900

Wilmington was the largest city in North Carolina until 1910. It was a major port and railroad center, and its fine opera house was second to none in the state. Many of the most celebrated actors in America played on its stage. There were musical performances by John Phillip Sousa, Sir Harry Lauder, and opera singer Lillian Nordica. Tom Thumb appeared in a variety show, and Oscar Wilde lectured on decorative arts.

Between engagements, the theatre was rented for local events, including community concerts, recitals, meetings, graduations, and exhibitions. In the latter part of the century, amateur dramatic clubs, such as the Wilmington Dramatic Club, gave performances at the Wilmington Opera House.

Volunteer groups, mostly made up of women, presented large pageants consisting of tableaux, illustrative scenes, and dancing. One of the most elaborate was the *Story of the Reformation*, with a cast of 150, presented by the Ministering Circle. In 1897, to raise money for the Cornelius Harnett Monument, the Colonial Dames produced a dramatization of Ouida's novel *Under Two Flags*. In the production, the British army was portrayed by the Wilmington Light Infantry, and the French soldiers were depicted by the Wilmington Naval Reserves. The Arabs and the dancing girls were played by the Colonial Dames. The highlight of the evening was when Annie de Rosset rode a horse across the stage.

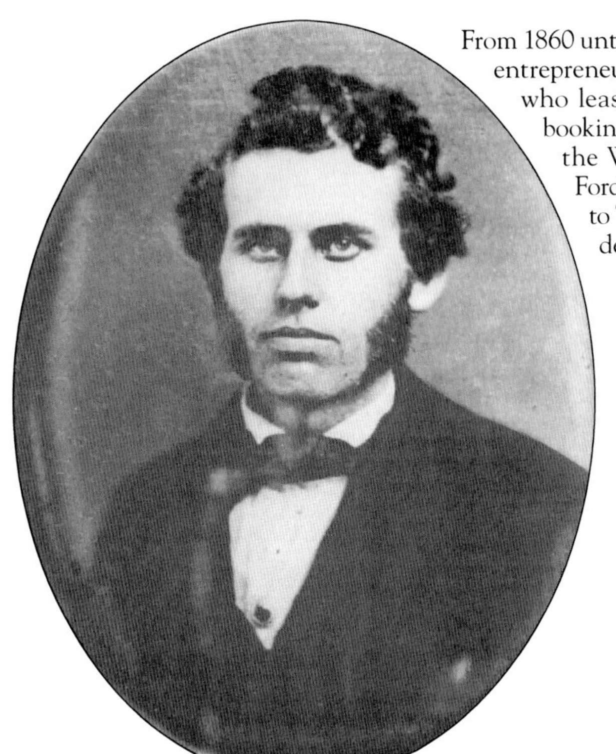

From 1860 until 1936, the theatre was leased to private entrepreneurs. The most famous was John T. Ford, who leased the theatre in 1869 and served as booking agent until 1873. He renamed the venue the Wilmington Opera House. His famous Ford's Theatre in Washington, though similar to Thalian Hall, is not a copy, nor were they designed by the same architect.

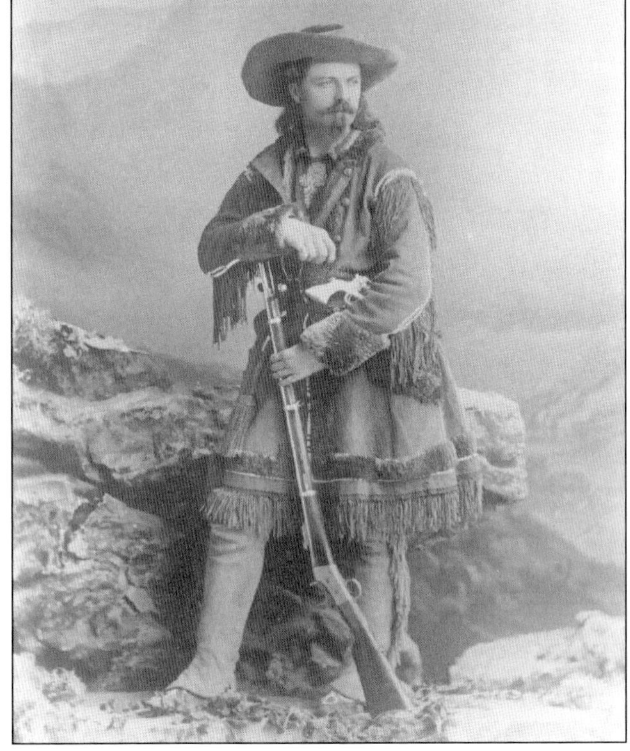

Under the management of John T. Ford, "Buffalo Bill" Cody appeared at the Wilmington Opera House for two nights in October 1878 as the star in *May Cody, or Lost and Won*, a play loosely based on his life. The performance concluded with a display of his prowess as a marksman. (Buffalo Bill Center of the West, Cody, Wyoming, U.S.A.)

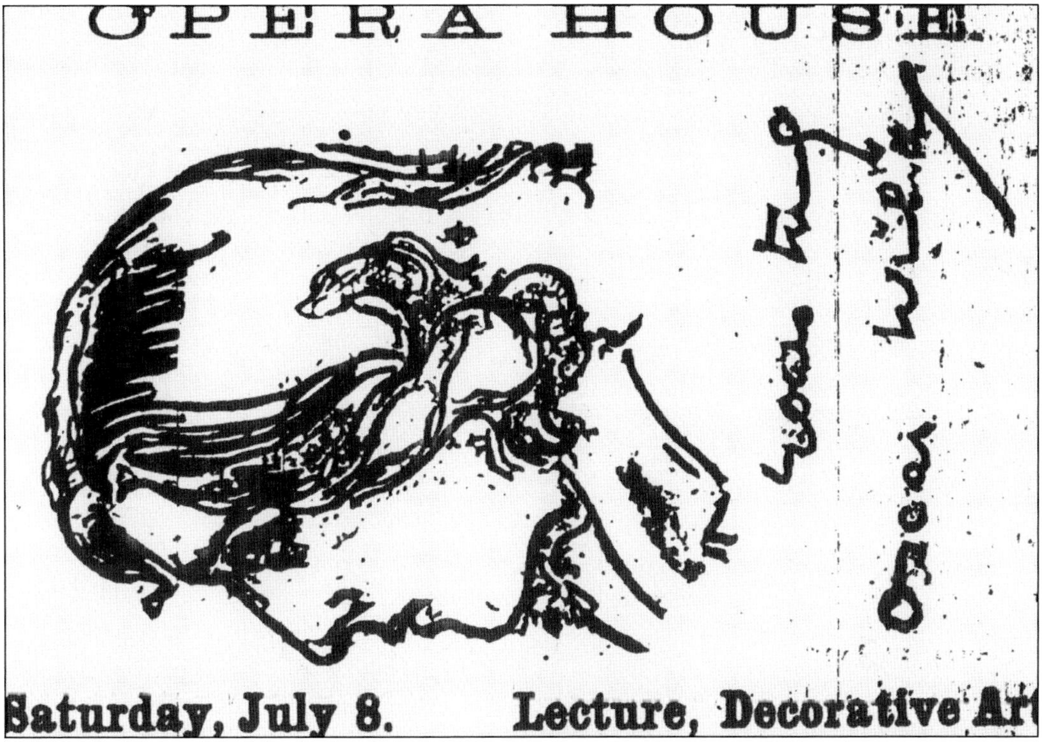

OPERA HOUSE

Saturday, July 8. Lecture, Decorative Art

This advertisement for Oscar Wilde's lecture on the decorative arts appeared on the front page of the *Wilmington Star*. On July 8, 1882, Wilde spoke at Thalian Hall. He remained in Wilmington for two days. (*Wilmington Star-News*, NHCPL.)

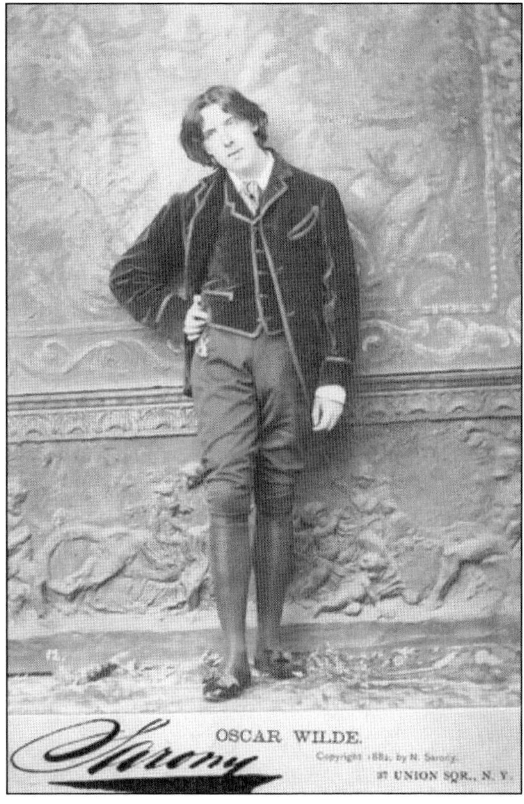

While he was staying at the Purcell Hotel on Front Street, Wilde accepted an invitation to visit Manning's Pine Grove Resort on Wrightsville Sound. He spent the day there socializing with many of the residents. In the afternoon, a party of young men took Wilde by boat to the beach, where he participated in a footrace. That evening, he had dinner at Stedman's Park, an estate on the sound that became the Gray Gables Restaurant in the 1970s.

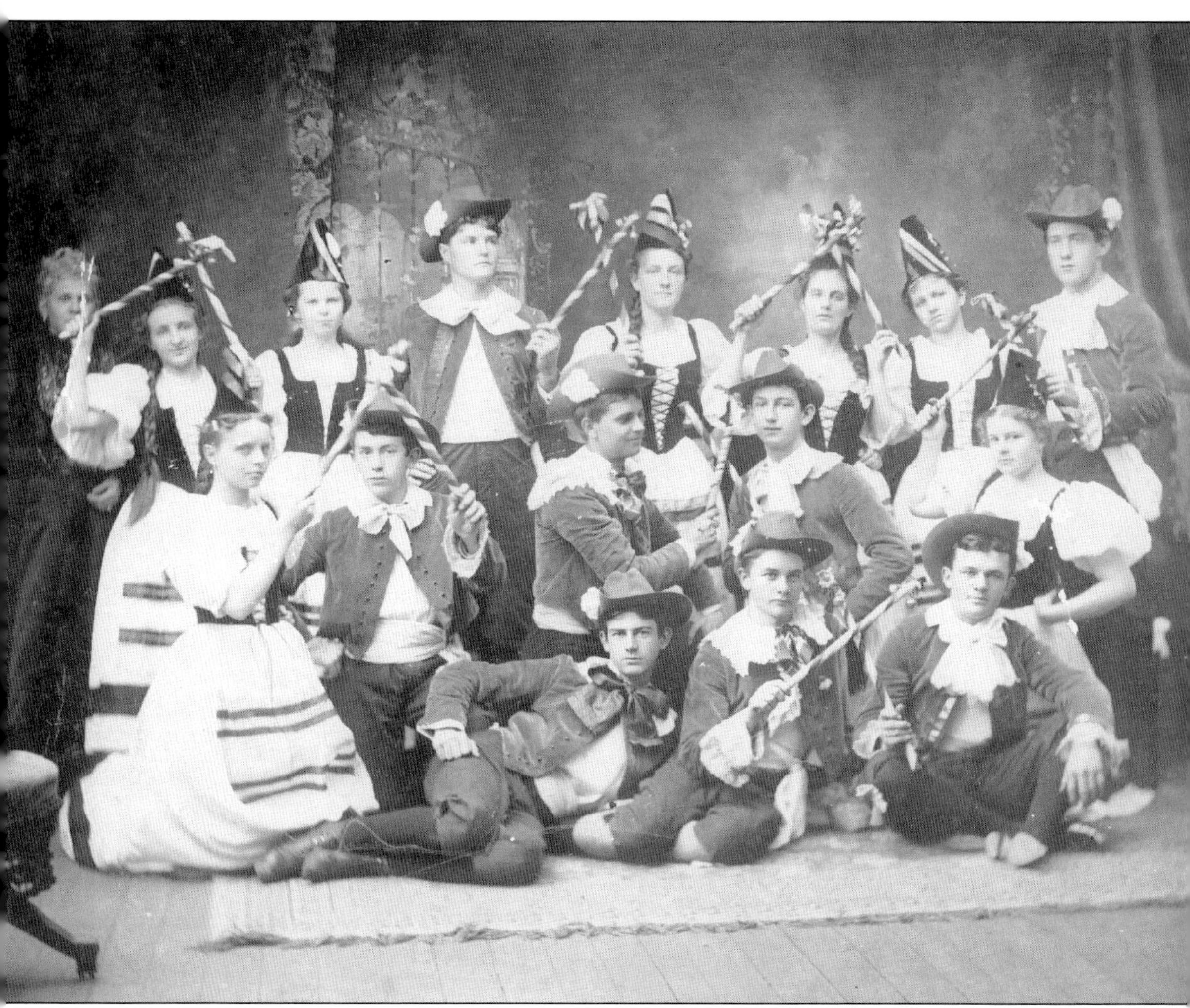

In the 1890s, amateur dramatic performances flourished at the opera house. Pageants, put on by volunteer groups of women, consisted of tableaux, illustrative scenes, and dancing. The high point was reached in 1896, when a cast of 200 presented *The Kirmess* for four evenings. Costumes were brought in from New York. During the run, two nights were designated for New Bern and Fayetteville, which sent contingents down by train. City hall was turned into the "Kirmess Inn," and the hallways were fitted out with booths selling food and items from different nations. In this scene, entitled "A Swedish Christmas Eve," are, from left to right (in front) Will Crow, Louis Cutlar, and James Stevenson; (kneeling) Mildred Davis, Tom Davis, Tom Meyers, Robert Nash, and Jeanie Peck; (standing) Lucille Wright Murchison, Alice Smallbones, Beulah Armstrong, Dawson Latham, Martha Williams, Sue Meares, Sue McQueen, and Fred Dick. Proceeds were used to fund the erection of the Cornelius Harnett Monument on Market Street. (Ministering Circle.)

As a young actor, Joseph Jefferson performed in the old Innes Academy. After achieving fame in New York in *Our American Cousin*, he became world famous for his production of *Rip Van Winkle*, which played the opera house in 1880 and in 1897. He also appeared there in *The Rivals* with Mrs. John Drew, grandmother of the famous Barrymores. (THCPA.)

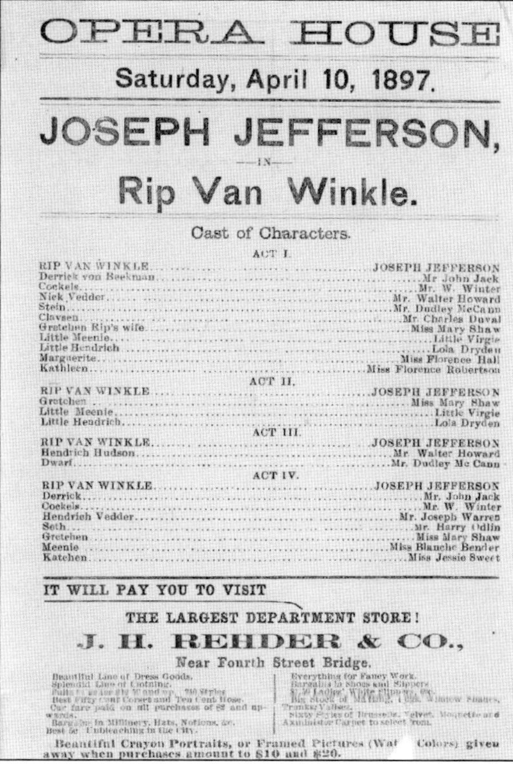

OPERA HOUSE

Saturday, April 10, 1897.

JOSEPH JEFFERSON,

—IN—

Rip Van Winkle.

Cast of Characters.

ACT I.

RIP VAN WINKLE	JOSEPH JEFFERSON
Derrick von Beekman	Mr John Jack
Cockels	Mr. W. Winter
Nick Vedder	Mr. Walter Howard
Stein	Mr. Dudley McCann
Clavsen	Mr. Charles Duval
Gretchen Rip's wife	Miss Mary Shaw
Little Meenie	Little Virgie
Little Hendrich	Lola Dryden
Marguerite	Miss Florence Hall
Kathleen	Miss Florence Robertson

ACT II.

RIP VAN WINKLE	JOSEPH JEFFERSON
Gretchen	Miss Mary Shaw
Little Meenie	Little Virgie
Little Hendrich	Lola Dryden

ACT III.

RIP VAN WINKLE	JOSEPH JEFFERSON
Hendrich Hudson	Mr. Walter Howard
Dwarf	Mr. Dudley Mc Cann

ACT IV.

RIP VAN WINKLE	JOSEPH JEFFERSON
Derrick	Mr. John Jack
Cockels	Mr. W. Winter
Hendrich Vedder	Mr. Joseph Warren
Seth	Mr. Harry Odlin
Gretchen	Miss Mary Shaw
Meenie	Miss Blanche Bender
Katchen	Miss Jessie Sweet

IT WILL PAY YOU TO VISIT

THE LARGEST DEPARTMENT STORE!

J. H. REHDER & CO.,

Near Fourth Street Bridge.

Beautiful Line of Dress Goods.
Splendid Line of Clothing.
[illegible]
Best Fifty Cent Corsets and Ten Cent Hose.
Car fare paid on all purchases of $2 and upwards.
Bargains in Millinery, Hats, Notions, &c.
Best 5c Unbleaching in the City.

Everything for Fancy Work.
Bargains in Shoes and Slippers.
[illegible]
Big Stock of [illegible] Window Shades, Trunks, Valises.
Sixty Styles of Brussels, Velvet, Moquette and Axminster Carpet to select from.

Beautiful Crayon Portraits, or Framed Pictures (Wat[illegible] Colors) given away when purchases amount to $10 and $20.

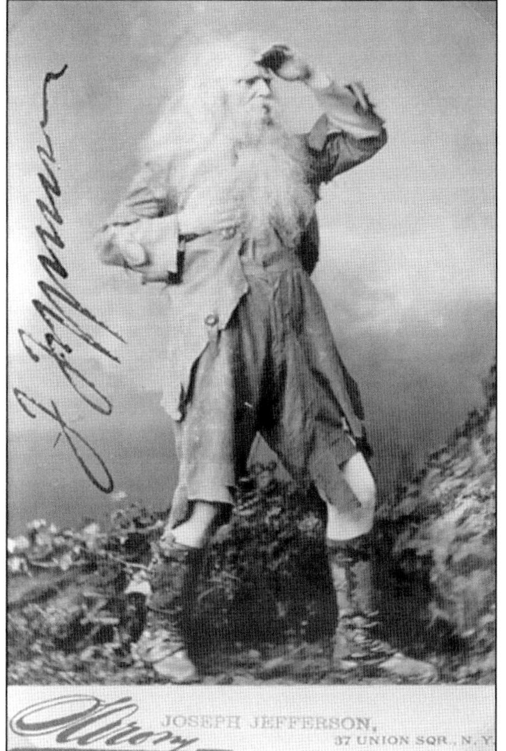

This souvenir card shows Joseph Jefferson as Rip Van Winkle. Following his performance in 1884 as Bob Acres in *The Rivals*, a special reception was held in the mayor's rooms in Wilmington City Hall with the former members of the antebellum Thalian Association. (J. Willis Sayre Photographs, University of Washington.)

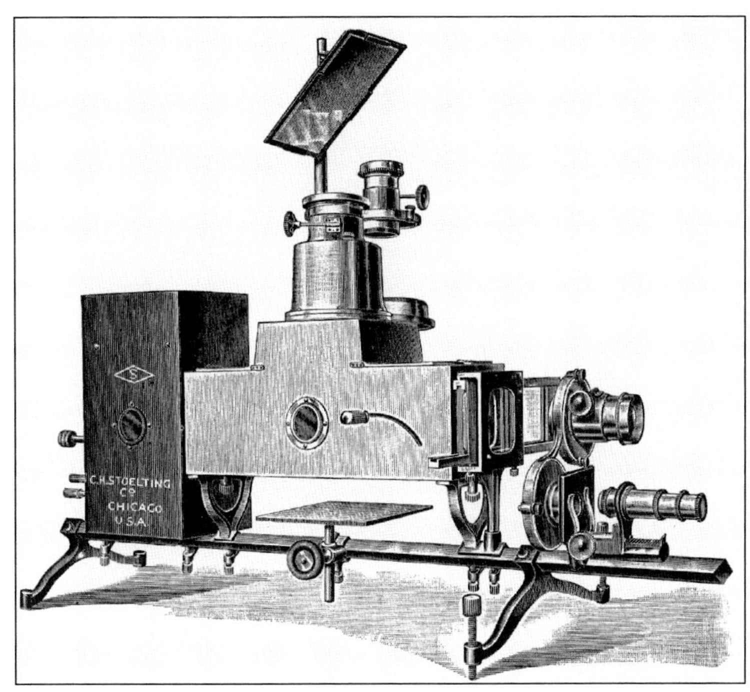

On March 9, 1897, the Wilmington Electric Company was at work all day wiring the opera house for a five-day demonstration of Thomas Edison's newest wonder, the projectoscope. The device allowed audiences to experience speeding trains, horse-drawn fire engines, and people rushing to and fro, all projected on a silver screen. Edison himself would visit Wilmington two years later, staying at the Orton Hotel on Front Street.

Owing to the great desire of our colored citizens to witness the "Projectoscope" at the Opera House, the dress circle will be reserved for them to-night. The entire lower floor will be held for whites.

Matinee to-day and to-night's performance is your last chance to see the "Projectoscope."

At the end of the 19th century, Wilmington had one of the most viable and prosperous African American communities in the nation. The community flourished until the race riots of November 1898. This advertisement in the *Wilmington Messenger* of March 20, 1897, indicates the importance of the African American community while at the same time denoting their second-class treatment. (NHCPL.)

Four

Academy Tonight 1900–1928

At the beginning of the 20th century, commercial theatre was a booming business all across America. As North Carolina's most populous city, with over 20,000 residents, Wilmington provided ample audiences for theatre performances, which usually exceeded over 100 annually. At this time, the theatre came under the control of Wilmington's influential S.A. Schloss, the representative of the Southern Theatre Managers Association. In 1909, he undertook a major renovation of Thalian Hall, including a new proscenium, the removal of the side balconies, and the installation of electric stage lighting.

Through the 1920s, Wilmington audiences had the choice of a wide variety of comedies, historical plays, and musical comedies. The repertoire of stock companies continued to supply a large part of the day-to-day entertainment between the appearances of hit plays and star performers. In 1913, Schloss's death ended Wilmington's close connection with New York theatre. The following year, the Victoria Theatre, with 1,100 seats, opened, and most of the major road shows performed there. Other competition came from the movie theatres; by the 1920s, the Bijou, the Grand, and the Royal were presenting vaudeville and motion pictures. Though theatrical performances dropped off markedly, repertory companies, African American touring performers, sporting events, and classical concerts continued to play the Academy of Music through the 1920s. One of the last major road shows was the Ziegfeld Follies of 1928.

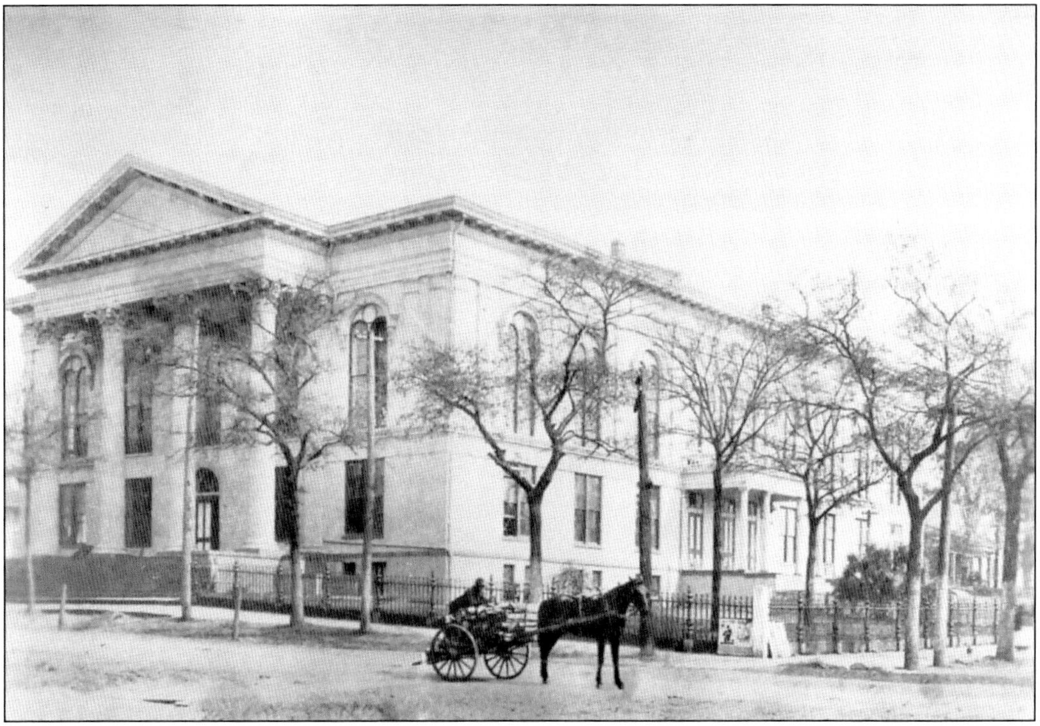

The 1893 Chicago Exposition spawned a new municipal architecture, consisting of classical design with gleaming white exteriors. In Wilmington, all that was needed was a new coat of white paint, and the Italianate Revival building matched the style. (NHCPL.)

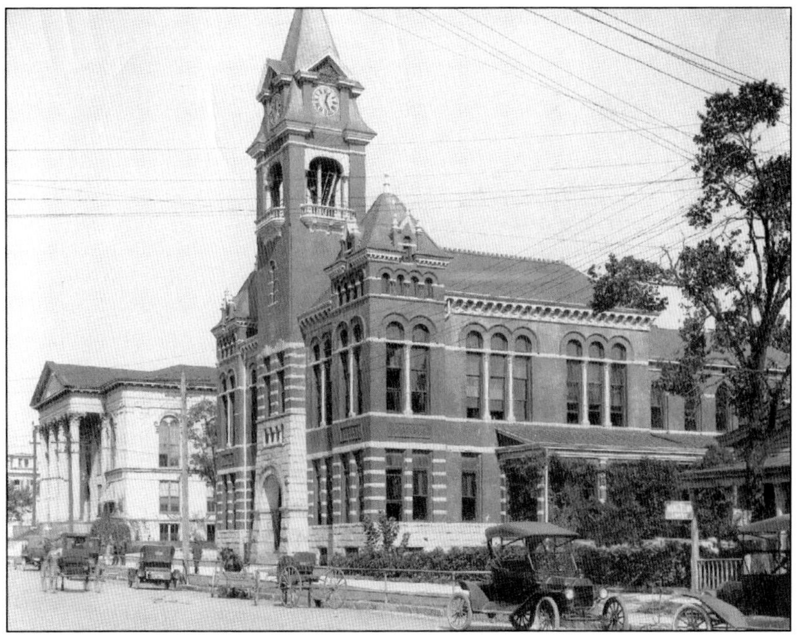

In 1892, a new courthouse was built on the southeast corner of Third and Princess Streets. This photograph was taken about 1915. For many years, a blacksmith's shop stood on this site across from Thalian Hall. (NHCPL.)

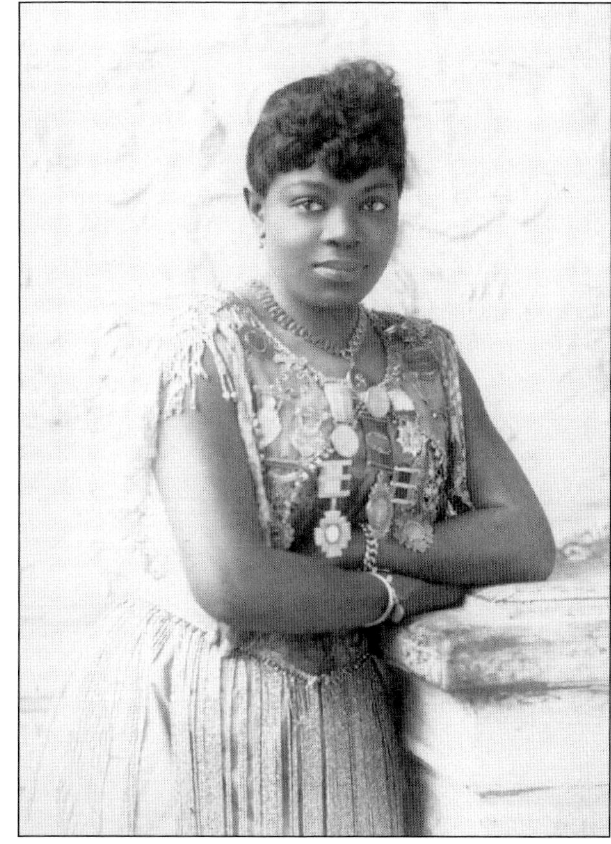

Sissieretta Jones, popularly known as "The Black Patti," was a distinguished African American soprano who toured America and Europe, playing for Queen Victoria and four American presidents. Her 40-member company, known as the Black Patti Troubadours, played the Academy of Music on September 13, 1907. (Library of Congress.)

This photograph, taken on the steps of city hall around 1910, shows members of the brass band from a Wild West show called *Buckskin Ben's Family*. The show featured cowboys, Indians, ropers, and riders, as well as trained horses, dogs, and monkeys. (CFM.)

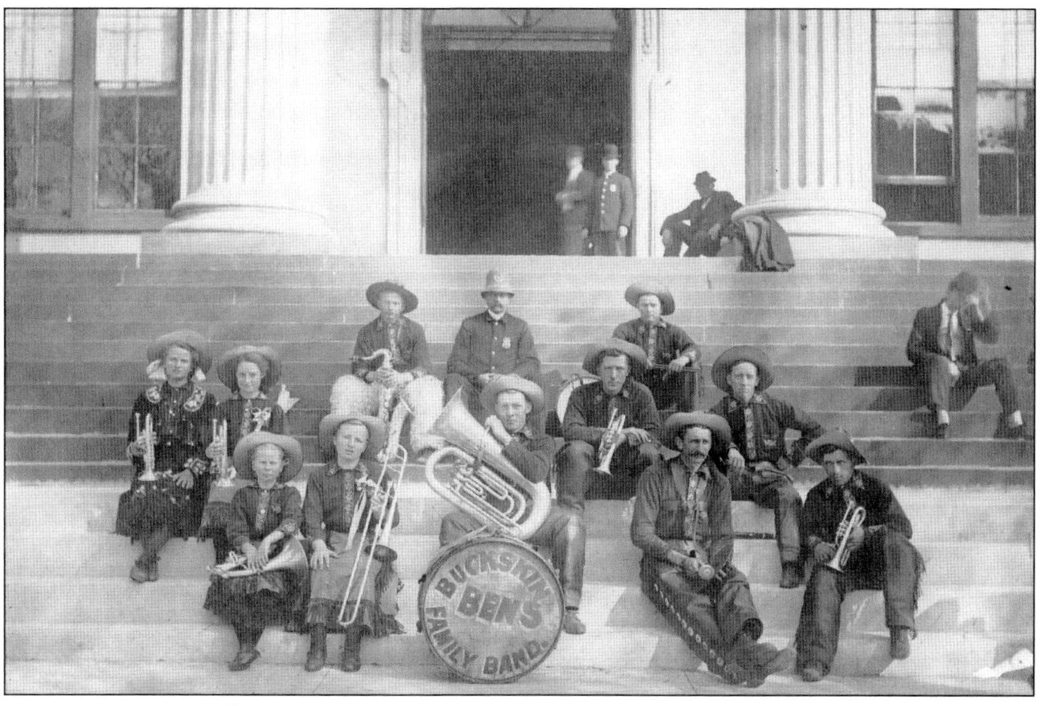

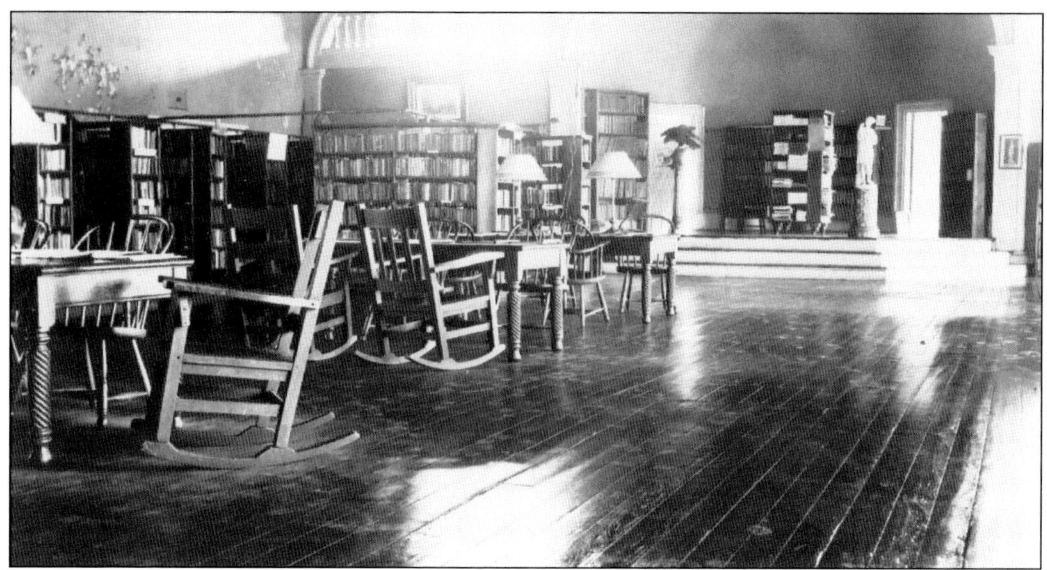

By 1906, the North Carolina Sorosis established Wilmington's first public library in the large second-floor room in Wilmington City Hall. The space, originally known as the Lecture Room, was used as an assembly hall until the library was created. It was not used for town meetings until 1990. (THCPA.)

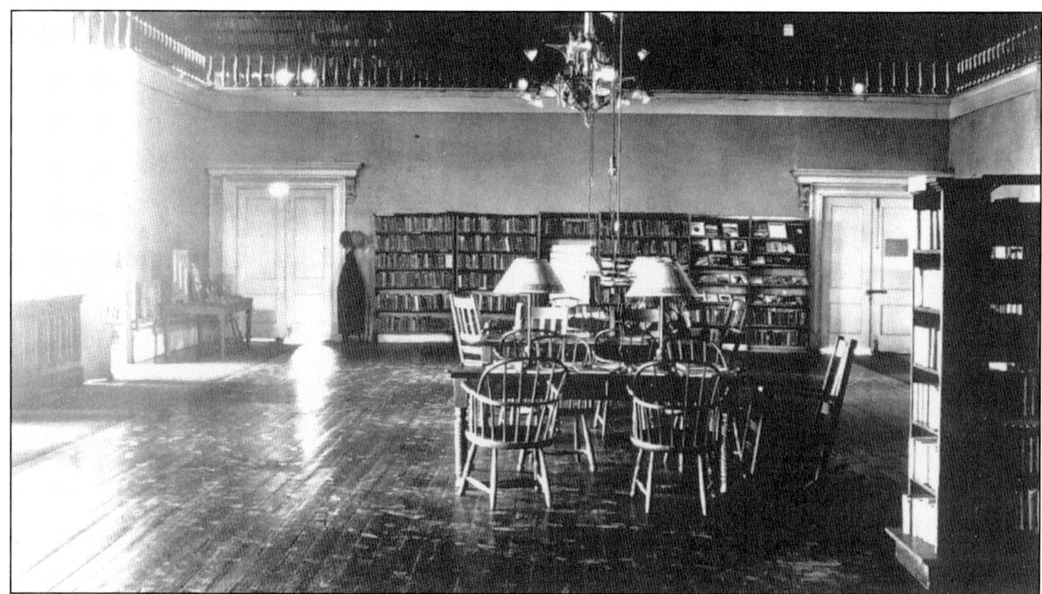

This is another view of the Wilmington Public Library, looking north toward Chestnut Street. For many years, the original tables and chairs, seen here, provided the seating in the Local History Room at the New Hanover County Library. (THCPA.)

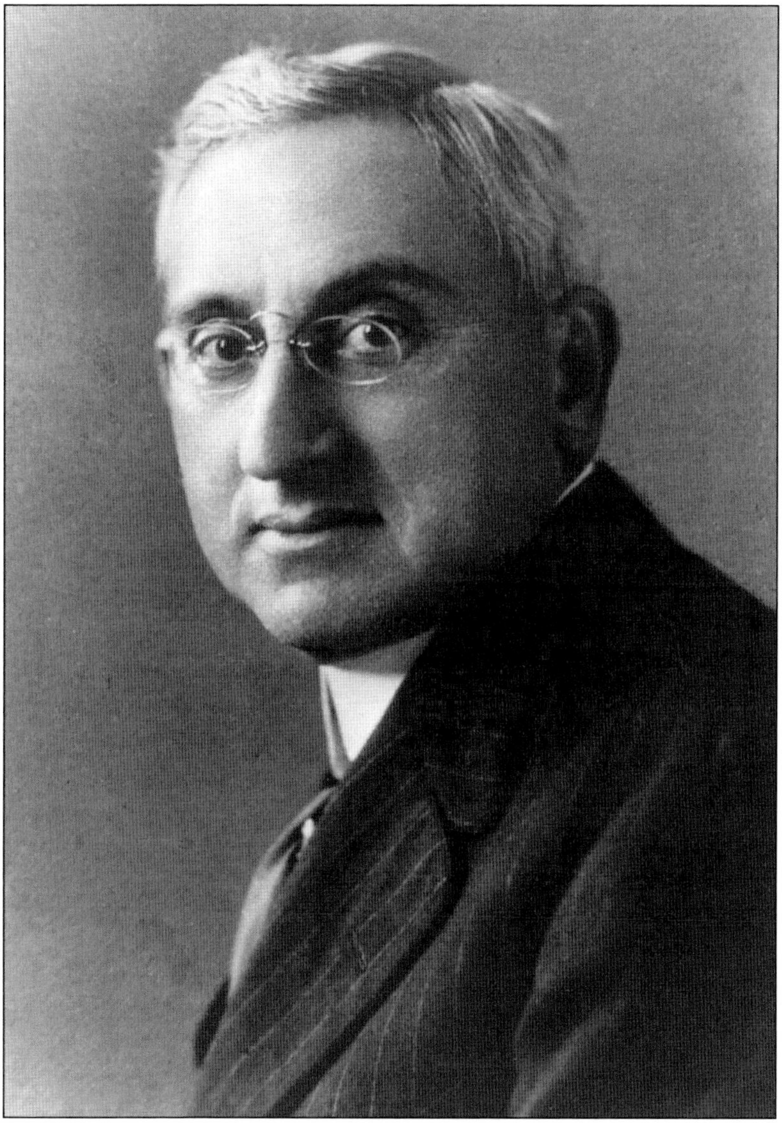

Simeon Archibald Schloss held the lease for Thalian Hall for almost two decades, until 1915 when his theatrical circuit was sold following his death. Schloss was a talented musician, and as a young man he traveled as a member of an orchestra. (NHCPL.)

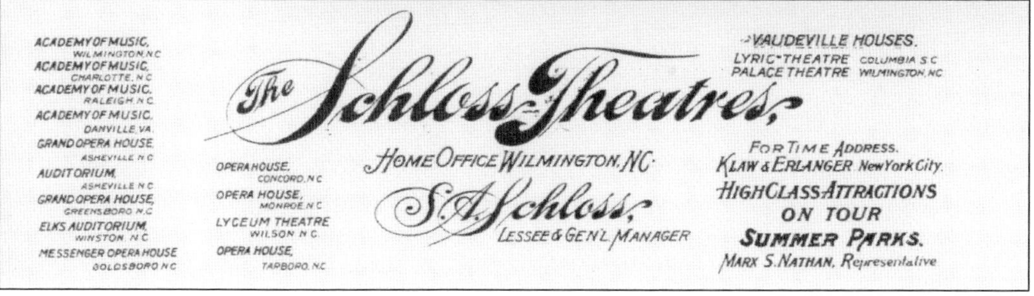

Throughout his life, Schloss established a number of successful commercial enterprises, but he made his mark in show business. His theatre circuit, based in Wilmington, operated as many as 14 theatres in North Carolina and South Carolina. He was also the representative of the Southern Theatre Managers Association to the New York Theatre Syndicate. (Paul Wilson.)

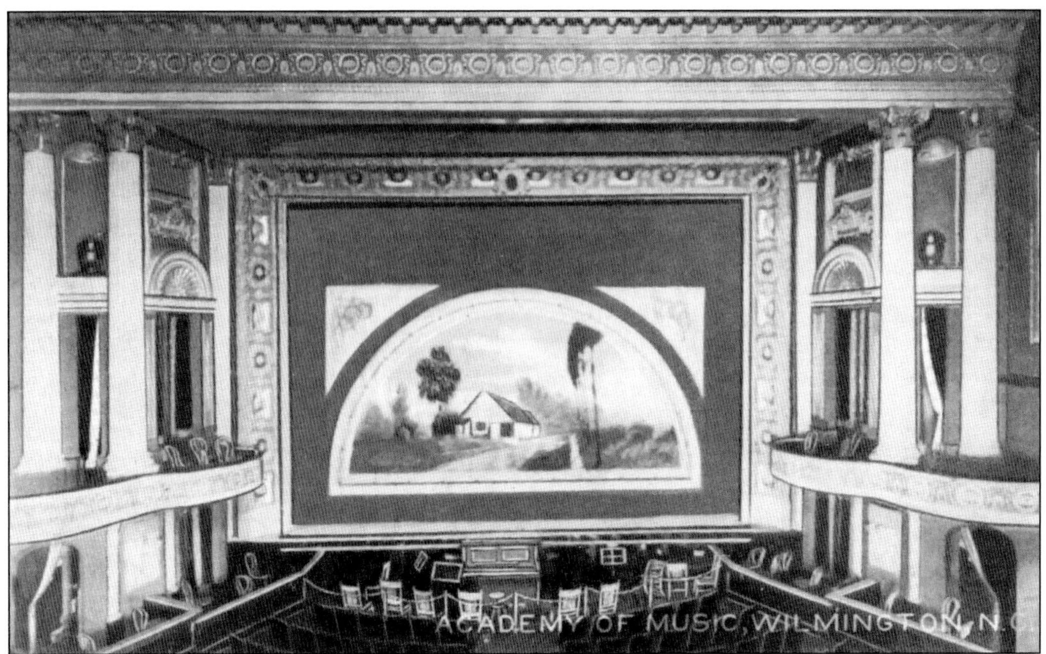

This hand-tinted postcard appeared in 1909, offering the earliest view of the interior of Thalian Hall. It was created from a photograph taken after major changes were made to the 1858 auditorium and proscenium. Another change was the removal of sections of the first balcony on either side of the auditorium and the creation of the decorative stenciling. (THCPA.)

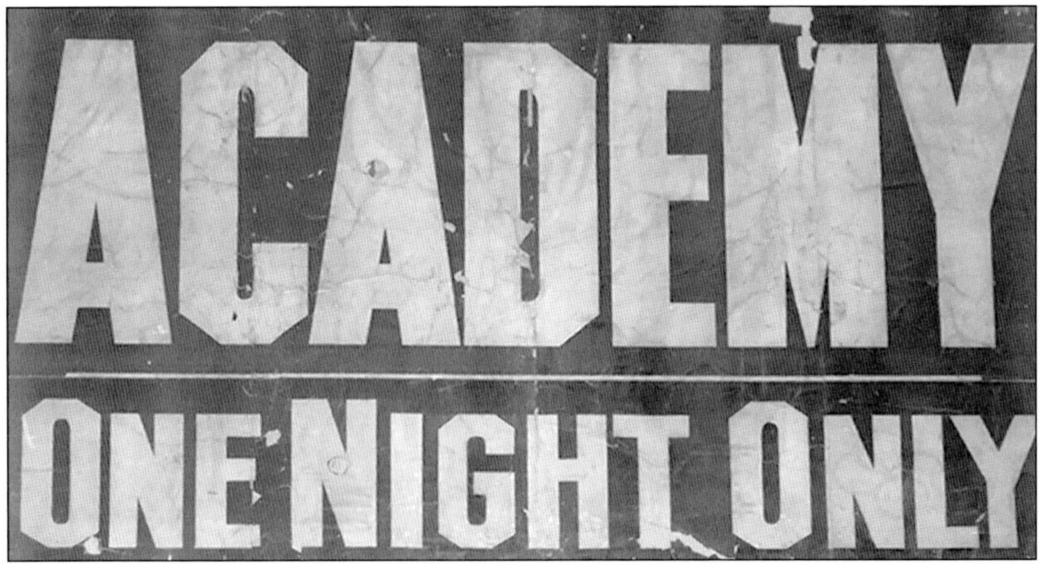

The various names for Thalian Hall were determined by what was in vogue at the time. During the Civil War, it was advertised as the Wilmington Theatre. In 1871, John T. Ford renamed it the Wilmington Opera House, and in 1902 the leaseholders changed it to the Academy of Music. This original sign dates from the 1920s. In 1932, the city adopted the name Thalian Hall at the request of the Thalian Association. (THCPA.)

The Greek Revival structure in this 1914 photograph was located behind the Thalian Hall stage. Built by the Odd Fellows as a school in 1843, it was purchased by Levin Meginney as a part of the land transaction leading to the building of the new town hall in 1854. He used it as a school and residence, and his family sold it to the city in 1925. (CFM.)

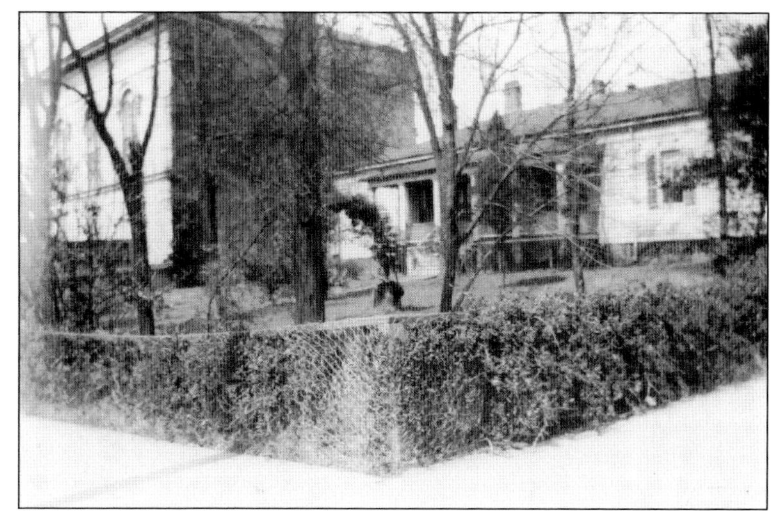

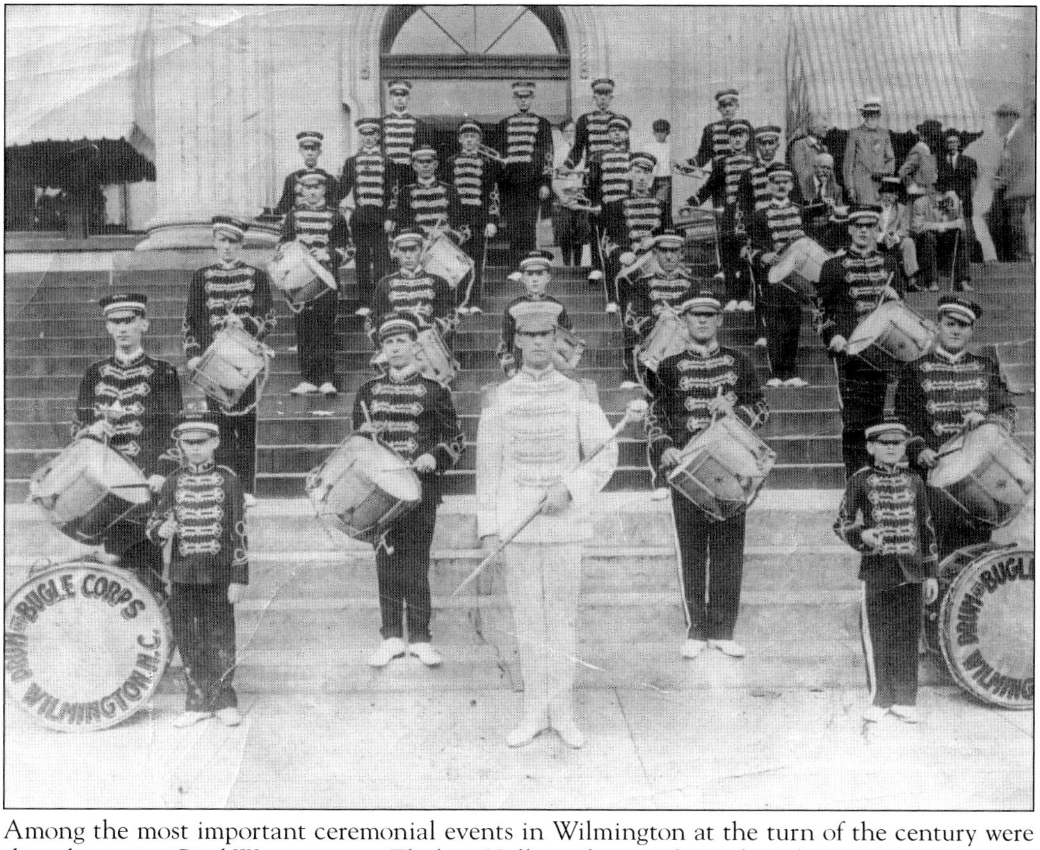

Among the most important ceremonial events in Wilmington at the turn of the century were those honoring Civil War veterans. Thalian Hall was frequently used on these occasions. In this c. 1914 photograph, the Wilmington Drum and Bugle Corps poses on the steps of city hall. Visible at upper right are Confederate veterans wearing their commemorative medals. (HSLCF.)

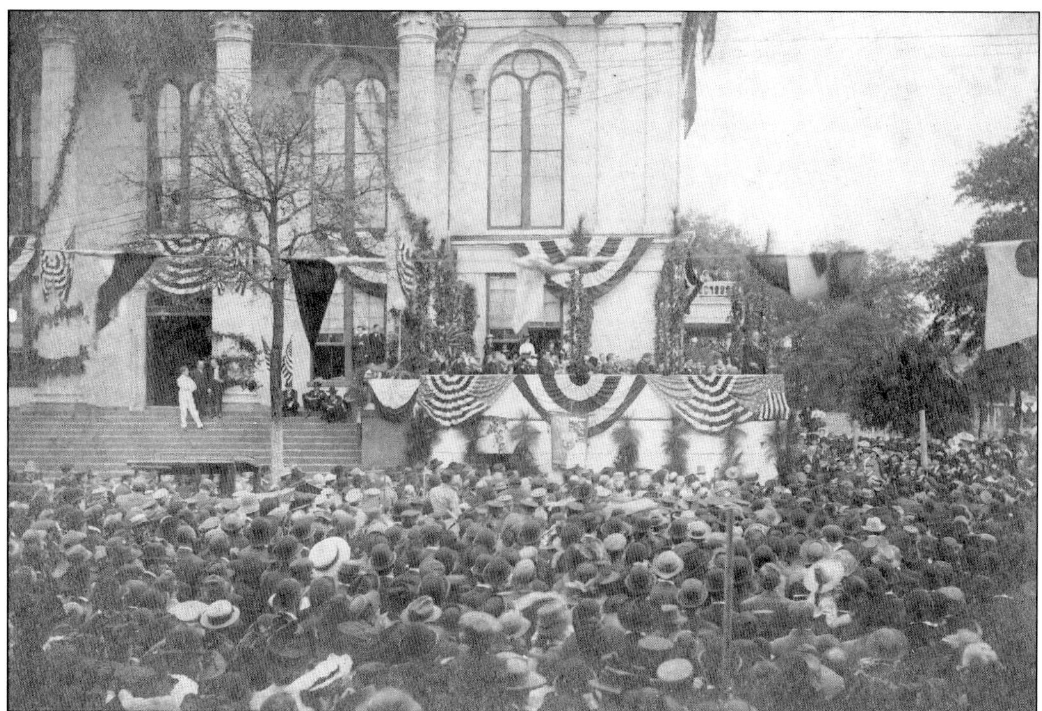

Pres. William Howard Taft spoke in Wilmington. A large platform was constructed for the occasion, and Taft made his address from the corner of it. Directly below the spot where Taft made his speech, a granite marker was installed to commemorate the occasion. It is located to the right of the main steps leading up to Wilmington City Hall. (CFM.)

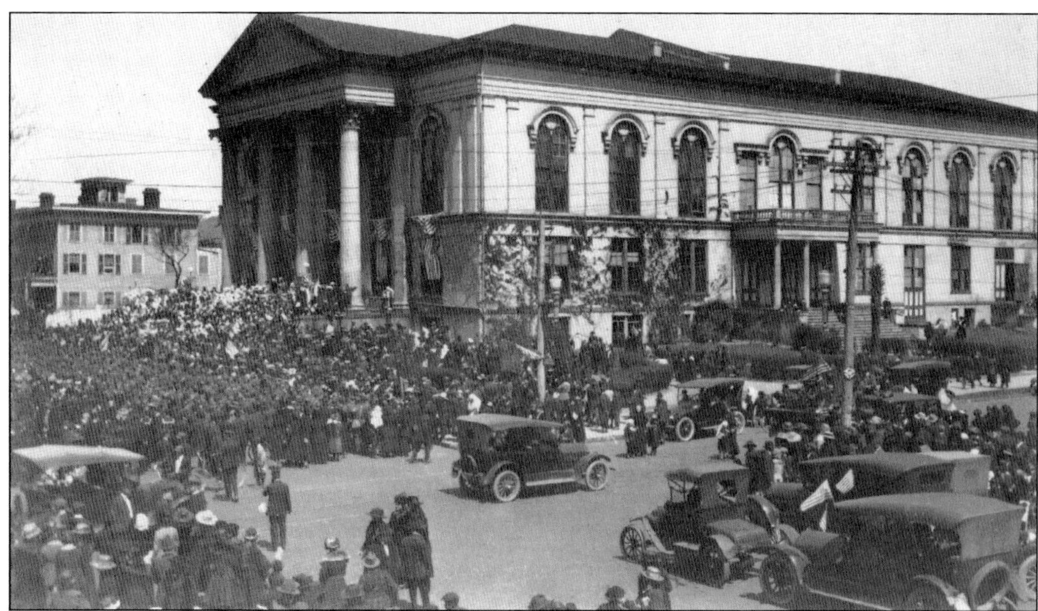

This photograph shows the citizens of Wilmington as they gather on Third Street to celebrate the end of World War I with the signing of the Armistice on November 11, 1918. (CFM.)

This is an example of the many road shows that played the Academy of Music after World War I and through the 1920s. At the end of the decade, the number of performances decreased with the decline of touring shows. The genre disappeared from many cities by the 1930s. (James H. McKoy Theatre Collection, NHCPL.)

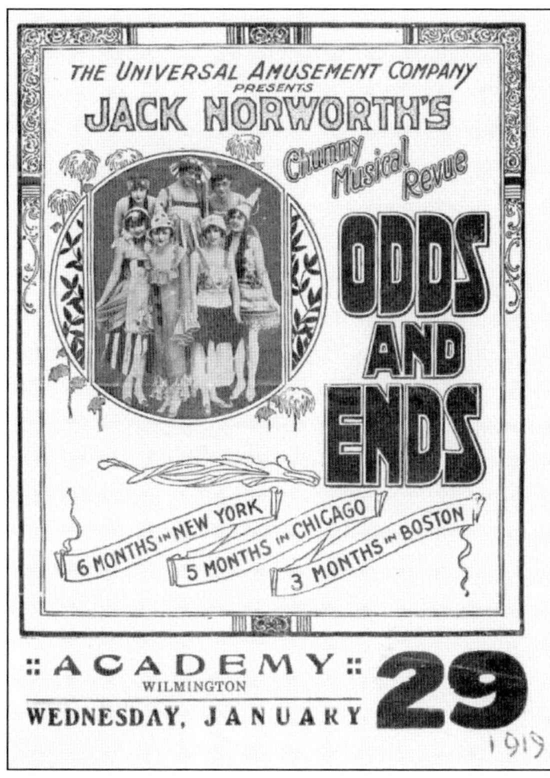

On May 24, 1922, Ethel Waters appeared on the stage of the Academy of Music as the headliner in the Black Swan Company. This is a much later photograph, taken in the 1940s. The *Wilmington Dispatch* stated, "Ethel Waters' blues numbers closed the program with her jazz masters under perfect control and rendering jazz music that is only possible with Negro artists, she backed all colored competitors who have ever appeared here completely off the boards." (University of Washington Digital Collections.)

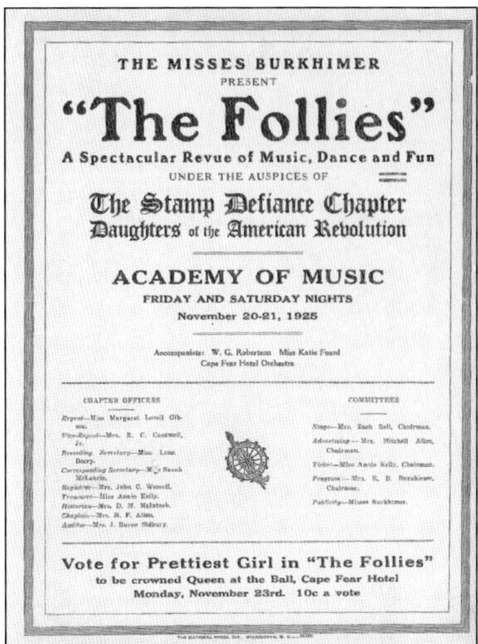

THE MISSES BURKHIMER
PRESENT
"The Follies"
A Spectacular Revue of Music, Dance and Fun
UNDER THE AUSPICES OF
The Stamp Defiance Chapter
Daughters of the American Revolution

ACADEMY OF MUSIC
FRIDAY AND SATURDAY NIGHTS
November 20-21, 1925

Accompanists: W. G. Robertson Miss Katie Feard
Cape Fear Hotel Orchestra

CHAPTER OFFICERS

Regent—Miss Margaret Lovell Gibson.
Vice-Regent—Mrs. R. C. Cantwell, Jr.
Recording Secretary—Miss Leon Beery.
Corresponding Secretary—Miss Sarah McLaurin.
Registrar—Mrs. John C. Wessell.
Treasurer—Miss Annie Kelly.
Historian—Mrs. D. M. McIntosh.
Chaplain—Mrs. M. F. Allen.
Auditor—Mrs. J. Buren Sidbury.

COMMITTEES

Stage—Mrs. Zack Bell, Chairman.
Advertising—Mrs. Mitchell Allen, Chairman.
Ticket—Miss Annie Kelly, Chairman.
Program—Mrs. E. B. Burkhimer, Chairman.
Publicity—Misses Burkhimer.

Vote for Prettiest Girl in "The Follies"
to be crowned Queen at the Ball, Cape Fear Hotel
Monday, November 23rd. 10c a vote

The 1920s saw extravagant amateur events like *The Pageant of the Lower Cape Fear* and *The Feast of the Pirates*. In 1925, the Daughters of the American Revolution produced a spectacular show called *The Follies*. The show, with over 100 players in its cast, featured the Cape Fear Hotel orchestra and scenes from *Peter Pan*, *Cleopatra's Court*, and *Madame Butterfly*. (THCPA.)

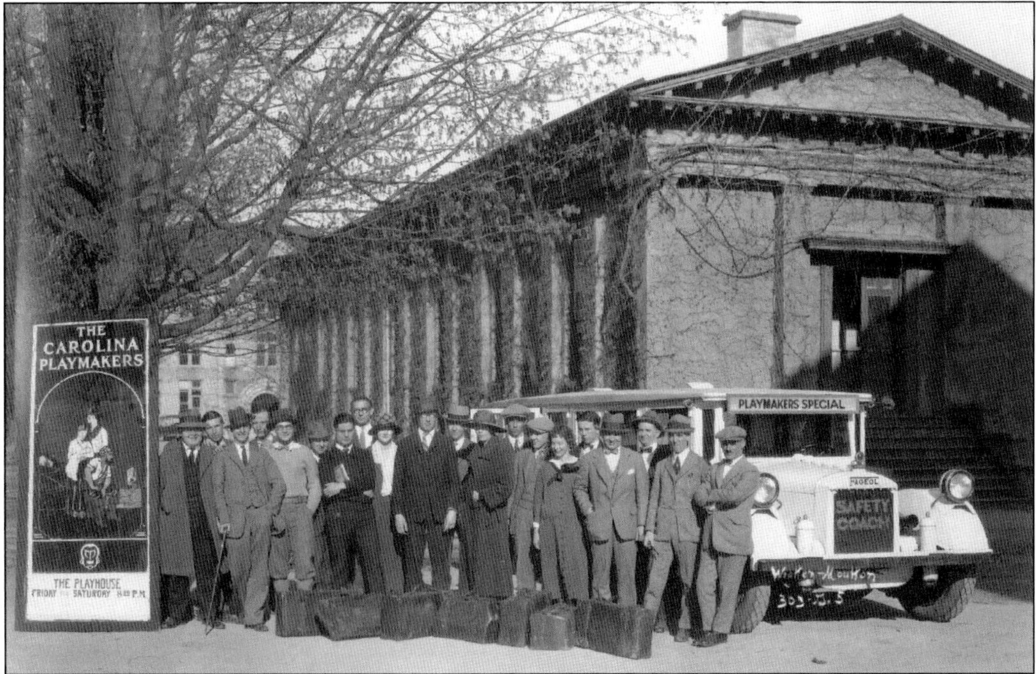

Members of the Carolina Playmakers and their tour bus are seen here in front of Playmakers Theatre. Frederick H. Koch established both the drama department and the Playmakers at the University of North Carolina at Chapel Hill in 1918. This would have a profound influence on the development of the little theatres in cities across the state, including Wilmington. By 1928, the Playmakers were touring theatrical productions, and the Academy of Music was a regular stop. (Carolina Playmakers, Louis Round Wilson Special Collections Library, University of North Carolina at Chapel Hill.)

Five

THE ARTS AND THE COMMUNITY 1928–1940

By the 1920s, competition from the movies was having an effect on the number of road shows touring the nation. In 1924, Wilmington's Victoria Theatre at Second and Market Streets was converted solely to movies. At the same time, many citizens became interested in art as opposed to entertainment. The Wilmington Art League was formed in 1923; the following year, the Thursday Morning Music Club was established. A major influence on community theatre was the establishment of the Carolina Playmakers in Chapel Hill and their touring productions. In 1928, a group of Wilmingtonians organized a little theatre group, and after a public meeting in March 1929 the Wilmington Thalian Association was reborn. In May, the association presented a production of one acts at the Academy of Music.

The same year, the Wilmington Concert Association was formed, with an initial membership of 700 people. During the 1920s, a number of classical concerts were held at the academy under the sponsorship of the Rotary Club, but the creation of the concert association began an annual season of regularly scheduled performances. Most of the early concerts were performed in Thalian Hall, which had been renamed in 1932.

In 1936, George Bailey of Howard & Wells Amusements relinquished his lease, and responsibility for upkeep passed to the city. In 1938, the city received a grant from the Public Works Administration for the renovation of Wilmington City Hall and the library, as well as improvements to Thalian Hall. When workmen were excavating for a new elevator, the sandy ground shifted and the north wall of city hall collapsed. This began a major debate on the survival of the building; many people felt it was time to demolish the 80-year-old structure and build a new city hall, library, and auditorium. After engineering studies determined that city hall was fundamentally sound, additional funds were made available from the PWA, and the project continued. The work was completed at the end of 1940, and the theatre reopened with the Thalian Association as the leaseholder.

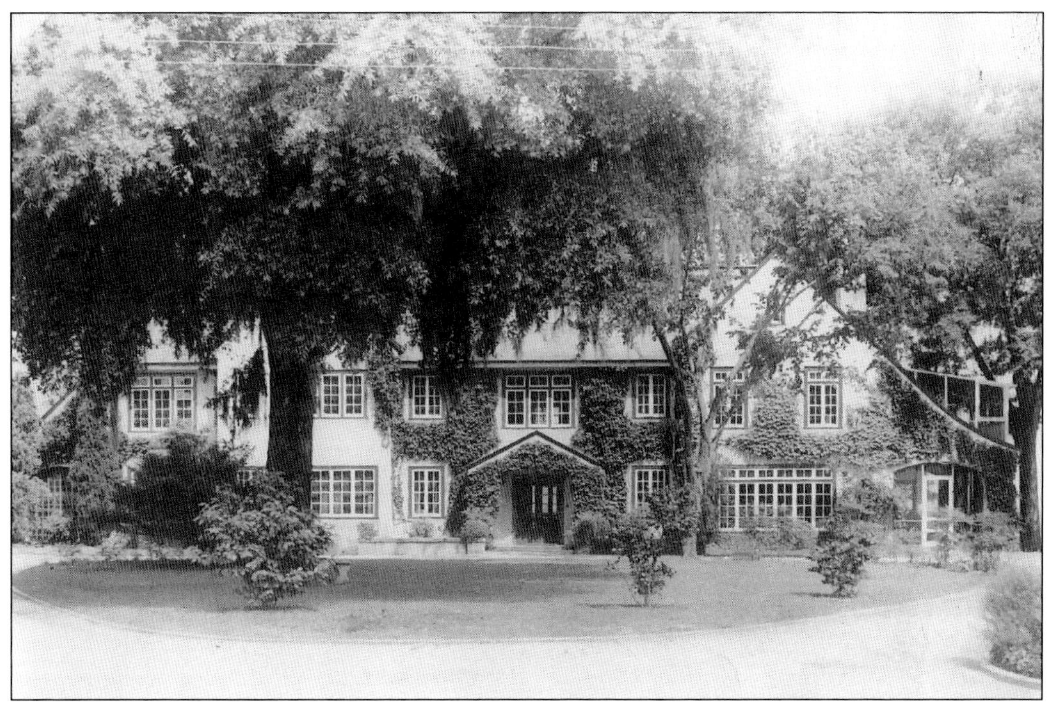

On December 18, 1928, at the Greenville Sound residence of Walter P. Sprunt, a group of Wilmingtonians presented three one-act plays to an invited audience. So much enthusiasm was generated that the next month the Little Theatre Guild of Wilmington was organized at the chamber of commerce. Following a February performance at the Guild Hall of St. James, a decision was made to ask Prof. Hubert Heffner of the Carolina Playmakers to speak and provide assistance. (Walter P. Sprunt family.)

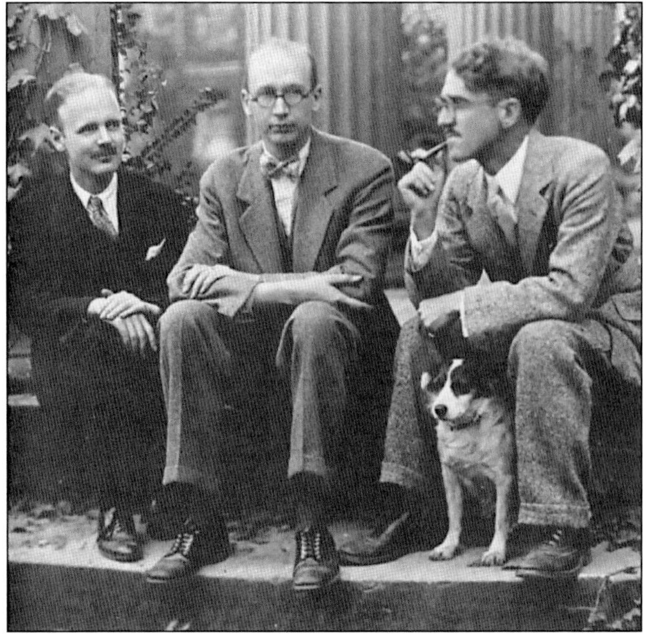

Sitting in front of Playmakers Theatre in Chapel Hill are Sam Seldon (left), Hugh Heffner (center), and Frederick Koch. On March 7, 1929, an audience of over 100 people gathered at the YWCA to hear Professor Heffner speak about the creation of a community theatre for Wilmington. He proposed the name "thalian" as preferable to "little theatre guild" in recognition of the history of antebellum Thalians. A motion was unanimously passed to adopt the name Thalian Association. (Carolina Playmakers, Louis Round Wilson Special Collections Library, University of North Carolina at Chapel Hill.)

The first performance under the name of the Thalian Association was presented not in Wilmington but in Tarboro, as seen in this program. The first performance in Wilmington was at the Academy of Music on May 31, 1929. On that evening, the association presented *The Robbery*, *The Valiant*, and *The Beau of Bath*. One of the performers was Louise Washburn, who had been instrumental in the first performance at Greenville Manor. (THCPA.)

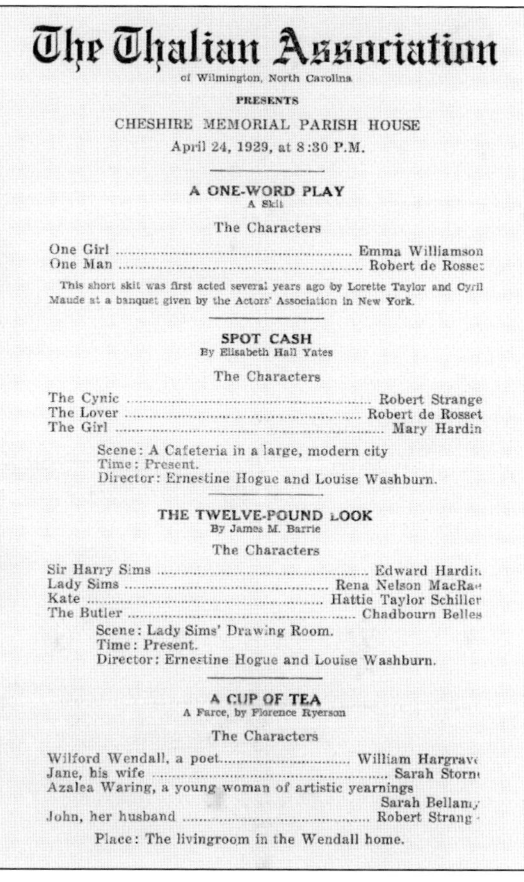

The Thalian Association

of Wilmington, North Carolina

PRESENTS

CHESHIRE MEMORIAL PARISH HOUSE

April 24, 1929, at 8:30 P.M.

A ONE-WORD PLAY

A Skit

The Characters

One Girl .... Emma Williamson
One Man .... Robert de Rosset

This short skit was first acted several years ago by Lorette Taylor and Cyril Maude at a banquet given by the Actors' Association in New York.

SPOT CASH

By Elisabeth Hall Yates

The Characters

The Cynic .... Robert Strange
The Lover .... Robert de Rosset
The Girl .... Mary Hardin

Scene: A Cafeteria in a large, modern city
Time: Present.
Director: Ernestine Hogue and Louise Washburn.

THE TWELVE-POUND LOOK

By James M. Barrie

The Characters

Sir Harry Sims .... Edward Hardin
Lady Sims .... Rena Nelson MacRae
Kate .... Hattie Taylor Schiller
The Butler .... Chadbourn Belles

Scene: Lady Sims' Drawing Room.
Time: Present.
Director: Ernestine Hogue and Louise Washburn.

A CUP OF TEA

A Farce, by Florence Ryerson

The Characters

Wilford Wendall, a poet .... William Hargrave
Jane, his wife .... Sarah Storm
Azalea Waring, a young woman of artistic yearnings .... Sarah Bellamy
John, her husband .... Robert Strange

Place: The livingroom in the Wendall home.

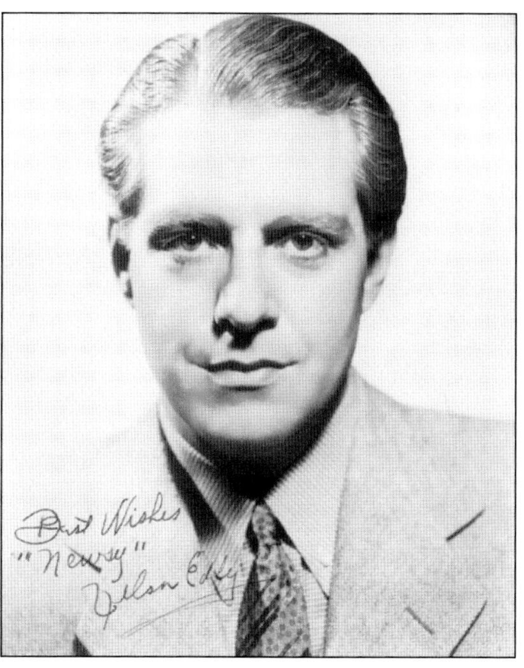

Also in 1929, the Wilmington Concert Association was organized. Most of its early concerts were given in the Academy of Music. Lawrence Tibbett of the Metropolitan Opera appeared there in the first season. Another of the early artists brought in by the group was a former resident, Nelson Eddy (pictured). When he was a young man, his father, John R. Eddy, worked for Wilmington's Tidewater Power Company. Nelson was a tenor soloist at St. James Church. (J. Willis Sayre Photographs, University of Washington Digital Collections.)

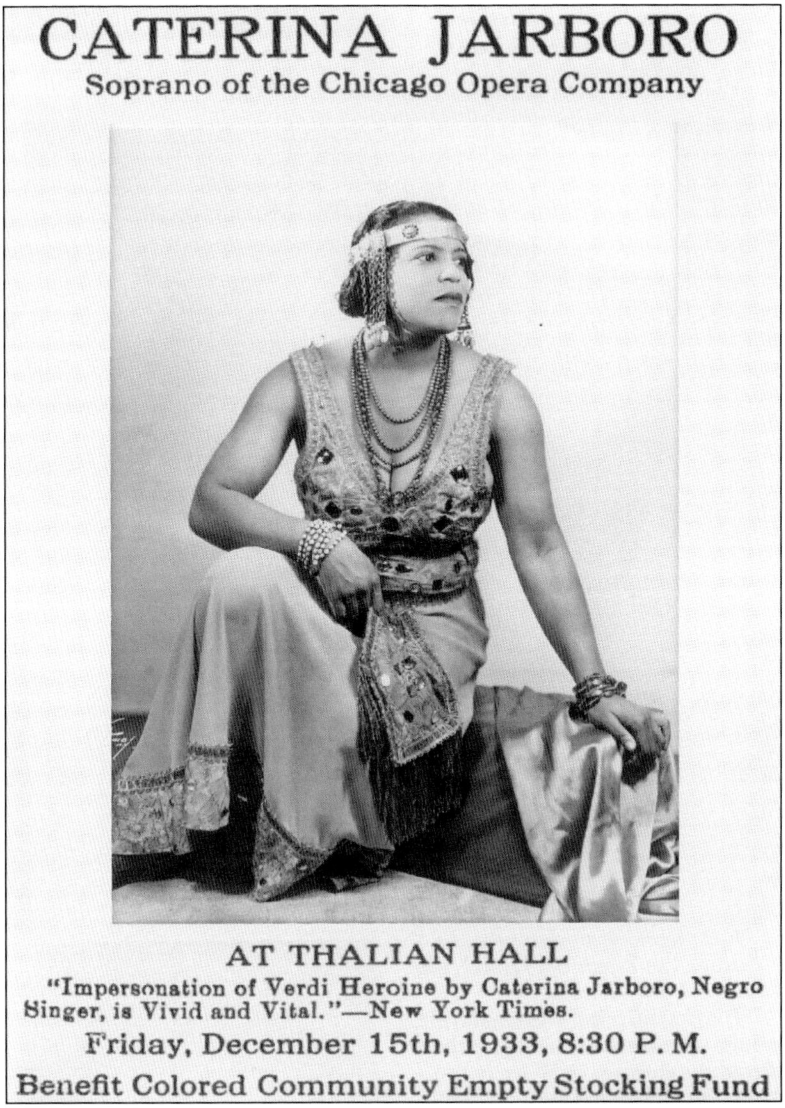

CATERINA JARBORO

Soprano of the Chicago Opera Company

AT THALIAN HALL

"Impersonation of Verdi Heroine by Caterina Jarboro, Negro Singer, is Vivid and Vital."—New York Times.

Friday, December 15th, 1933, 8:30 P. M.

Benefit Colored Community Empty Stocking Fund

Caterina Jarboro was the first African American singer to appear with an all-white opera company. She is seen here in the role of Aida when she performed with the Chicago Lyric in New York. Jarboro was born Katherine Yarborough in 1898. When she was 13, she moved to Brooklyn, New York, to live with an aunt and to study music. She also studied in Paris and Italy. Following her 1929 debut as Aida at the Milan Opera House, she made concert tours throughout Europe. (THCPA.)

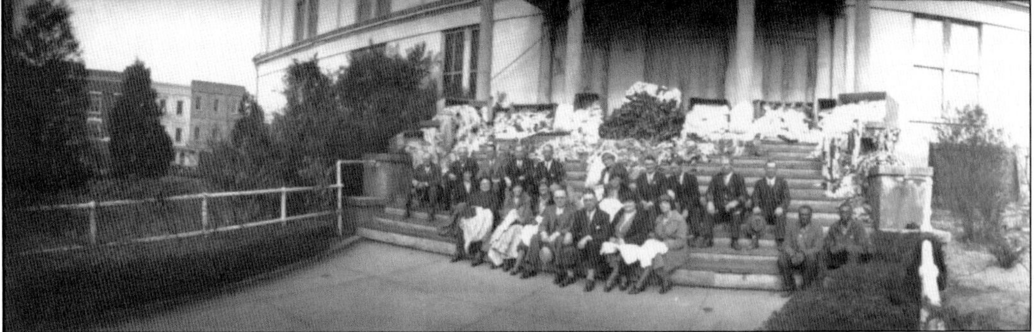

This photograph was staged on the steps of the Academy of Music. Taken in the midst of the Great Depression, the portrait documents a clothing drive to help the less fortunate. (Louis T. Moore Collection, NHCPL.)

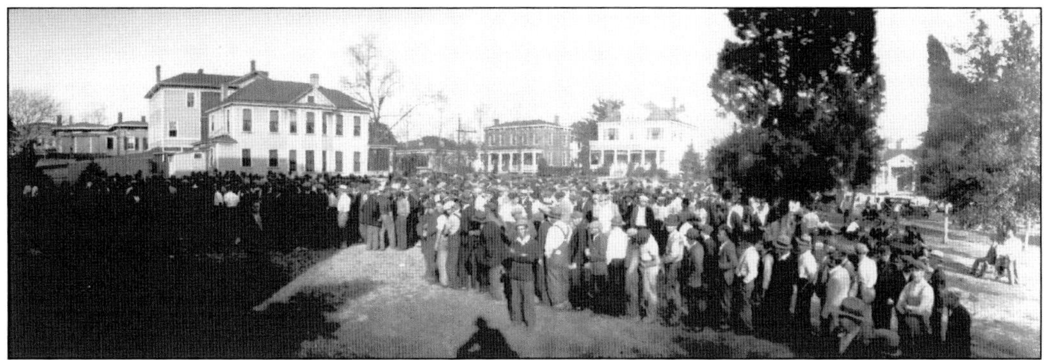

In the park behind the theatre at the corner of Fourth and Princess Streets, laborers gather to receive their wages. They were part of the public-works projects funded by the Works Progress Administration in the 1930s. (Louis T. Moore Collection, NHCPL.)

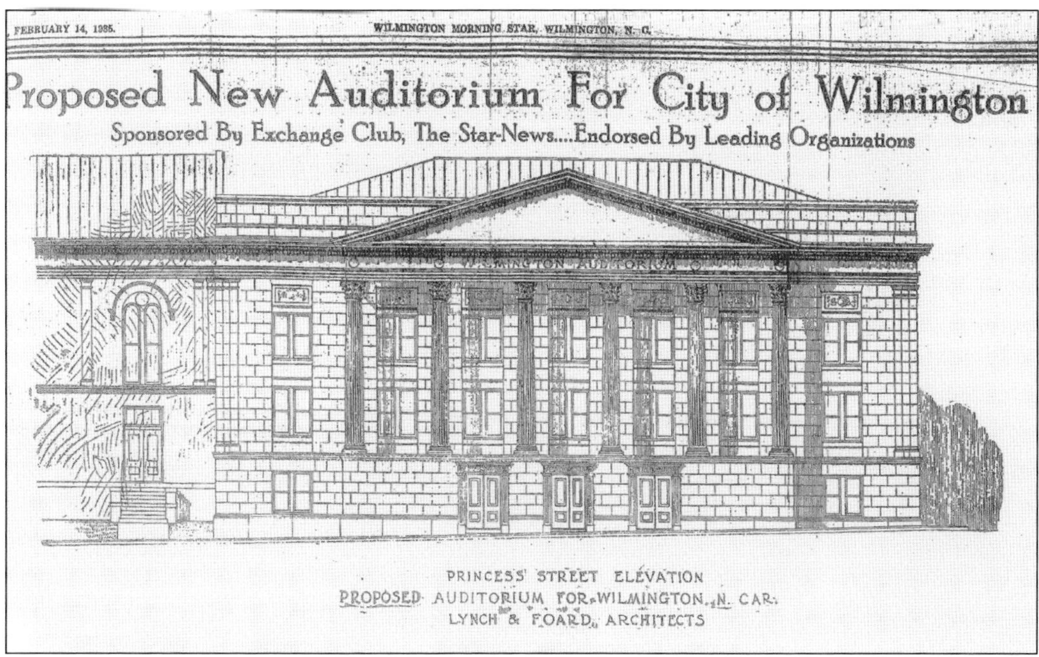

FEBRUARY 14, 1935. WILMINGTON MORNING STAR, WILMINGTON, N. C.

Proposed New Auditorium For City of Wilmington

Sponsored By Exchange Club, The Star-News....Endorsed By Leading Organizations

In 1935, a proposal was developed to build a new convention facility in the park behind the theatre. The proposed auditorium, as seen in this conjectural drawing, would seat 4,000 people. The ground floor was designed to serve as exhibition space and have seating for 2,000 people for banquets. The proposal also called for the complete rebuilding of Wilmington City Hall with modern steel construction and an elevator to the library. The total cost was $400,000. Though the new facility was never built, the city hall project was completed in 1941. (*Wilmington Star-News*, NHCPL.)

PATRONESSES:

MRS. HERBERT BLUETHENTHAL
MRS. GEORGE B. ELLIOTT
MRS. W. J. HUTAFF
MRS. GRAHAM KENAN
MRS. HUGH MACRAE
MRS. ALBERT PERRY
MRS. J. LAWRENCE SPRUNT
MRS. JESSIE KENAN WISE

COMMITTEES FOR THE PLAY

Casting:
MRS. CYRUS HOGUE

Costumes:
MRS. GEORGE KIDDER
MRS. WILLIAM PECK
MRS. WALTER STORM

Make-Up:
MISS VIRGINIA HERRIN
MISS EMMA GADE HUTAFF

Properties:
MRS. J. FRANK HACKLER
MISS MILDRED HUTAFF
MRS. ROBERT TAPP

Social:
MRS. WILLIAM BROADFOOT

Stage Manager:
J. DOUGLAS TAYLOR

Technical Director:
EVERETT HUGGINS

Properties by Courtesy of
Belk-Williams Co.
Will Rehder
Wilmington Electric Supply Co.
Wilmington Furniture Co.

THE THALIANS
PRESENT
THROUGH THE COURTESY OF THE FEDERAL THEATRE OF THE WORKS PROGRESS ADMINISTRATION

"FIRST LADY"

BY
KATHERINE DAYTON AND GEORGE S. KAUFMAN
Directed by HOWARD GANSTIER
Assisted by J. PADDISON PRETLOW

THALIAN HALL
Thursday, February 3, 1938

SCENES

ACT I
Living Room in the Secretary of State's Home, Washington, D. C. December.

ACT II
Scene 1. Cater Hibbard's Study. January.
Scene 2. The Secretary of State's Home. February.

ACT III
Again the Secretary's Home. March.

CAST

SOPHY PRESCOTT	RUTH GRAFFLIN DAVIS
CHARLES	EDWARD C. SNEAD
EMMY PAIGE	SUE BRENT CALDER
LUCY WAYNE CHASE	MARGARET V. GIBBONS
STEPHEN WAYNE	ERNEST F. BEALE
BELLE HARDWICK	RENA NELSON MACRAE
MRS. IVES	LOUISE WORTH WASHBURN
ANN FORRESTER	MARY ORMAND
A CONGRESSMAN'S WIFE	LITA L. WHITEHEAD
HER FRIEND	AGNES HARDIN CARY
THE BARONESS	GLADYS PROCTOR
SENOR ORTEGA	HENRY J. MACMILLAN
MR. CHANG	W. L. BURKHEIMER
HIS LADY	KATHERINE LANEY
A GENERAL	WILLIAM VANDYKE OCHS
MRS. CREEVY	MARGARET HOLT ROBERTSON
MRS. DAVENPORT	MARGARET HERRING
SENATOR KEANE	DAVID SINCLAIR
TOM HARDWICK	WILLIAM G. ROBERTSON
IRENE HIBBARD	ERNESTINE L. HOGUE
BLEEKER	CHARLES HOPKINS
CARTER HIBBARD	MORTIMER GLOVER
GEORGE MASON	J. FRANK HACKLER
ELLSWORTH T. GANNING	W. L. HUMPHREY
JASON FLEMING	ROBERT F. FOSTER
HERBERT SEDGWICK	H. EDMUND RODGERS

GUESTS AT THE RECEPTION, BUTLERS, ETC.

GERALDINE BRADBURY	EMMA WILLIAMSON
ELIZABETH BRIDGERS	ROSEMARY YOUNG
BELLE DUFFY	WALLACE BARBER
MONIMIA MACRAE	JOHN HOGGARD
ALICE OCHS	WILLIAM PECK, SR.
ALICE PECK	WILLIAM ROBERTSON, JR.

In 1938, through the WPA Federal Theatre project, the Thalian Association secured one of its first professional directors, Howard Ganstier. His initial production in Thalian Hall was *First Lady*, a comedy about powerful women in politics. Ganstier would spend the rest of his life in Wilmington, and he directed many theatrical productions. (THCPA.)

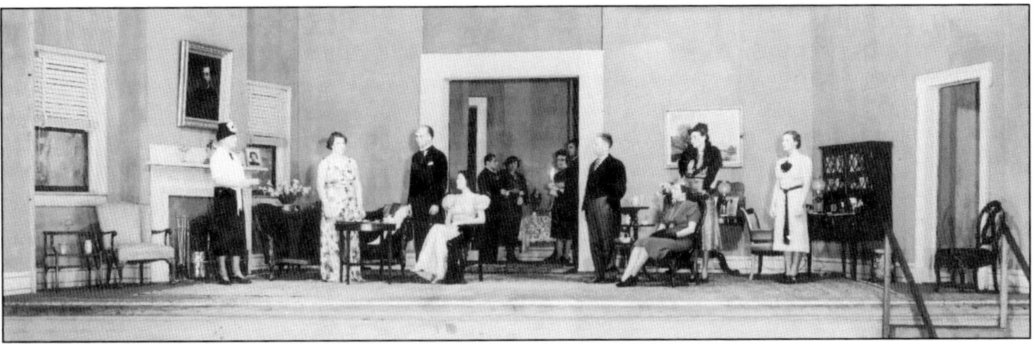

The production of *First Lady* had a large cast, with 25 speaking roles. The scene in this photograph on the Thalian Hall stage depicts the Washington home of the secretary of state. The players are, from left to right, Rena McRae, Margaret V. Gibbons, Ernest F. Beale, Sue Brent Calder, W.L. Burkeimer, Geraldine Bradbury, Belle Duffy, John Hoggard, William G. Robertson, Louise Washborn, Mary Ormand, and Ruth Grafflin Davis. (THCPA.)

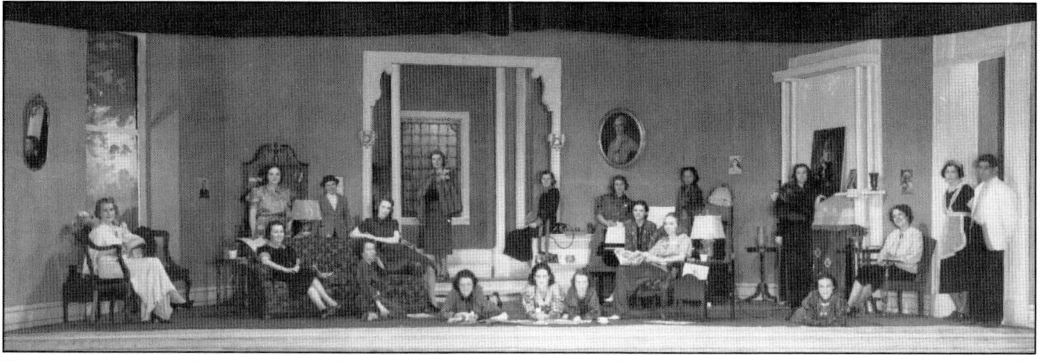

For his second production in the historic theatre, Ganstier chose *Stage Door*, the comedy about single girls in show business. Once again, a huge cast was assembled for the production, as can be seen in the program for the production in this publicity shot on the Thalian Hall stage. (THCPA.)

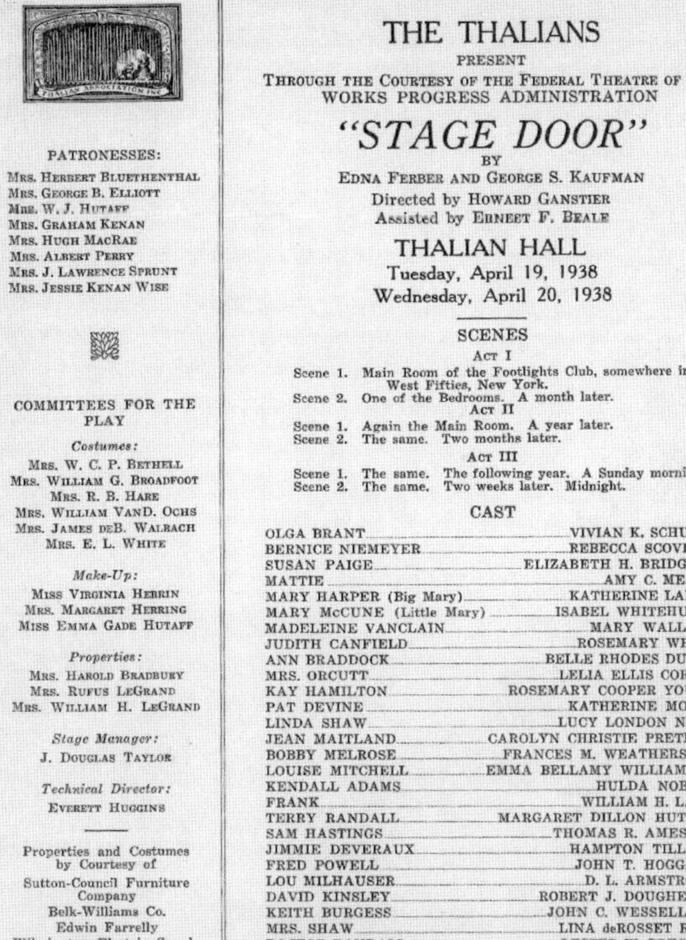

PATRONESSES:

MRS. HERBERT BLUETHENTHAL
MRS. GEORGE B. ELLIOTT
MRS. W. J. HUTAFF
MRS. GRAHAM KENAN
MRS. HUGH MACRAE
MRS. ALBERT PERRY
MRS. J. LAWRENCE SPRUNT
MRS. JESSIE KENAN WISE

COMMITTEES FOR THE PLAY

Costumes:
MRS. W. C. P. BETHELL
MRS. WILLIAM G. BROADFOOT
MRS. R. B. HARE
MRS. WILLIAM VAND. OCHS
MRS. JAMES DEB. WALBACH
MRS. E. L. WHITE

Make-Up:
MISS VIRGINIA HERRIN
MRS. MARGARET HERRING
MISS EMMA GADE HUTAFF

Properties:
MRS. HAROLD BRADBURY
MRS. RUFUS LEGRAND
MRS. WILLIAM H. LEGRAND

Stage Manager:
J. DOUGLAS TAYLOR

Technical Director:
EVERETT HUGGINS

Properties and Costumes by Courtesy of
Sutton-Council Furniture Company
Belk-Williams Co.
Edwin Farrelly
Wilmington Electric Supply Company

THE THALIANS
PRESENT
THROUGH THE COURTESY OF THE FEDERAL THEATRE OF THE WORKS PROGRESS ADMINISTRATION

"STAGE DOOR"
BY
EDNA FERBER AND GEORGE S. KAUFMAN
Directed by HOWARD GANSTIER
Assisted by ERNEST F. BEALE

THALIAN HALL
Tuesday, April 19, 1938
Wednesday, April 20, 1938

SCENES

ACT I
Scene 1. Main Room of the Footlights Club, somewhere in the West Fifties, New York.
Scene 2. One of the Bedrooms. A month later.

ACT II
Scene 1. Again the Main Room. A year later.
Scene 2. The same. Two months later.

ACT III
Scene 1. The same. The following year. A Sunday morning.
Scene 2. The same. Two weeks later. Midnight.

CAST

OLGA BRANT	VIVIAN K. SCHULTZ
BERNICE NIEMEYER	REBECCA SCOVILLE
SUSAN PAIGE	ELIZABETH H. BRIDGERS
MATTIE	AMY C. MEADE
MARY HARPER (Big Mary)	KATHERINE LANEY
MARY McCUNE (Little Mary)	ISABEL WHITEHURST
MADELEINE VANCLAIN	MARY WALLACE
JUDITH CANFIELD	ROSEMARY WHITE
ANN BRADDOCK	BELLE RHODES DUFFY
MRS. ORCUTT	LELIA ELLIS CORBIN
KAY HAMILTON	ROSEMARY COOPER YOUNG
PAT DEVINE	KATHERINE MORSE
LINDA SHAW	LUCY LONDON NASH
JEAN MAITLAND	CAROLYN CHRISTIE PRETLOW
BOBBY MELROSE	FRANCES M. WEATHERSBEE
LOUISE MITCHELL	EMMA BELLAMY WILLIAMSON
KENDALL ADAMS	HULDA NOBLES
FRANK	WILLIAM H. LAND
TERRY RANDALL	MARGARET DILLON HUTAFF
SAM HASTINGS	THOMAS R. AMES, JR.
JIMMIE DEVERAUX	HAMPTON TILLERY
FRED POWELL	JOHN T. HOGGARD
LOU MILHAUSER	D. L. ARMSTRONG
DAVID KINSLEY	ROBERT J. DOUGHERTY
KEITH BURGESS	JOHN C. WESSELL, JR.
MRS. SHAW	LINA deROSSET ROSS
DOCTOR RANDALL	LESTER W. PRESTON
ELLEN FENWICK	MARGARET McCLAMMY
TONY GILLETTE	ISABEL JAMES
LARRY WESTCOTT	ADDISON HEWLETT, JR.
BILLY	CLAUDE HOWELL
ADOLPH GRETZL	HARRY M. SOLOMON

One of the cast members of *Stage Door* was Claude Howell, acclaimed North Carolina artist and founder of the UNCW art department. In his 1938 journal, he wrote, "The play was a great success and everyone was elated. Mr. Edmund Rogers, an elderly dignified lawyer, was working backstage and had a little too much to drink perhaps, for he kept saying he had to 'sift sheenery.' When Elizabeth Bridgers went by he coyly pinched her on the fanny." (THCPA.)

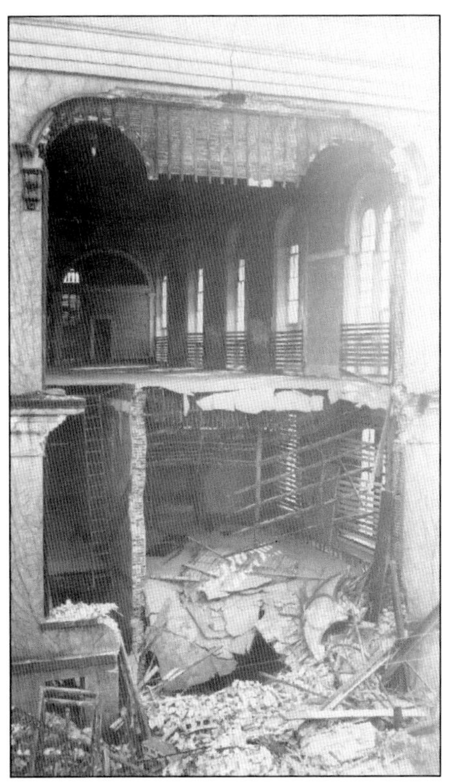

In 1938, the city received a grant from the Public Works Administration for the renovation of city offices and the library as well as structural work on the stage of Thalian Hall. During the excavation for the new elevator, the sand hill underneath the building shifted, causing the north wall of Wilmington City Hall to collapse. The result led to a public debate on the structural integrity of the building. (THCPA.)

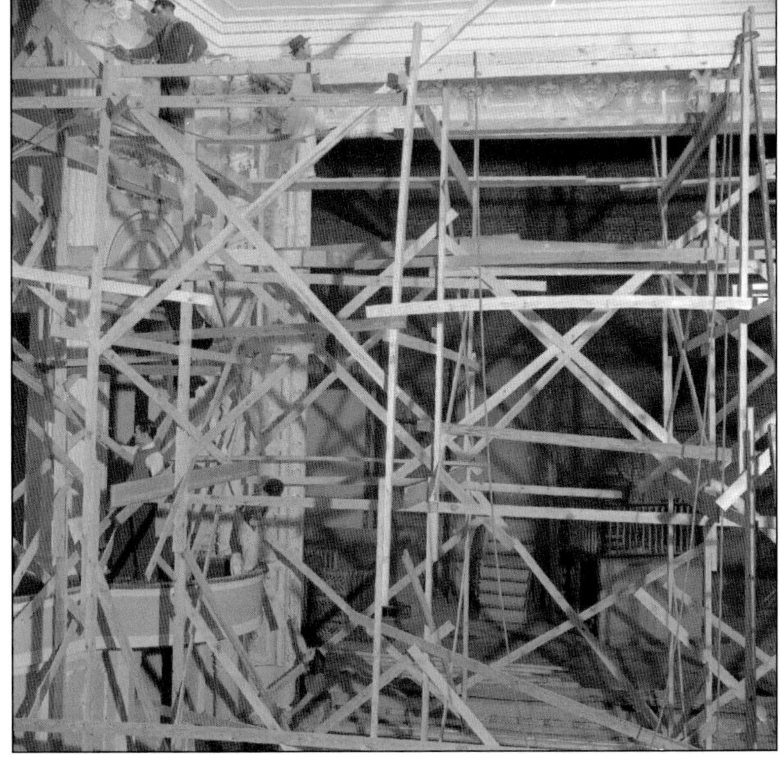

After much study, it was decided to continue the project. Additional funds were provided by the PWA. The total project, including city funds, cost $145,000. The interior of the theatre was painted according to a decorating scheme by Henry MacMillan. The walls were painted gray, and the proscenium and the balconies were painted white and pink. The plaster features were highlighted in gold paint. (CFM.)

Six

Saved, Condemned, Saved, and Celebrated 1940–1963

Thalian Hall reopened in March 1941 with a production of *Margin of Error.* At the same time, the US Army was completing the construction of Camp Davis for 20,000 soldiers at nearby Holly Ridge. To serve these men when in Wilmington on leave, a building known as the Woodrow Wilson Hut was constructed at the rear of Thalian Hall. Opened in June 1941, it has been credited with being the first recreation center built for enlisted men in the nation. In Thalian Hall, there were concerts, sporting events, and plays entertaining a community that had swelled in population due to the war effort. As part of a campaign to sell war bonds, *This Ain't the Army* was presented in Thalian Hall with a cast of soldiers from Camp Davis.

Following the war, the pace slowed down, and the Thalian Association announced three productions for the 1945–1946 season. However, by the end of that season, structural problems with the balconies had been discovered by the city's inspectors, and the building was condemned. In 1946, the entrances to the balconies were boarded up, and the building was closed.

With estimates as high as $200,000, the future of Thalian Hall became caught up in a greater discussion about building a new civic auditorium and convention center. Many members of the Thalian Association lobbied the city for support. During those years, theatre productions and concert performances moved to New Hanover High School. Through the efforts of Henry B. McKoy and Thomas H. Wright Sr., an engineering study was developed. It determined that the building was essentially sound. In 1949, a $50,000 citywide bond issue was passed by the voters. After two years of construction, the theatre reopened in 1952, and productions resumed. In 1958, the theatre's centennial was celebrated with a series of vignettes saluting its history.

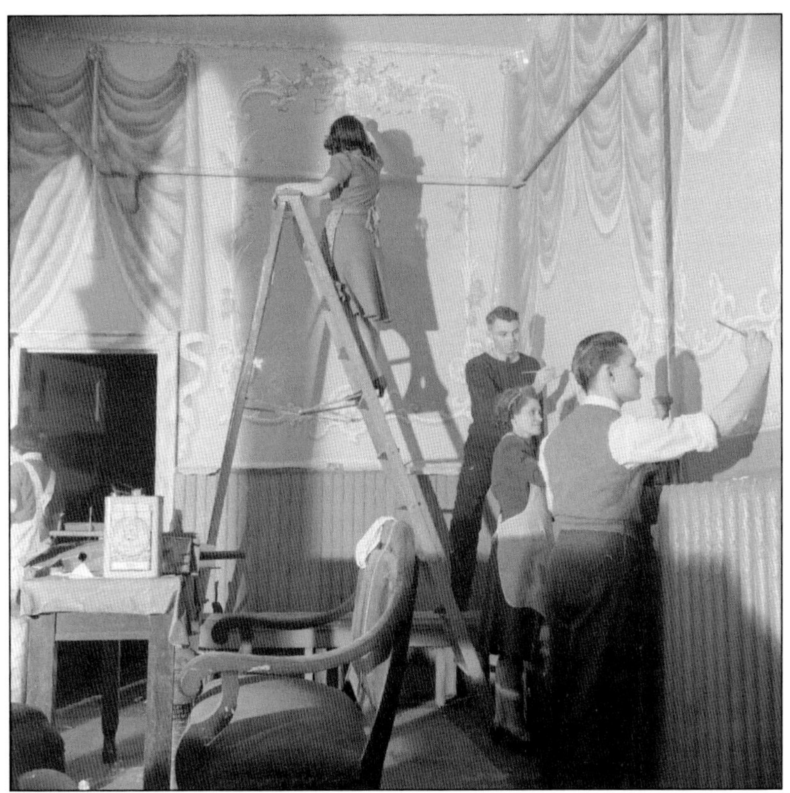

During the 1939–1941 renovation of city hall and the theatre, the Thalian Association undertook the repainting of the auditorium. Under the direction of Henry MacMillan, a series of Victorian murals were designed and painted on the walls of the lobby by members of the Wilmington Art Museum. Shown here are, from left to right, Elizabeth Bridgers, Helen MacMillan, Henry MacMillan, Ruth Willoughby, and William Turner. (CFM.)

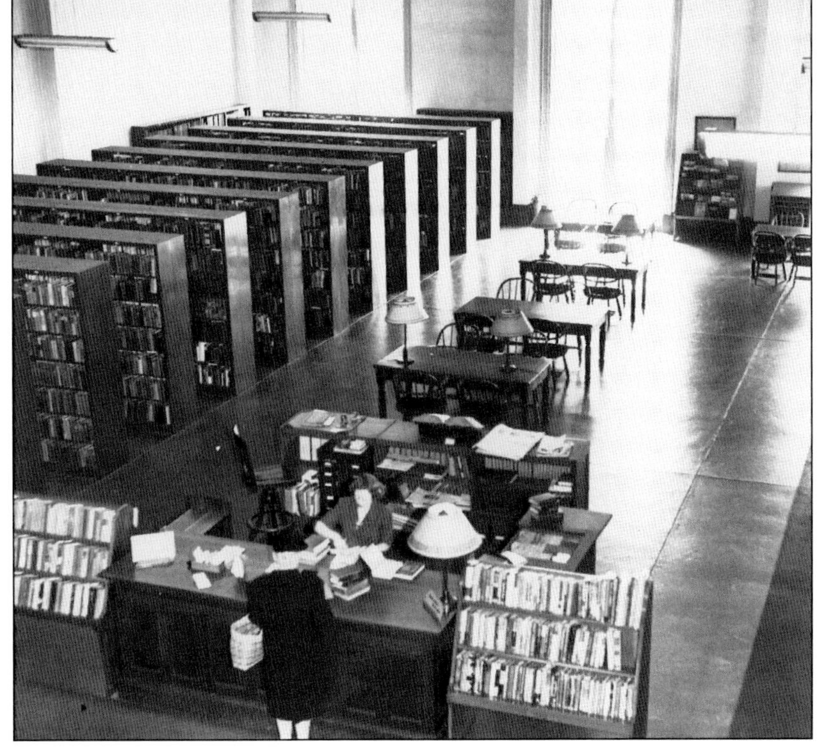

The city hall renovation was completed by the end of 1940. This photograph looks south toward Princess Street. The Wilmington Public Library would continue to occupy the second floor of city hall until 1956, when it was relocated to the Wilmington Light Infantry Building, next to First Baptist Church on Market Street. (NHCPL.)

On December 3, 1943, the British ambassador to the United States, Viscount Halifax, reviewed a parade of 350 British anti-aircraft troops from a flag-draped stand on the steps of Wilmington City Hall. He is shown here on the platform at center. Mayor Bruce Cameron is left of Halifax. Also on the stand are the commanding officers of Camp Lejeune and Camp Davis. (CFM.)

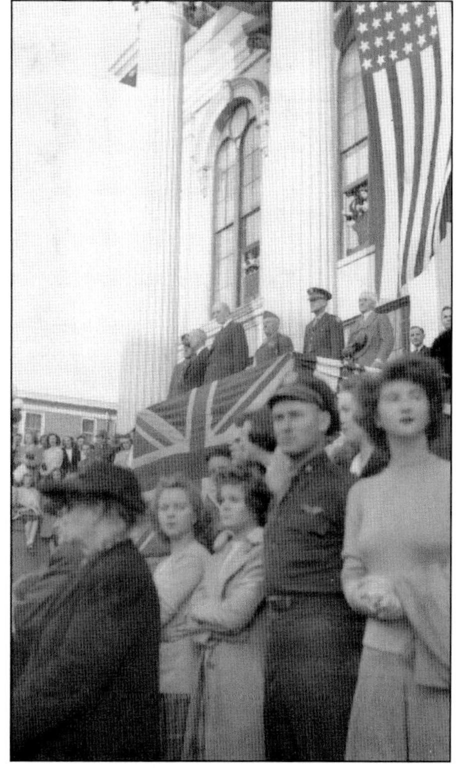

In the summer of 1943, a number of people turned out to view a group of British soldiers as they marched in front of city hall. The *Star-News* described them as "attired in their summer shorts, cocky overseas caps, and substantial socks." (CFM.)

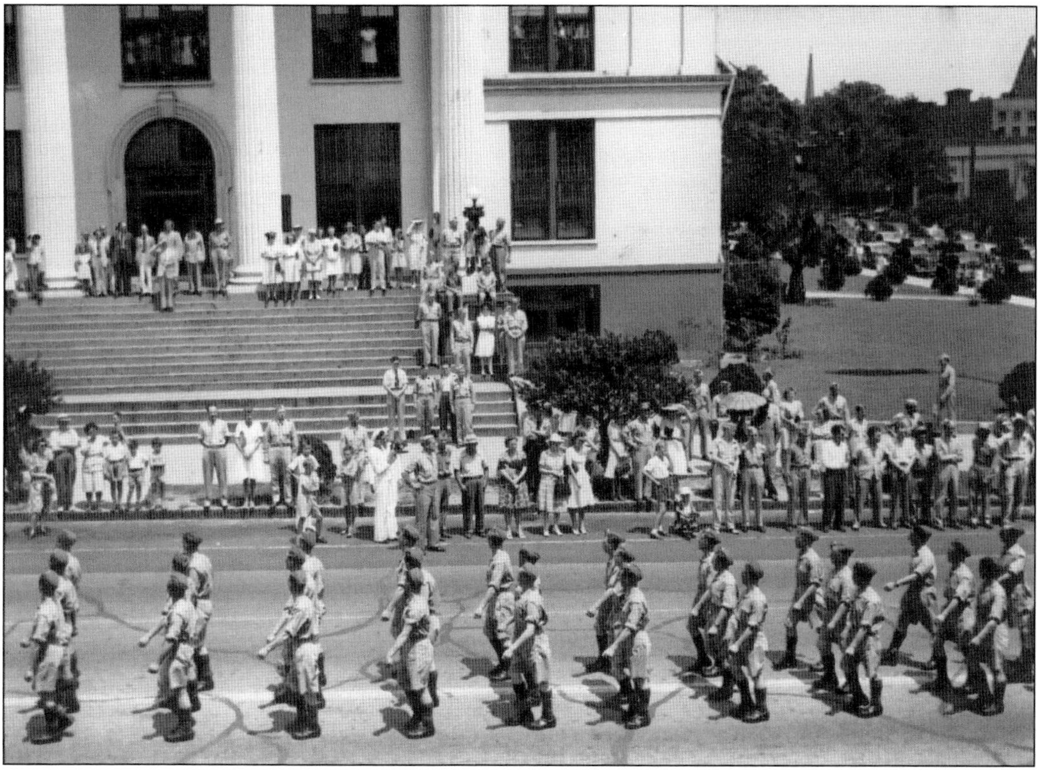

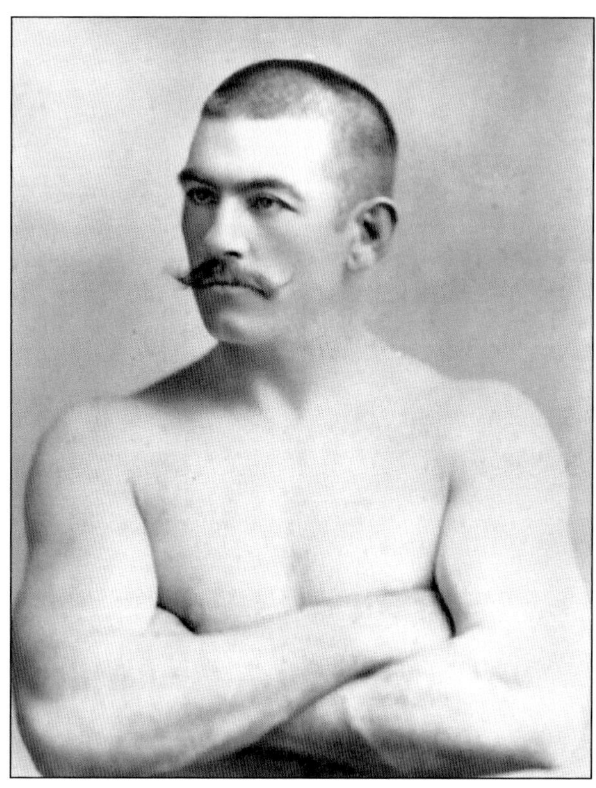

Athletes have been performing in Thalian Hall since 1858, when Charles Blondin, famous for his tightrope walk across Niagara Falls, ascended a rope from the theatre's stage to the ceiling. John L. Sullivan (pictured), the world-champion boxer, appeared at the Wilmington Opera House in 1891. His theatrical company performed *Honest Hearts and Willing Hands*. The action included a boxing match on stage.

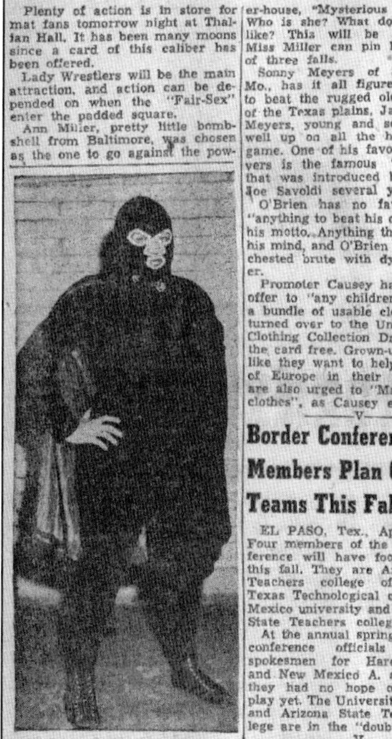

Thalian Card Dubbed Action In The Rough

Plenty of action is in store for mat fans tomorrow night at Thalian Hall. It has been many moons since a card of this caliber has been offered.

Lady Wrestlers will be the main attraction, and action can be depended on when the "Fair-Sex" enter the padded square.

Ann Miller, pretty little bombshell from Baltimore, was chosen as the one to go against the power-house, "Mysterious Miss Red". Who is she? What does she look like? This will be answered if Miss Miller can pin her two out of three falls.

Sonny Meyers of St. Joseph, Mo., has it all figured out, how to beat the rugged old war-horse of the Texas plains, Jack O'Brien. Meyers, young and scientific, is well up on all the holds of the game. One of his favorite maneuvers is the famous "drop-kick", that was introduced by Jumping Joe Savoldi several years ago.

O'Brien has no favorite hold, "anything to beat his opponent" is his motto. Anything that comes to his mind, and O'Brien is a barrell-chested brute with dynamic power.

Promoter Causey has issued an offer to "any children who bring a bundle of usable clothing to be turned over to the United Nations Clothing Collection Drive" to see the card free. Grown-ups who feel like they want to help the people of Europe in their predicament are also urged to "Make 'wid 'de clothes", as Causey expressed it.

—V—

'The Lady in Red'

Border Conference Members Plan Grid Teams This Fall

EL PASO, Tex., April 12—(AP)—Four members of the Border conference will have football teams this fall. They are Arizona State Teachers college of Flagstaff, Texas Technological college, New Mexico university and West Texas State Teachers college.

At the annual spring meeting of conference officials yesterday spokesmen for Hardin-Simmons and New Mexico A. and M. said they had no hope of resuming play yet. The University of Arizona and Arizona State Teachers college are in the "doubtful" class.

—V—

This *Wilmington Star-News* article from April 12, 1945, announces a "lady wrestling" match on the Thalian Hall stage between Ann Miller, the "Bombshell from Baltimore," and "Mysterious Miss Red" (pictured). Sporting events at Thalian Hall became popular in the 1920s and continued through World War II. The last major sports figure to appear on the Thalian Hall stage was Wilmington's Michael Jordan, who was awarded the key to the city in 1984 after the ceremony was rained out at Waterfront Park. (NHCPL.)

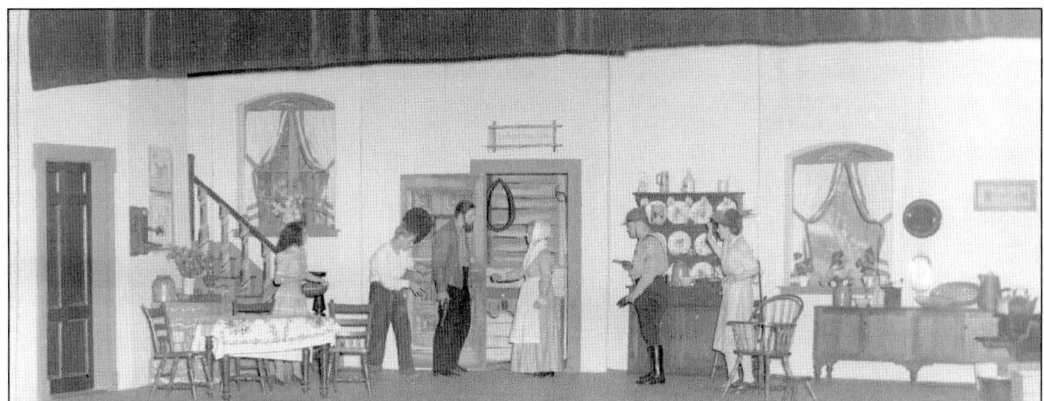

Shown here is a 1944 production of *Papa Is All,* a folk play set in Pennsylvania Dutch Country. The show was first presented for soldiers at the Camp Davis Hospital in Holly Ridge and then in Thalian Hall. The cast included, from left to right, Dorothy R. Arthur, Jimmy Burns, Charles Keane, Hester Donnelly, Thomas B. Hughes, and Elizabeth Williams. Hughes and Keen were in the military but had been film actors before coming to Wilmington. (THCPA.)

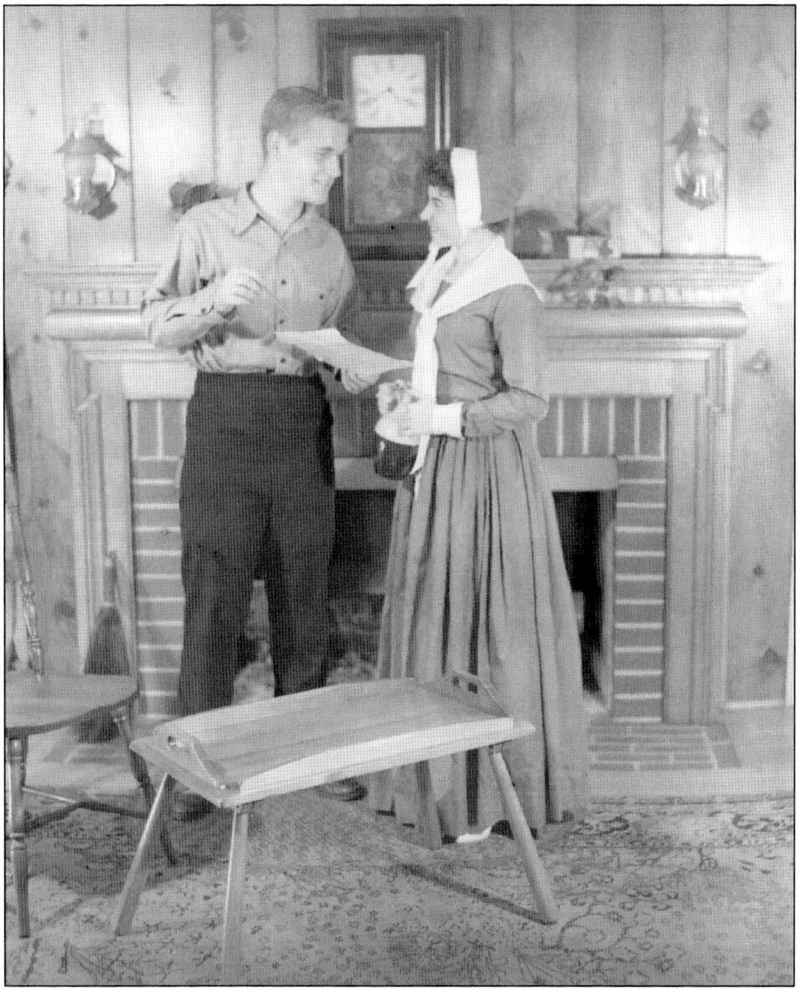

This promotional photograph for *Papa Is All* shows Jimmy Burns and Hester Donnelly. Burns would go on to study drama at Northwestern University. After graduation, he went into the military. During that time, he became a protégé of Mary Pickford. After performing in New York in several shows, he eventually returned to Wilmington and hosted a daily talk show on WECT-TV. (THCPA.)

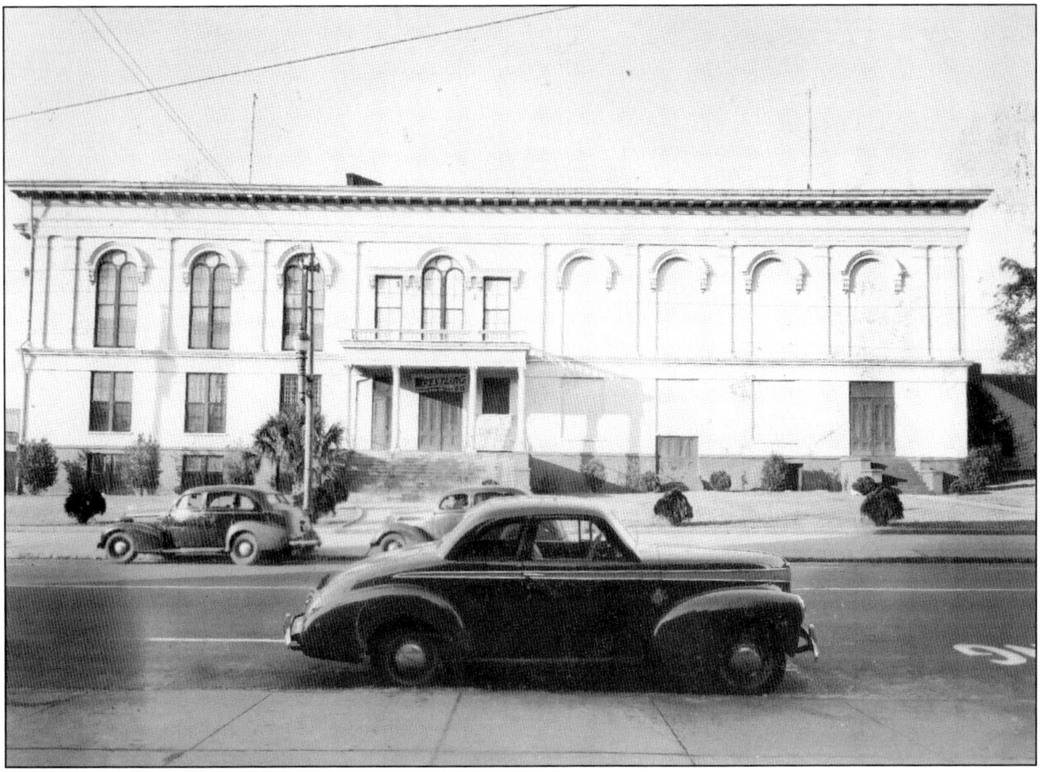

On February 21 and 22, 1946, the Thalian Association presented *The Doughgirls*, its last production on the historic stage for the next five years. The balcony and gallery had just been condemned, and the audience was only allowed on the lower floor. (THCPA.)

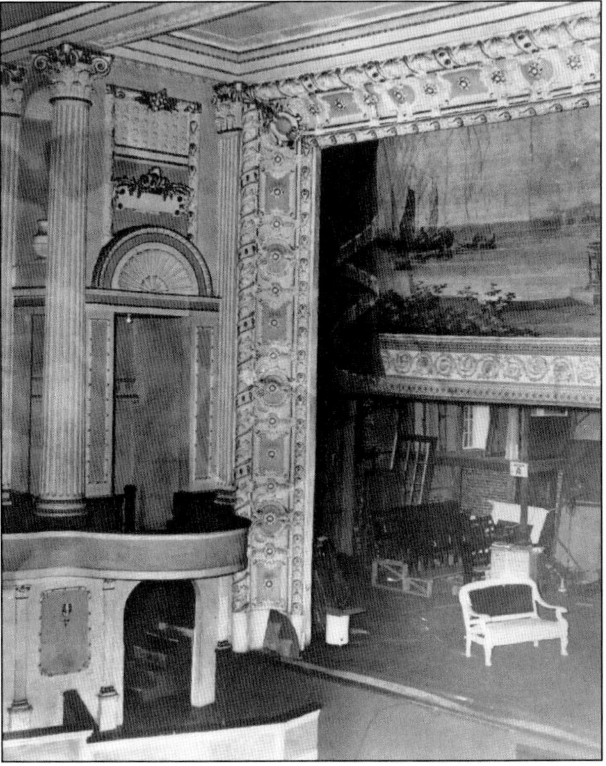

This 1947 photograph shows the stage after the theatre was closed. Also shown here is the original front curtain, which had served as a front border for theatrical productions. The theatre remained closed for six years, and productions moved to New Hanover High School. (THCPA.)

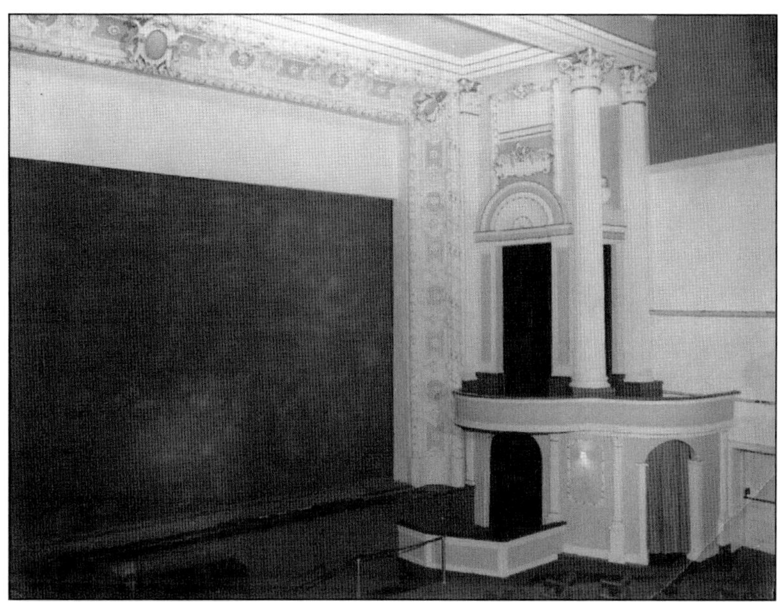

After a $50,000 city bond issue was passed in 1949, repairs began on the theatre. A major part of the renovation was the construction of a firewall separating the auditorium from the stage and the installation of new steel connections between the balconies and the outside walls. This photograph shows the interior in 1952, when the theatre reopened. (THCPA.)

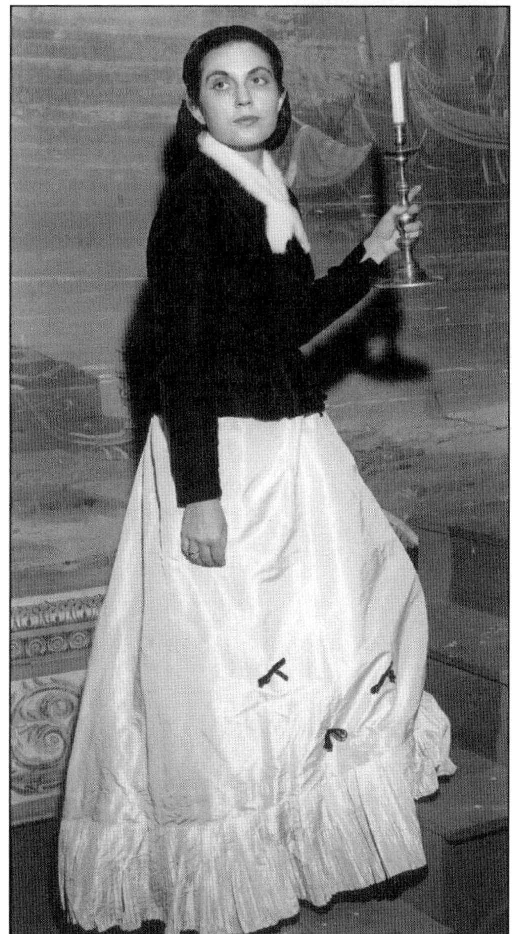

The play that opened the renovated Thalian Hall was *The Heiress*, with Betsy Pearsall in the title role. She was a former drama major who had performed in *Blithe Spirit* and *The Importance of Being Earnest*. This photograph was taken in 1958, when she reprised a scene from *The Heiress* for the Thalian Hall centennial. (THCPA.)

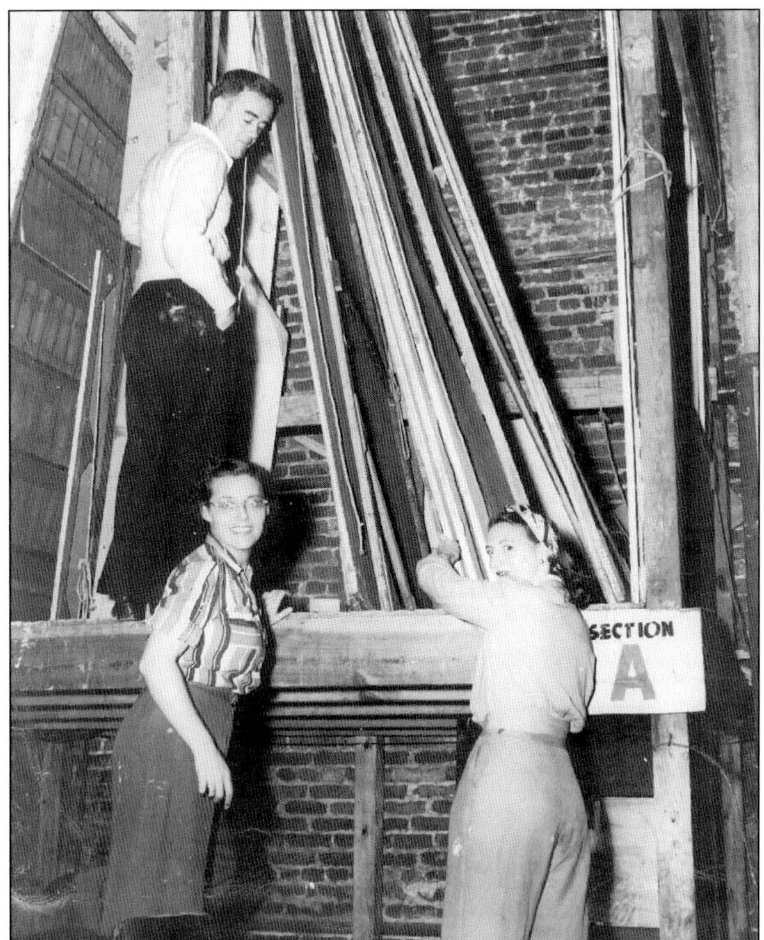

Hester Donnelly, seen here at center in 1946, designed and directed many productions. The scene dock was in a corner of the stage, built over a small winding stair that led to the downstairs dressing rooms. The sign "section A" refers to an area for seating when wrestling matches were held on the stage. Platforms with chairs would be arranged on the sides and the back wall surrounding the ring. (NHCPL.)

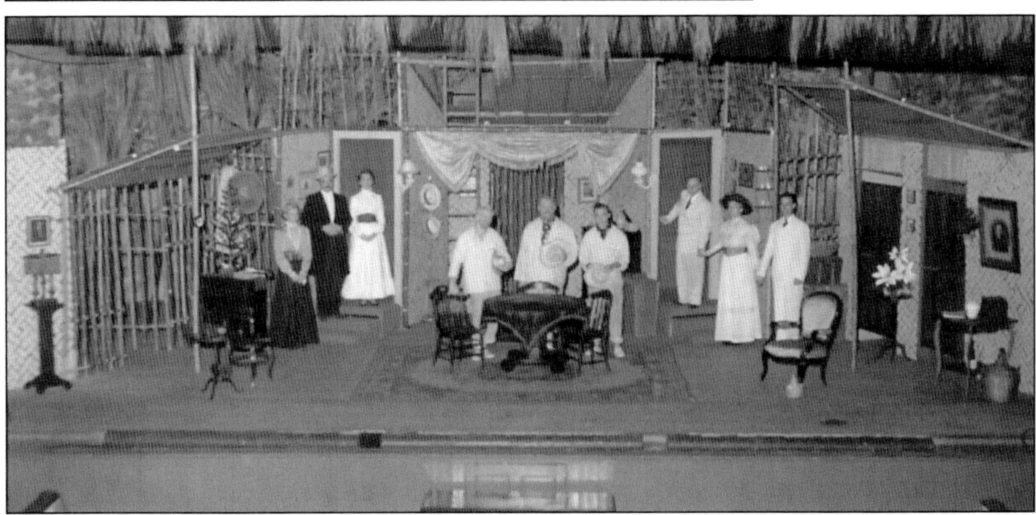

Local architects Herb McKim, Frank Ballard, and Robert Sawyer designed and built a number of sets for Thalian Association productions. A good example of their work is seen here in the play *My Three Angels*, presented for two nights in 1954. (THCPA.)

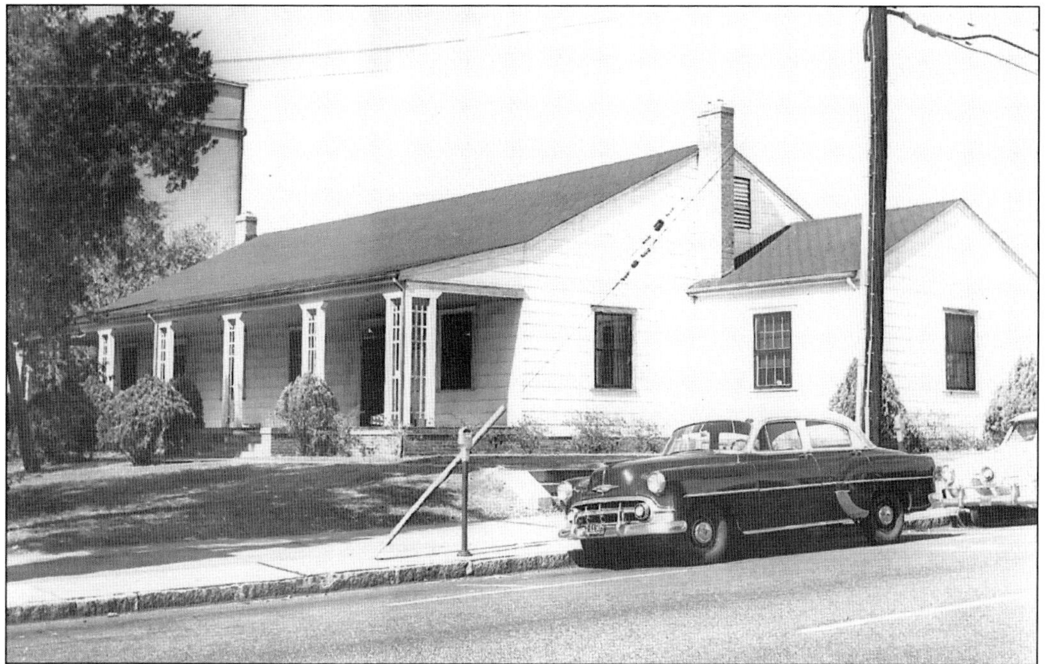

The Woodrow Wilson Hut was built in 1941 as a recreation center for enlisted men. Standing on the site of the old Meginney Hall, directly behind Thalian Hall, it contained an auditorium, reading room, and ladies lounge. After the war, it became the chamber of commerce building and the first office for the Azalea Festival. (NHCPL.)

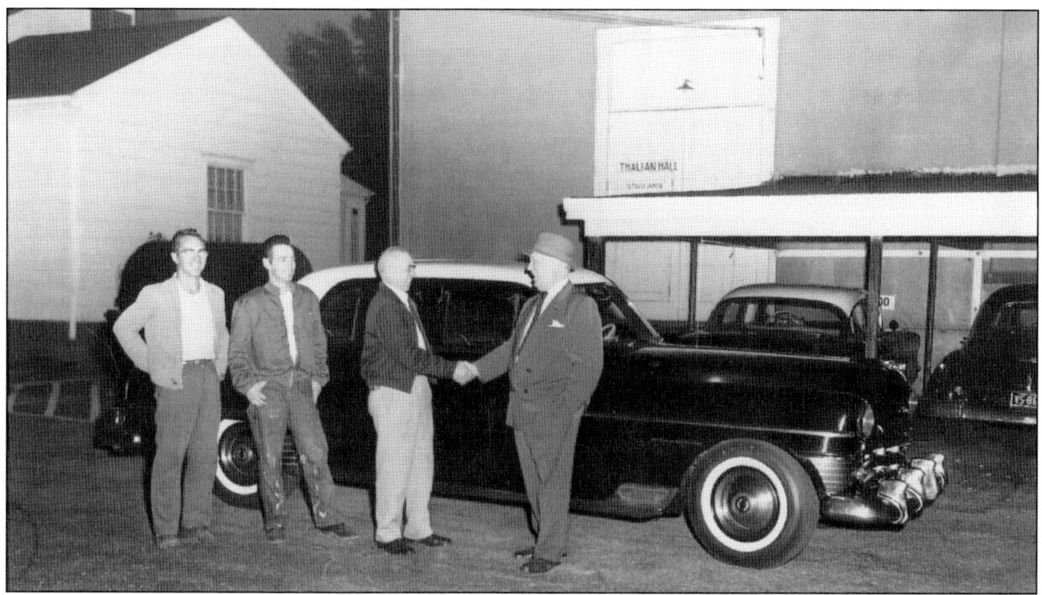

Standing to the right of the stage door is J.E.L. "Hi Buddy" Wade, one of Wilmington's most colorful mayors. As commissioner of public works in the 1930s, he was instrumental in the procuring of funds from the Public Works Administration for the renovation of Wilmington City Hall and Thalian Hall. (CFM.)

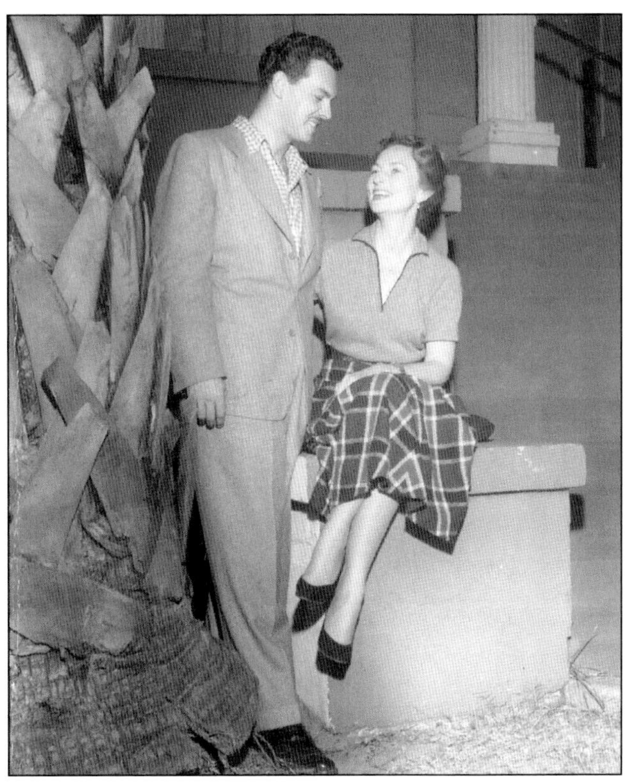

Agnes Moorehead and her company manager, Patrick Waltz, pose outside the entrance steps to Thalian Hall, where she appeared in *That Fabulous Redhead* on October 28, 1954. Moorehead was the first artist booked under a program spearheaded by James H. McKoy designed to present professional theatre personalities in addition to the regular Thalian season. (THCPA.)

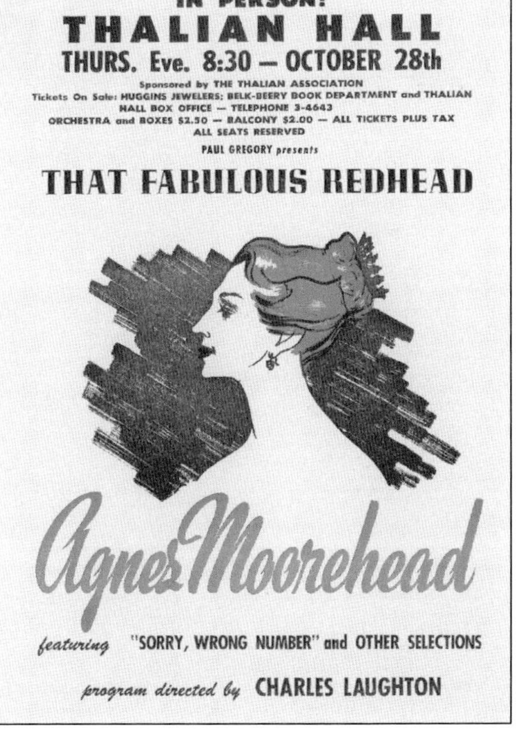

Moorehead's program included *Sorry, Wrong Number*, which was her famous solo radio drama. She also performed excerpts from the Bible: *Moses and the Bullrush, as Written by Her Nurse Daphne* and *Noah and the Ark*. Other selections were *Remembrance of Things Past* by Marcel Proust and *Some Like 'Em Cold* by Ring Lardner. (THCPA.)

The final show of the Thalian season in 1955 was a production of the Victorian thriller *Angel Street.* In this publicity photograph in front of city hall, police lieutenant Jack Moore pretends he is stopping Emma Bellamy (on ladder) and Jane Perry from making unauthorized changes to street names. (THCPA.)

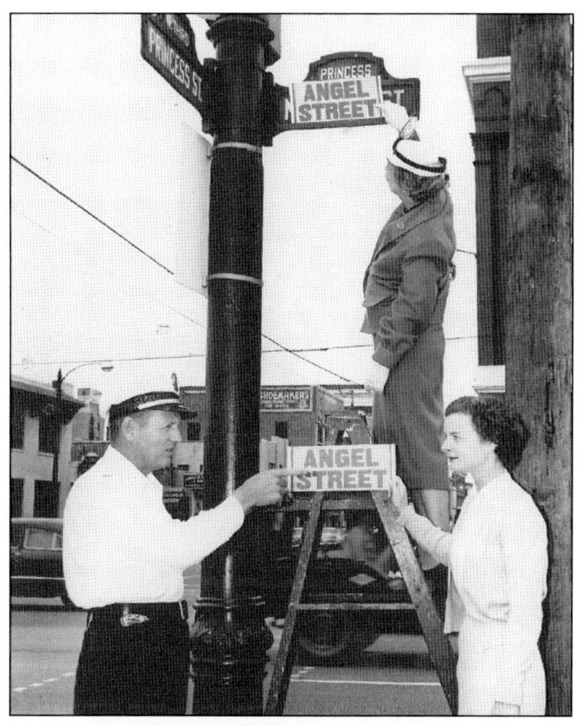

David Ruark (far left) was the director for *Angel Street.* The cast members are, from left to right, Dr. William Randall, Ethel Powers, Kay Ruark, Gar Falkner, and Jean Hickman. The part of Inspector Rough was played by Randall. He had worked as a young actor in Detroit before getting his degree in education at the University of Michigan. (THCPA.)

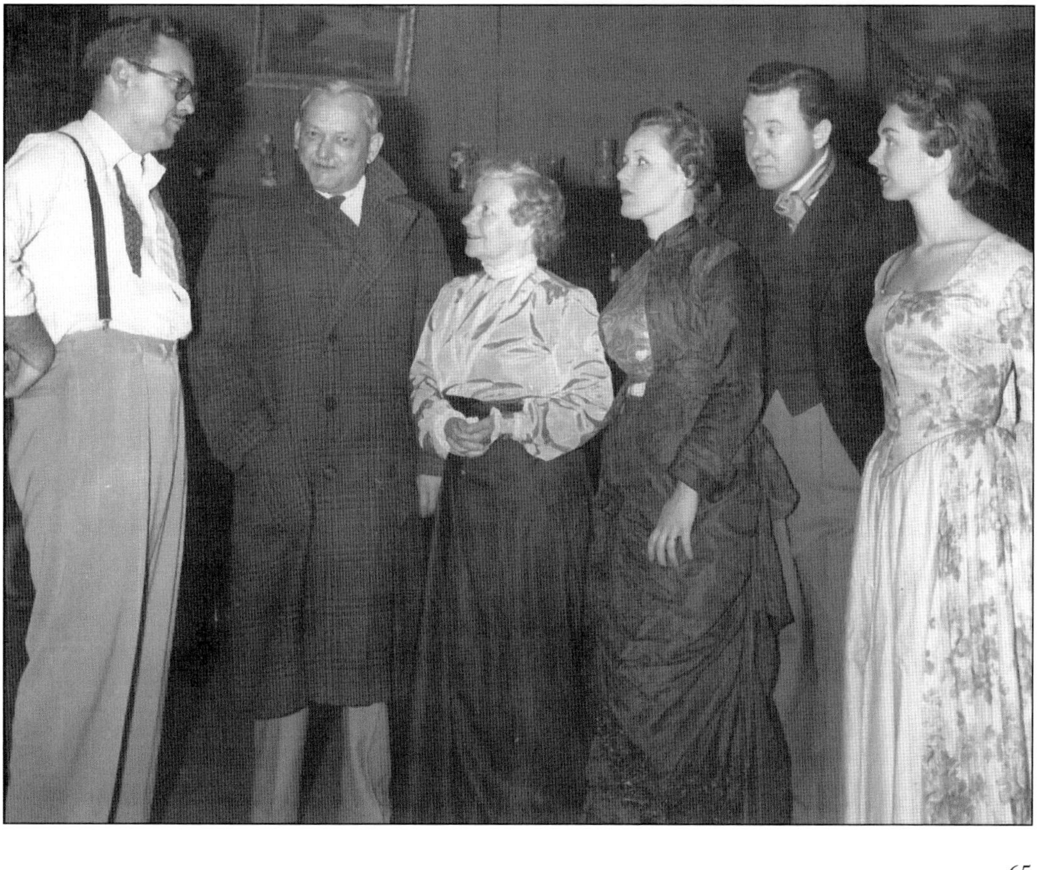

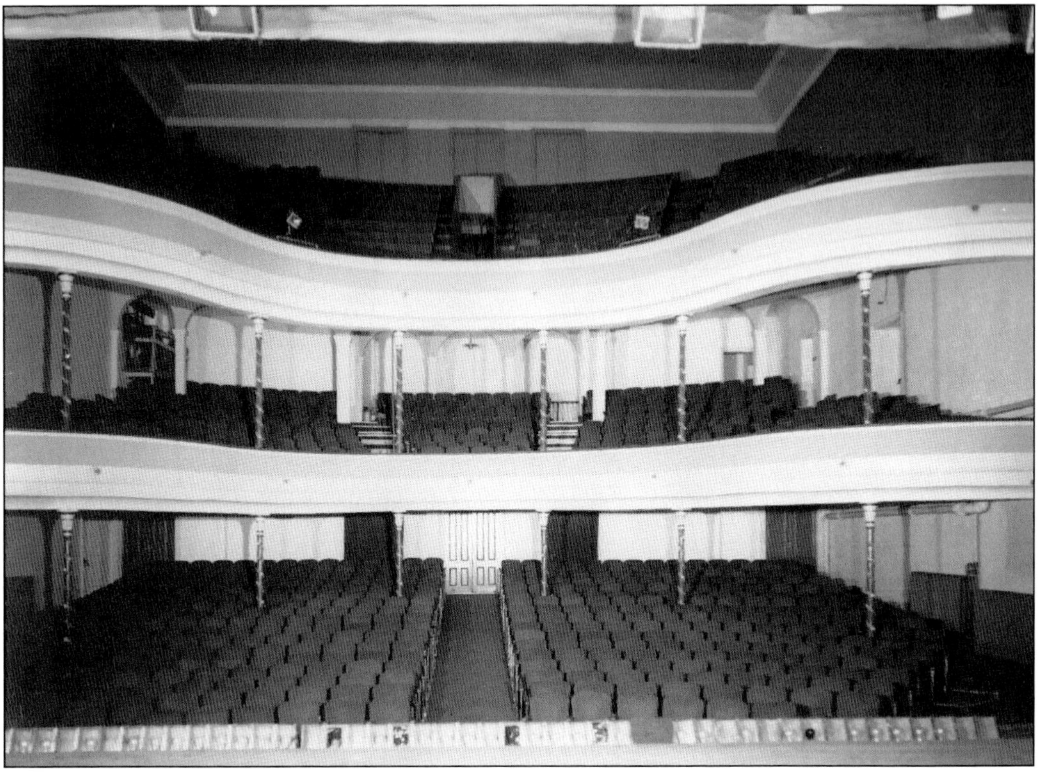

During the 1950s, there were concerts, foreign films, and on one occasion a dairy show in Thalian Hall. This is the auditorium as it appeared at that time. The center aisle and the footlight trough remained a feature of the theatre until the 1990 renovation. The large window fan on the left side of the balcony was the only air-conditioning until 1975. (THCPA.)

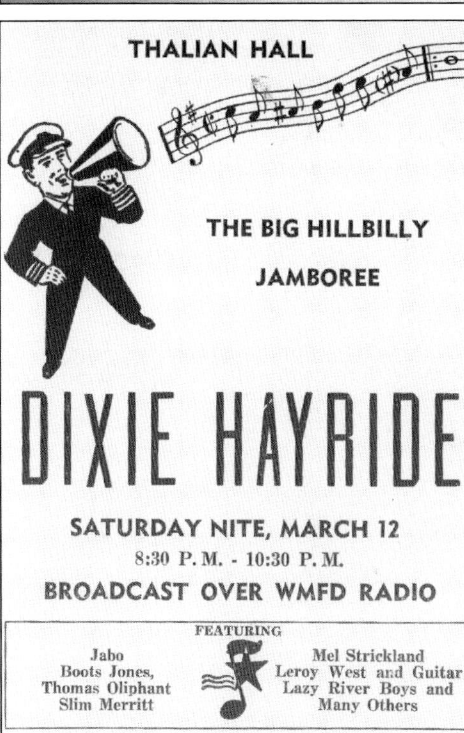

In 1954, a live radio show featuring country and western music became a weekly event on Saturday nights. The popularity of country music concerts at Thalian Hall continued throughout the 1950s, with shows like the *WSM Grand Ole Opry*, starring George Morgan and his Candy Kisses Kids. (James H. McKoy Collection, NHCPL.)

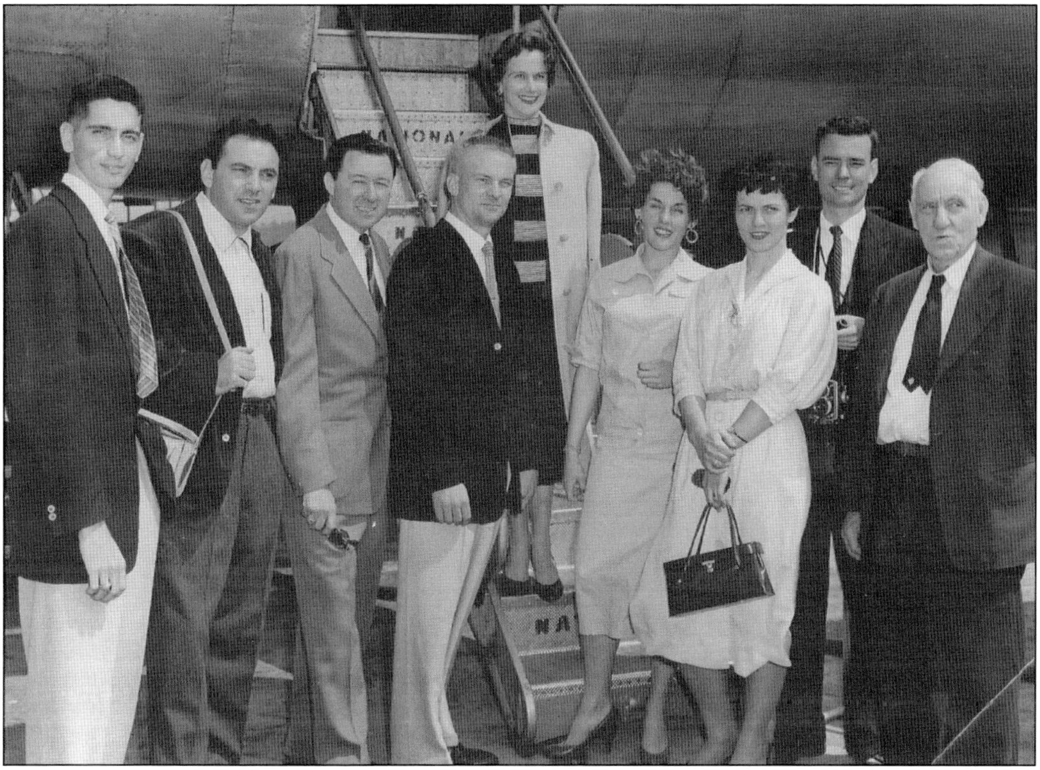

In February 1955, the Thalian Association presented the comic farce *See How They Run* with a local cast. Then, as a special addition to the Azalea Festival, James McKoy secured the appearance of actress Kim Hunter in the lead role for a second production of the play. Pictured here are, from left to right, unidentified, Frank Parker, Gar Falkner, unidentified, Kim Hunter, Lou Davenport, Nessie Henderson, unidentified, and Edmund Rogers. (THCPA.)

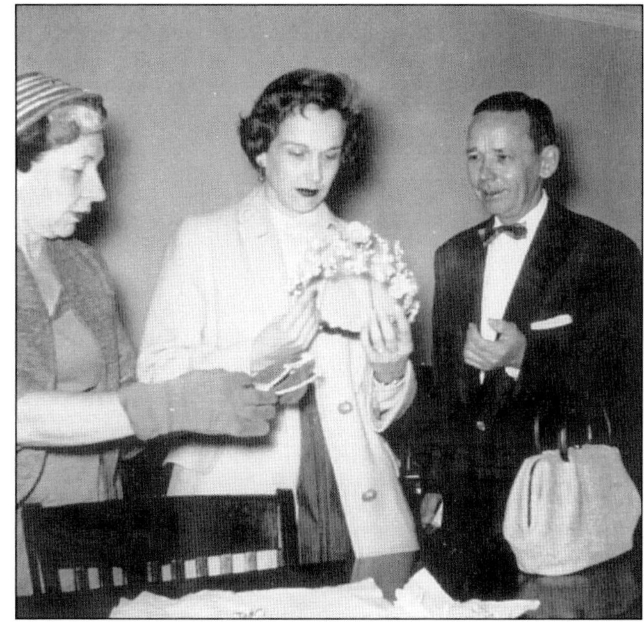

James McKoy (right), seen here with Kim Hunter (center), had returned to Wilmington after a career in theatre management. He opened St. John's Tavern, a popular restaurant during World War II. Hunter won the Oscar for best supporting actress for *A Streetcar Named Desire*. (THCPA.)

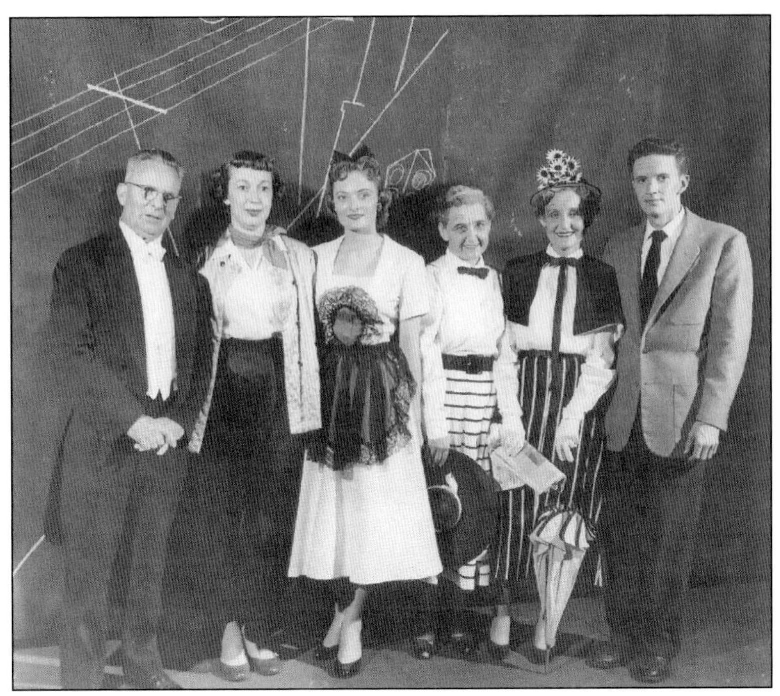

On March 17 and 18, 1955, two one-act operas by Gian-Carlo Menotti, *The Telephone* and *The Old Man and the Thief*, were performed at Thalian Hall. The production featured some of Wilmington's most talented musicians, including, from left to right, William G. Robertson, Betty Ware, Geraldyn Colkitt, Mildred Murdock, Mary Eunice Troy, and Page Shaw. (THCPA.)

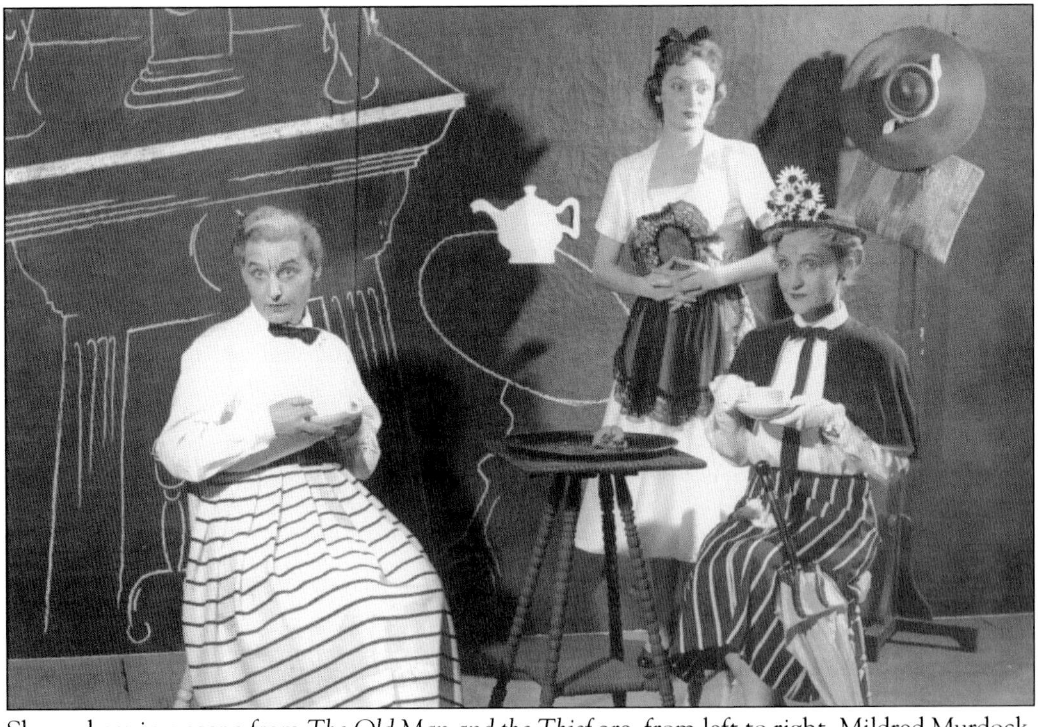

Shown here in a scene from *The Old Man and the Thief* are, from left to right, Mildred Murdock, Geraldyn Colkitt, and Mary Eunice Troy, all respected musicians. The whimsical cartoon sets seen here were designed and painted by local architects Herbert McKim, Frank Ballard, and Robert Sawyer. (THCPA.)

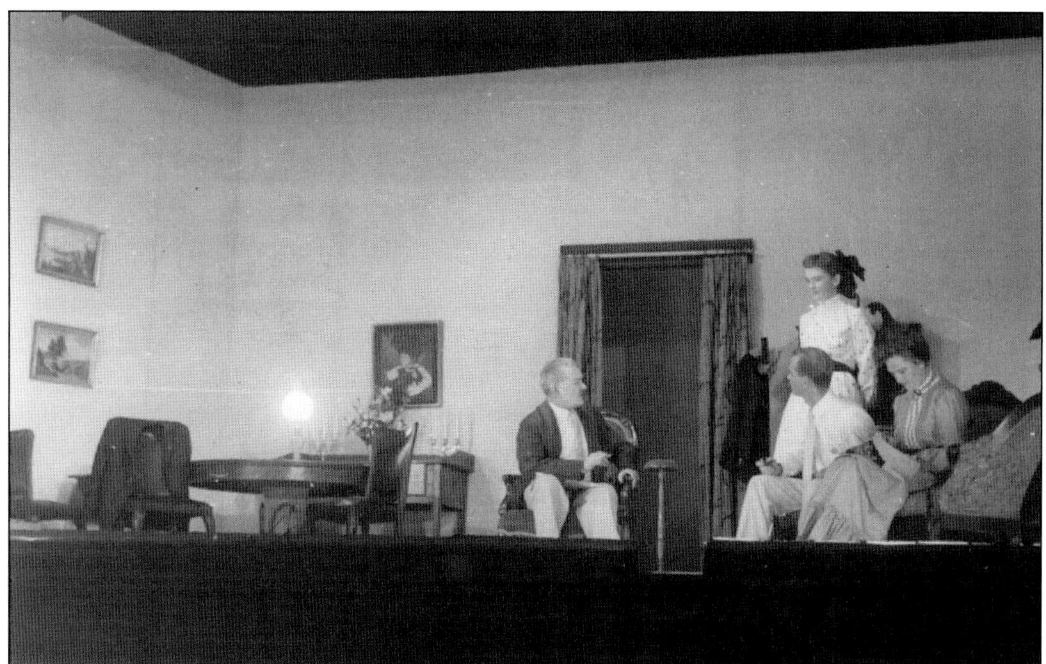

Ah, Wilderness by Eugene O'Neill, was presented in 1957. It featured, from left to right, Dr. William Randall, Rick Lindsey, Betty Black, and Edith Huggins. The following year, Randall was appointed president of Wilmington College. It was under his direction that the drama department under Doug Swink was established. (THCPA.)

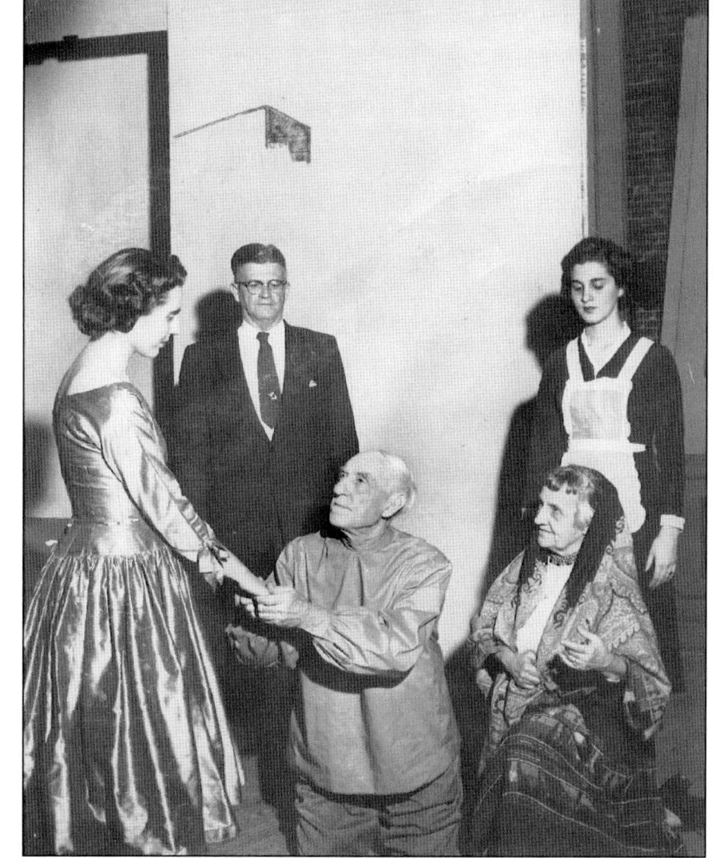

The cast of the 1957 performance of *Anastasia* included Betsy Pearsall (far left) in the title role. Also in the cast were, from left to right, Fred Holdsworth, Edmund Rogers, Fanny de Rosset, and a newcomer to the Thalian Hall stage, Dorothy Pastis. The production was directed by Howard P. Ganstier, who came to Wilmington under the Federal Theatre Project. (THCPA.)

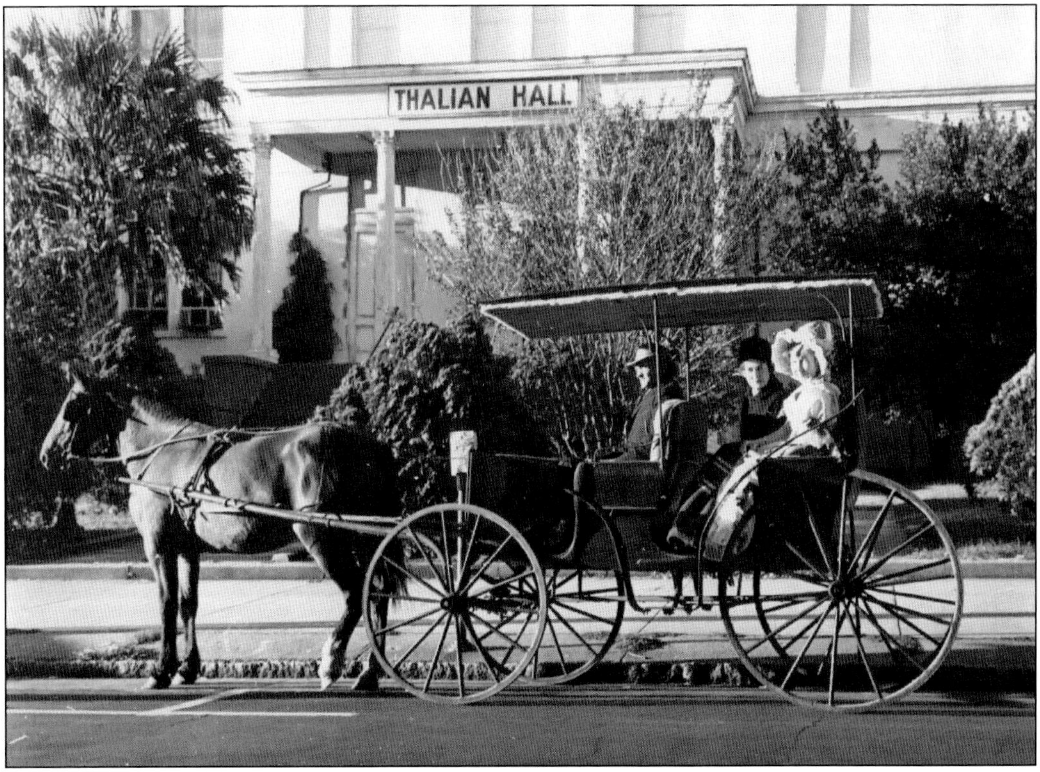

In 1958, the 100th anniversary of Thalian Hall was celebrated. In this publicity photograph, Elizabeth Bridgers (left) and Emma Bellamy Williamson arrive at the Princess Street entrance in an antique surrey. The women are dressed in 19th-century costumes. (THCPA.)

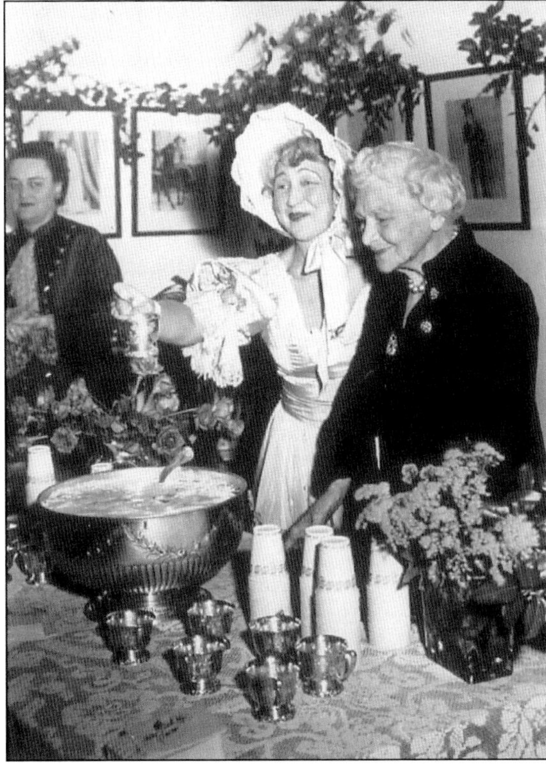

Emma Bellamy Williamson (center) and Rena McRae (right) serve punch in the lobby of Thalian Hall at the centennial reception. McRae had appeared as Diana in the 1896 extravaganza *The Kirmess*, and both women had appeared in the first performance of the Little Theatre Guild in 1929. They were passionate advocates for Thalian Hall, and both served as presidents of the Thalian Association. (THCPA.)

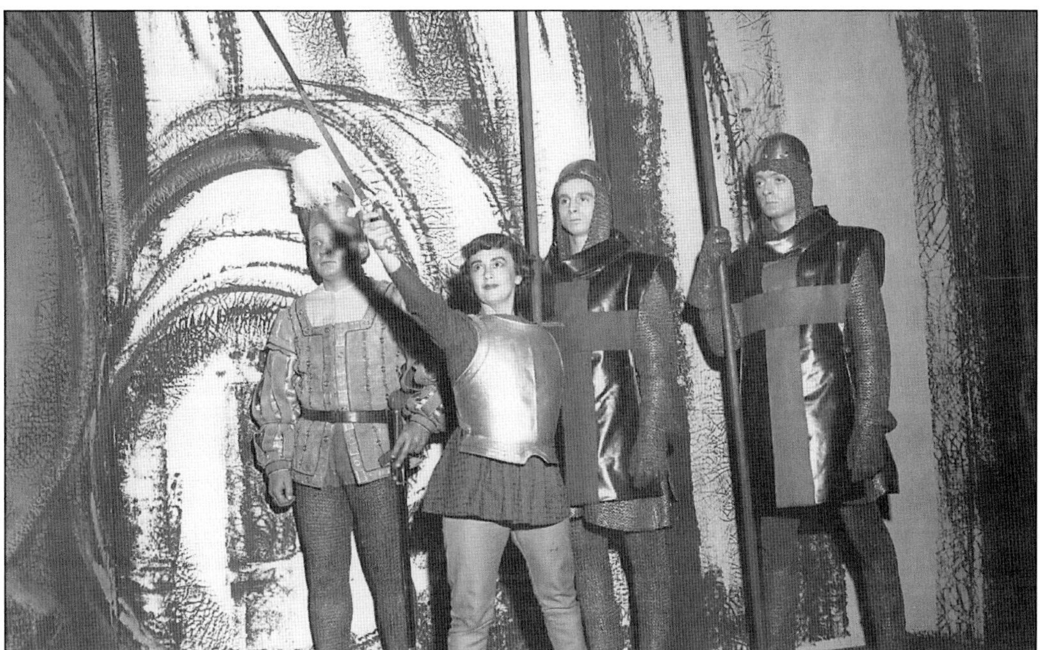

For the centennial season, a striking production of *The Lark* was presented for two nights in 1959. The part of Joan of Arc was played by Ruth Caplan. The abstract set, in brilliant colors, was designed and painted by Wilmington artist Neal Thomas, who lived at nearby Clarendon Plantation. (THCPA.)

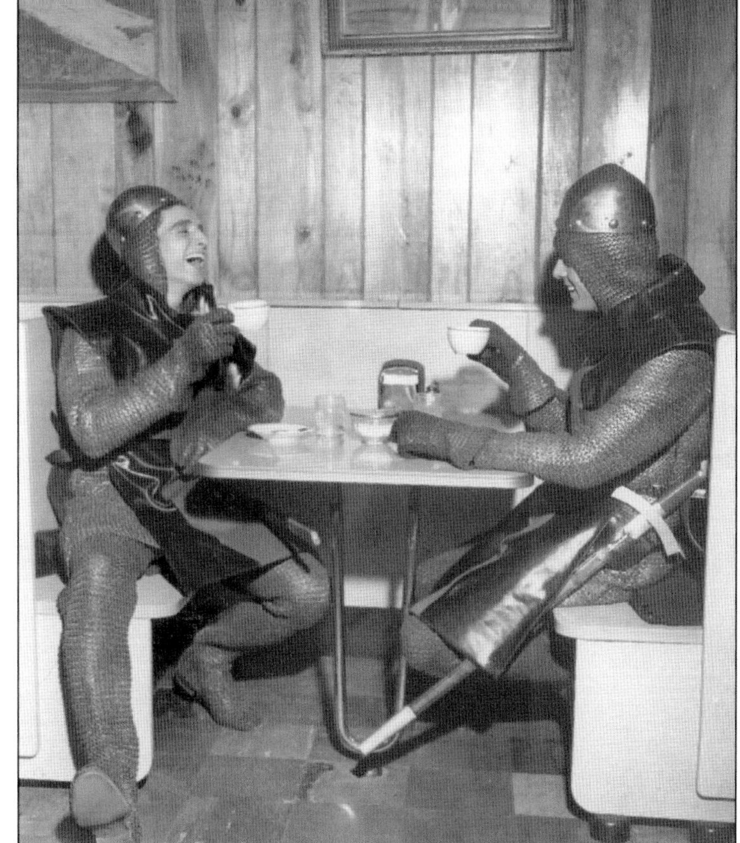

The guards in *The Lark*, George Wheelis (left) and George W. Knox, take a break and enjoy a cup of coffee in a very nonmedieval booth at Futrell's Drug Store on Princess Street. (THCPA.)

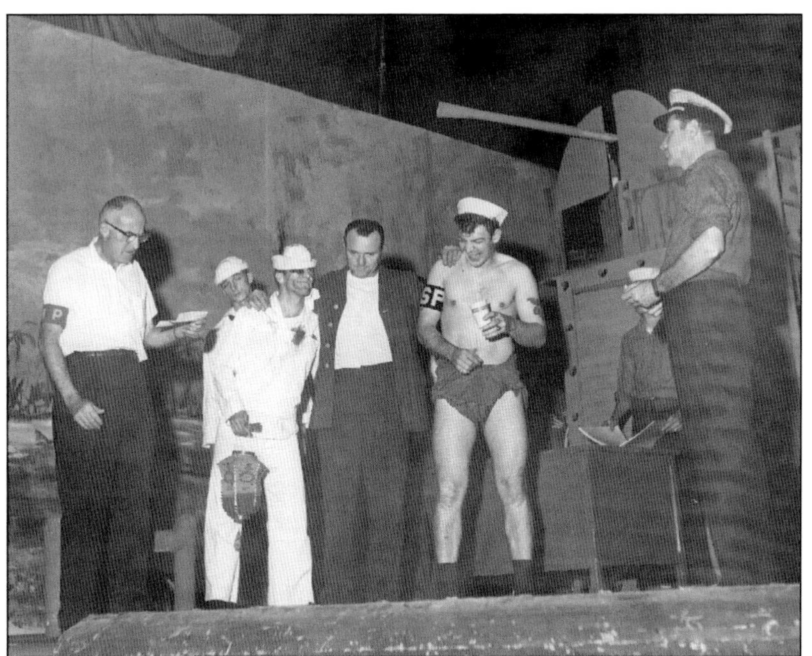

Members of the crew of a US Navy cargo ship return to the deck after a wild night of "liberty" in the 1961 production of *Mr. Roberts*. The cast included, from left to right, Tom Bradshaw, Jerry Sullivan, Frank Iole, Moe Kotler (who also served as director), Ray Pedro, and Alex Fonvielle Jr. in the title role. (THCPA.)

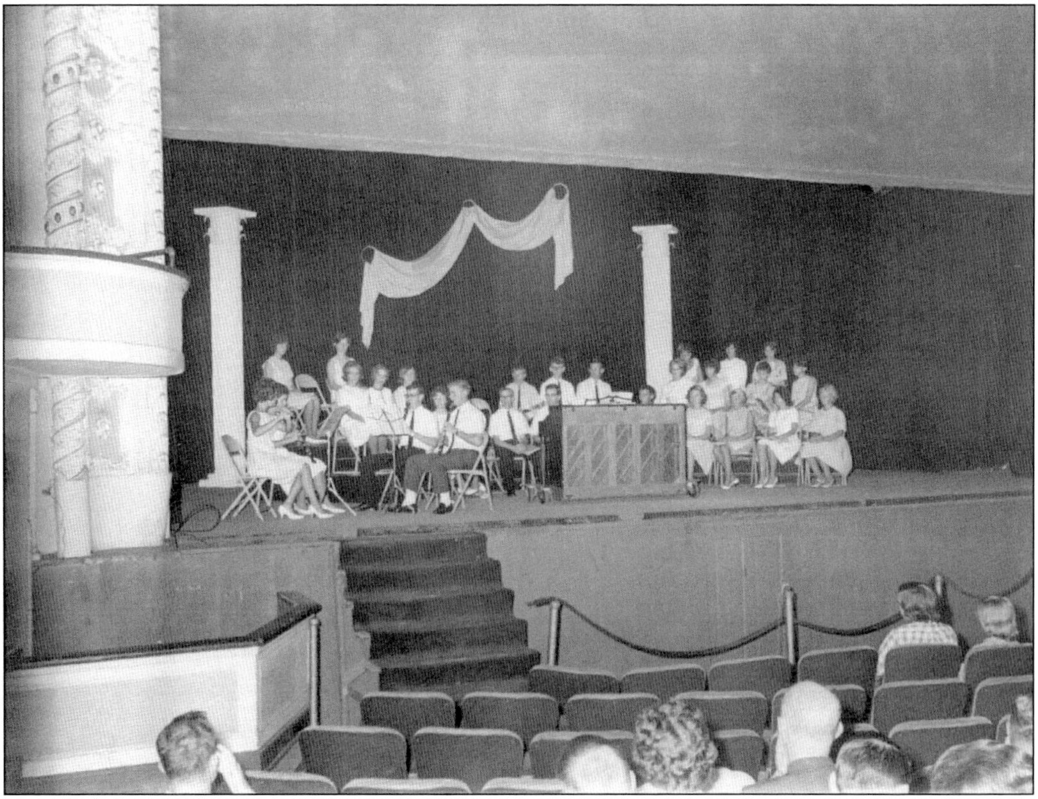

Thalian Hall has always been a popular location for local recitals and talent shows. Seen here is a performance by local musicians in the early 1960s. The lower side boxes were removed in the 1975 restoration. (THCPA.)

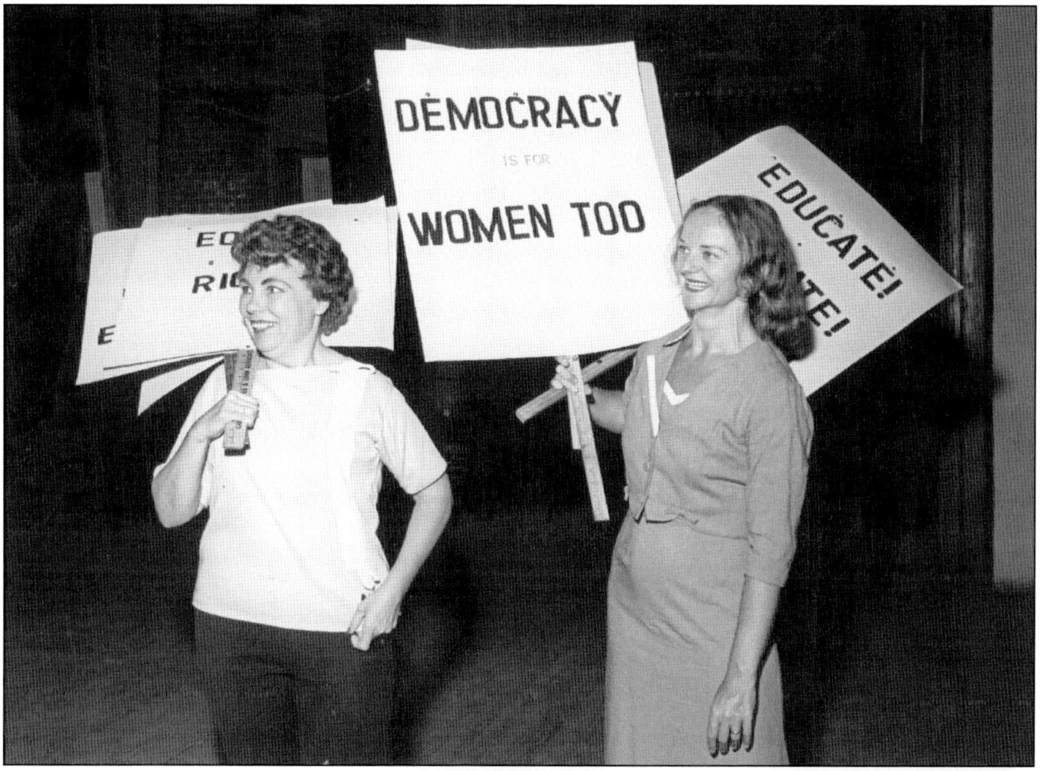

Shown here are Pearl West (left) and Dorothy Nesbitt. A community arts activist and dancer, Nesbitt wrote and directed this production of *The Suffragettes*, which appeared at Thalian Hall in 1962. Others in the cast included Dorothy Pastis, Ann Miller, Jane Hobbs, Roberta Schartz, Bidel High, and Bessie Andrews. (THCPA.)

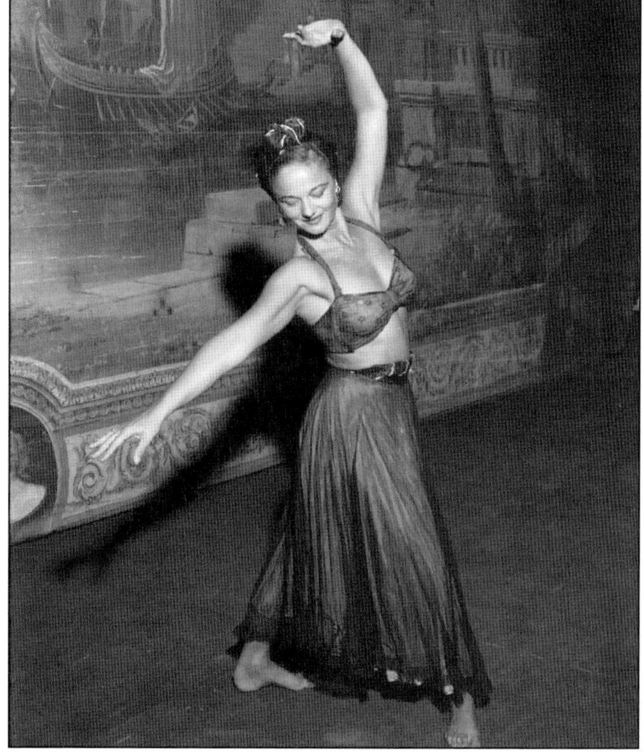

This photograph of Dorothy Nesbitt was taken in 1958 for the Thalian Hall centennial. She is seen portraying the famous modern dancer Ruth St. Dennis, who appeared at the Academy of Music in the 1928 Ziegfeld Follies. (THCPA.)

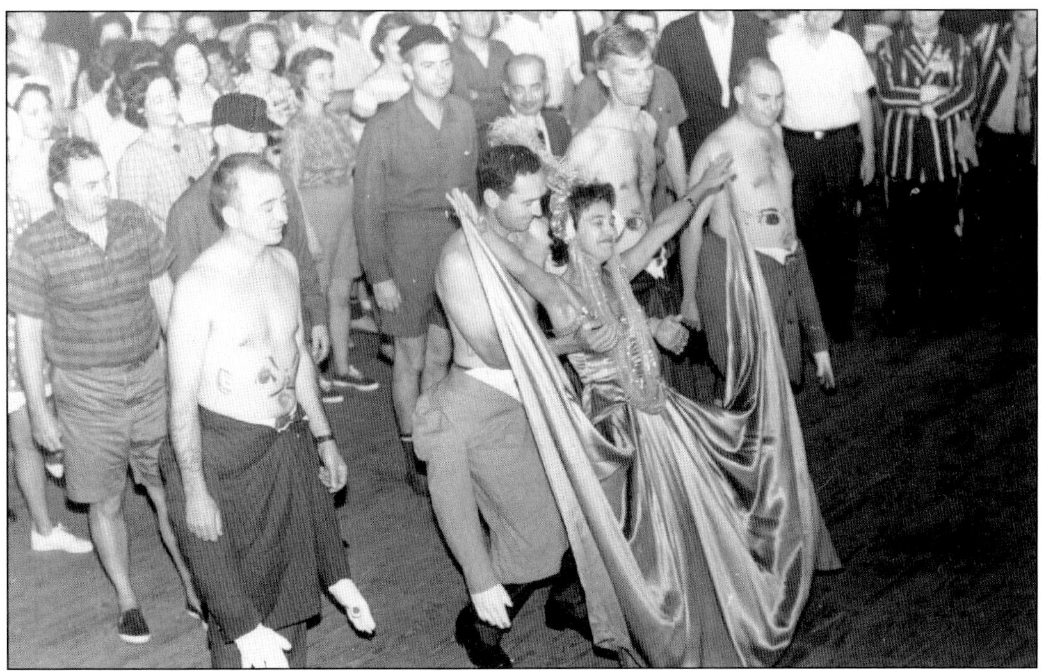

This is a rehearsal in Thalian Hall for the Junior League Follies. The revue, entitled *A La Carte*, was presented in the spring of 1962. Seen at center are Hugh McRae II and Virginia Van Velsor. The suit coat around McRae's waist is from a comic scene in one of the numbers, "The Martian Gentlemen." (THCPA.)

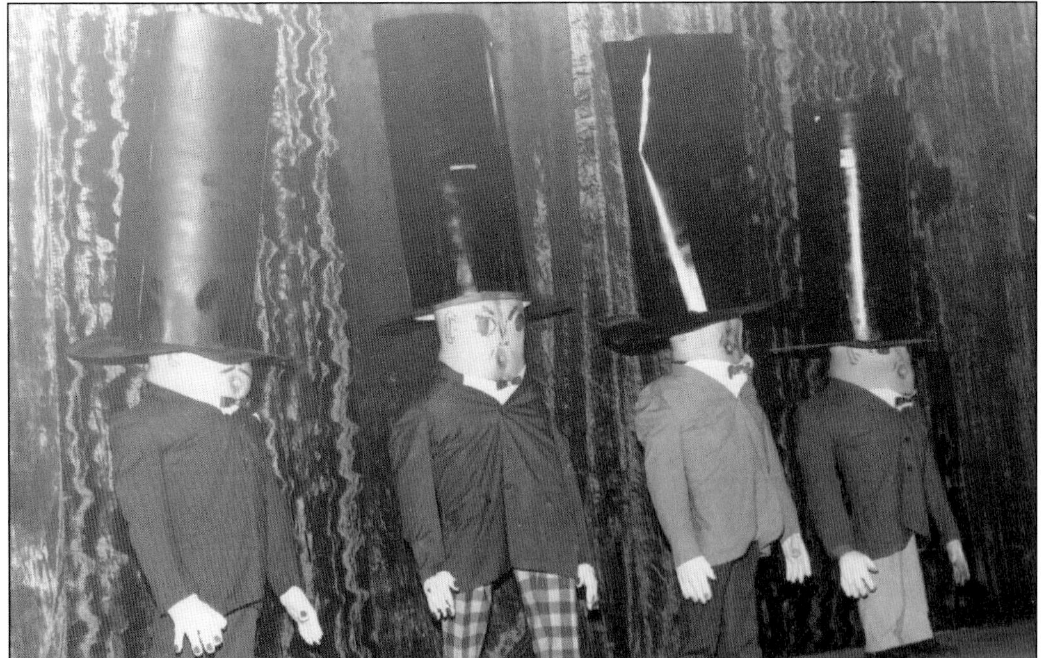

The actors portraying "The Martian Gentlemen" are seen in this photograph from the 1962 follies. Faces are drawn on their stomachs, and their coats are buttoned around their waists. Top hats cover their upper torsos. (THCPA.)

By 1963, Thalian Hall had become rather shabby, the carpet was worn, the interior needed repainting, the heating system was outmoded, and the theatre seats were over 40 years old. Following its production of *A La Carte*, the Junior League appointed a committee to undertake the formation of an organization whose purpose would be to restore Thalian Hall. (The Star-News Collection, NHCPL.)

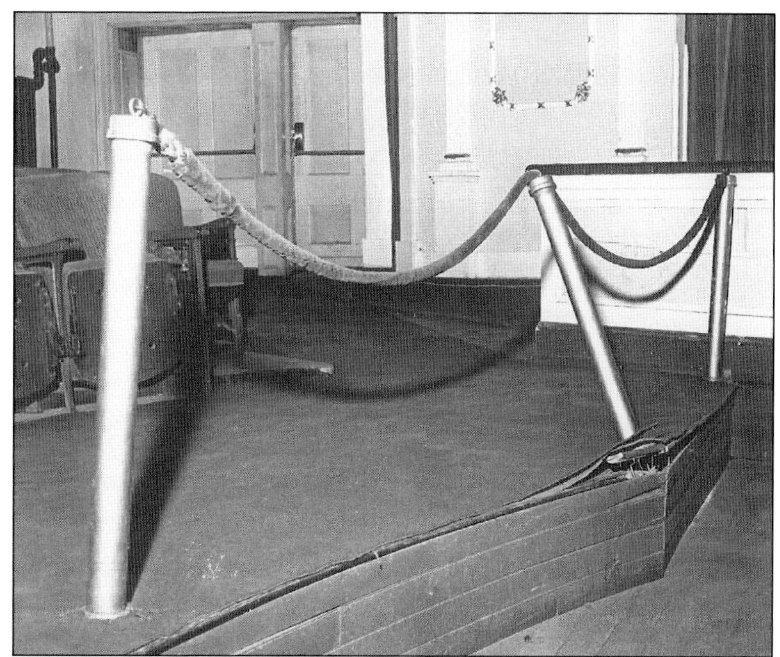

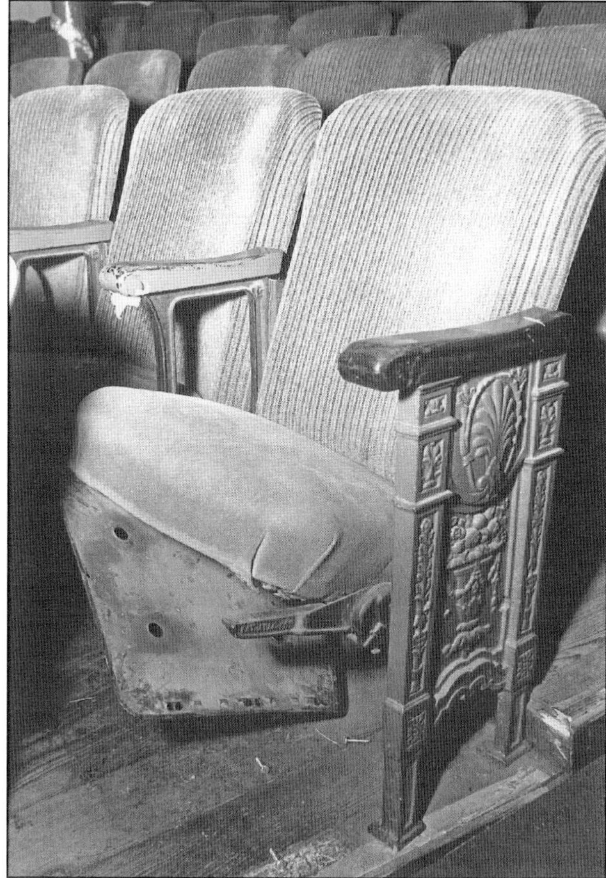

The Thalian Association had been managing the theatre for over 30 years, but limited financial resources allowed for only minimal maintenance. The league agreed to initially fund the new organization, which was chartered in 1963 under the name Thalian Hall Commission, Inc. (The Star-News Collection, NHCPL.)

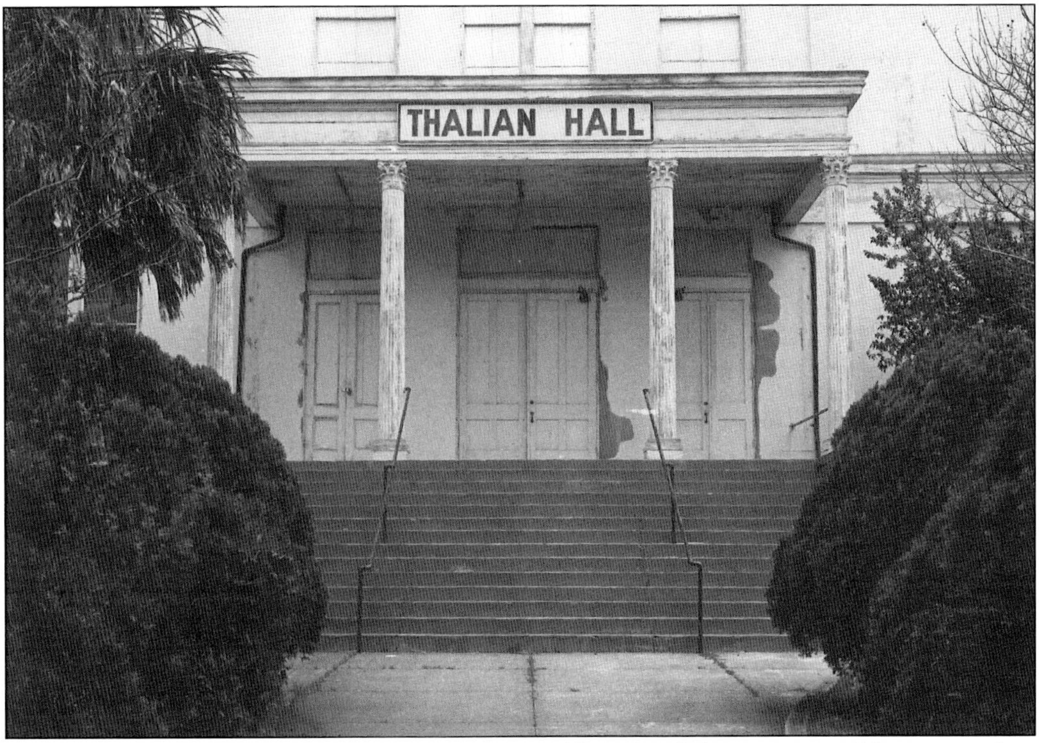

The members of the Thalian Hall Commission quickly realized the enormity of the project they had undertaken. They had to learn how to go about restoring a building, figure out where to get the money, and determine how it should be operated once it was restored. The historic theatre preservation movement was in its infancy, and there were few examples to study. (THCPA.)

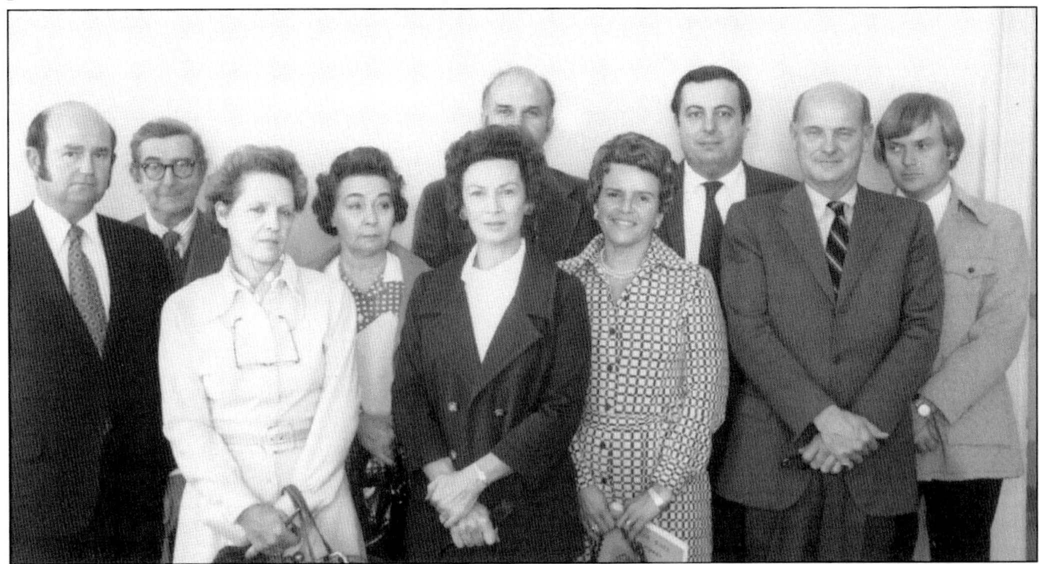

The members of the Thalian Hall Commission, Inc. and their consultants are seen here at Thalian Hall. Throughout the 1960s, plans were developed for the hall's restoration. The individuals in the first row were instrumental in the project. They are, from left to right, A.L Huneycutt, Isabel Williams, Jean Anne Sutton, Elizabeth Wright, and Thomas H. Wright Jr. (THCPA.)

Seven

The Community and the College 1963–1973

In September 1963, the Thalian Hall Commission, Inc. was chartered for the purpose of restoring Thalian Hall as a performing arts center for the region. There were several issues facing the commission. First, the city was still recovering from the 1960 departure of the Atlantic Coast Railroad and its financial impact on the community. Second, there were few historic theatre restorations to serve as examples. Third, the importance of Thalian Hall was not widely recognized, which made it difficult to develop the necessary support.

It was clear that there was a need for basic documentation so that the building could be listed as a historic site. A restoration committee was formed to create a preliminary history of the building to support grants for the project. The commission retained Milton Grigg, an architect who specialized in preservation projects. He began work on a study to provide estimates and future use.

Also in 1963, Dr. William Randall, president of Wilmington College, made an agreement with the Thalian Association to coproduce plays by the drama department under Doug Swink. For five years, Swink dominated the Thalian Hall stage, using casts made up of community actors and college students to present an exciting array of theatre. By 1968, the SRO Theatre had been created, and the drama department moved back to the campus. The Thalian Association continued to present shows at Thalian Hall.

At the same time, members of the Thalian Hall Commission spoke to civic groups, seeking their support for the project. In 1971, Thomas H. Wright Jr. agreed to chair the capital campaign. The commission was in the process of seeking funding sources when disaster struck.

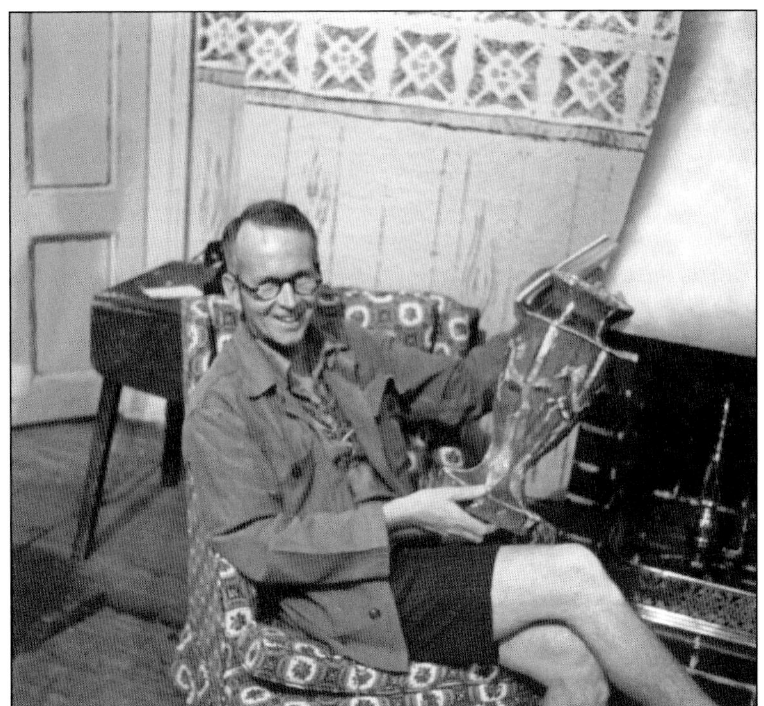

Doug Swink, founder of the Wilmington College drama department, is seen here on the set of *The Man in a Dog Suit*. He is holding one of his famous handmade props. He directed most of the 21 productions that were given at Thalian Hall from 1963 to 1968. (Swink Collection, THCPA.)

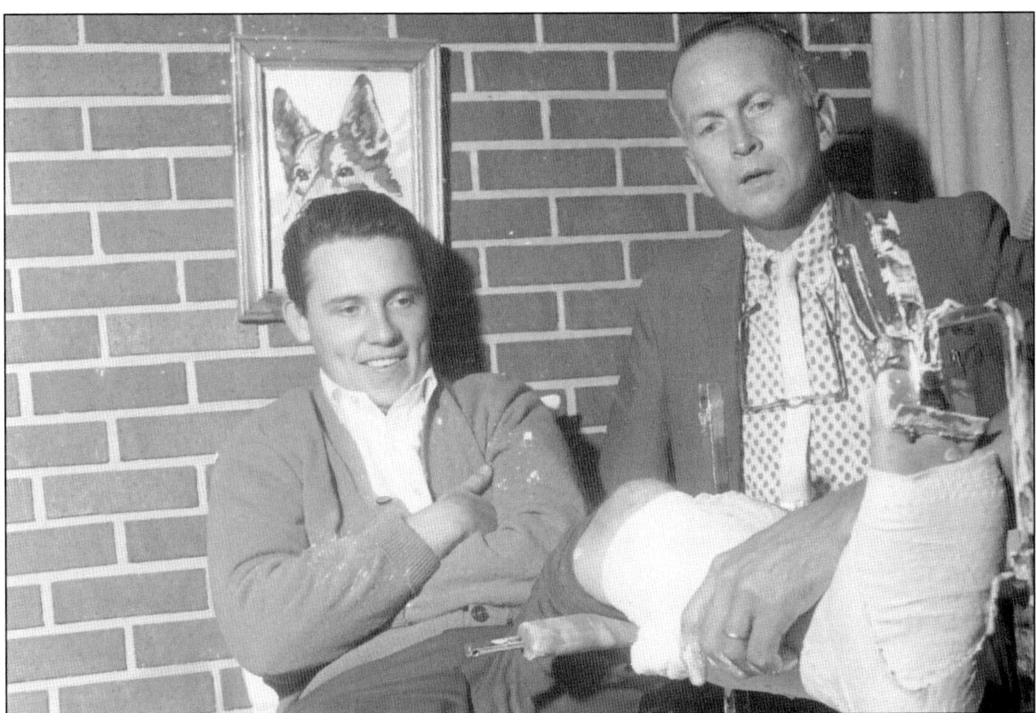

In the 1960s, George Deaton (left) was a well-known host on WECT's *Carolina in the Morning*. He appeared in many shows during this period. Here, he is seen with director Doug Swink as they put the finishing touches on Brick's cast for the 1966 production of *Cat on a Hot Tin Roof*. (Swink Collection, THCPA.)

The first coproduction by Wilmington College and the Thalian Association was *Teahouse of the August Moon*. At that time, the stage was very limited. Here, flats from previous productions are lined up against the back wall. The door on stage left was frequently opened during productions so that sets could be moved outdoors into Innes Park when they were not needed during a performance. (Swink Collection, THCPA.)

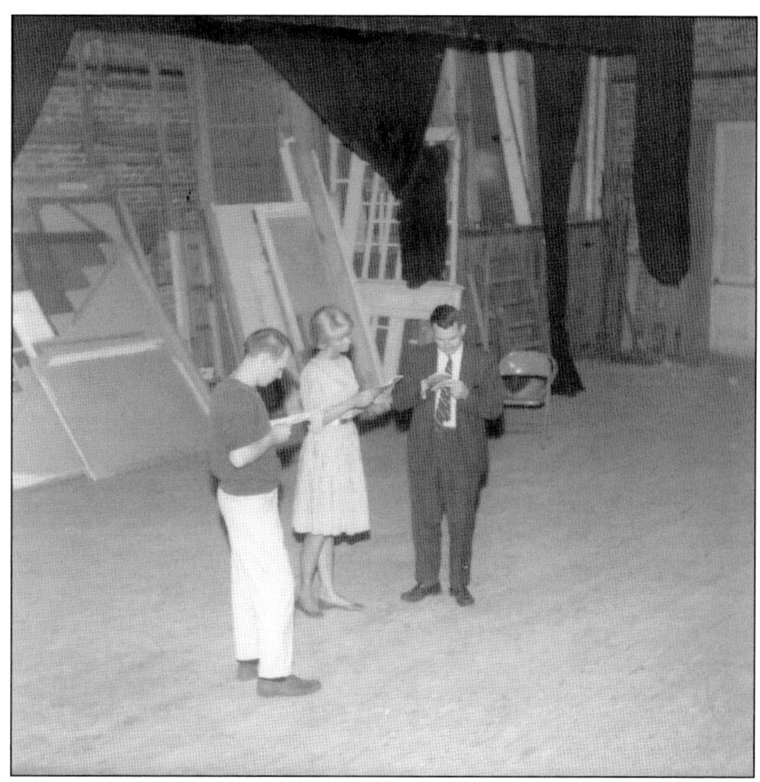

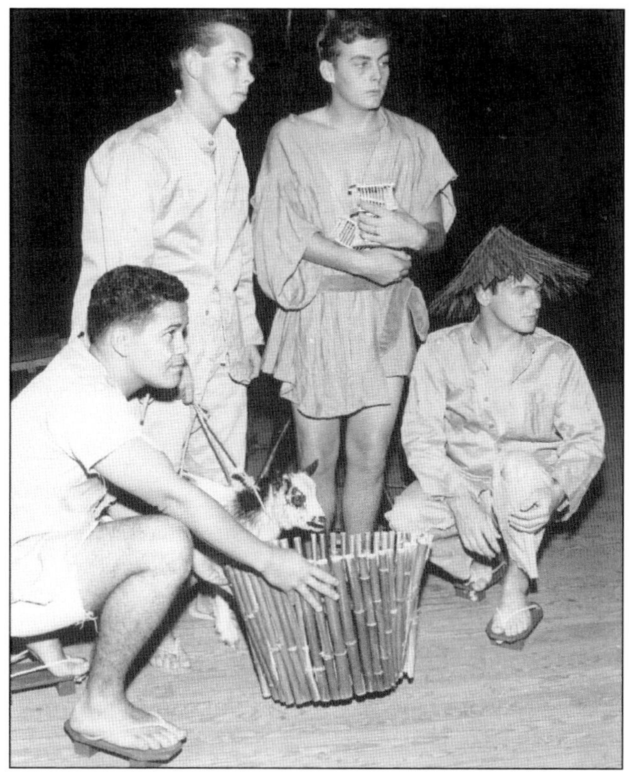

Teahouse of the August Moon was set in a village in Japan during the occupation after World War II. In this 1963 photograph, the skeptical villagers are played by, from left to right, Ray Oxendine, Paul Bainum, Wesley Ward, and Wayne Robinson. They are listening to plans to mass produce their one article of manufacture, artistic cricket cages. (Swink Collection, THCPA.)

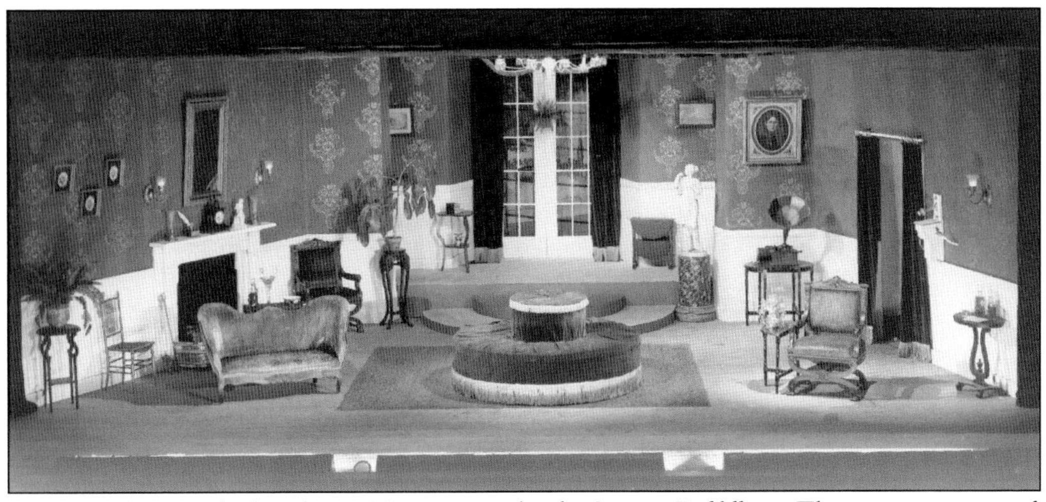

Doug Swink created a handsome Victorian parlor for *Strange Bedfellows*. The ottoman, or pouf, was originally purchased for the lobby in 1909. It was found in the attic and used in this 1963 production. It has since been refurbished and is back in the lobby. (THCPA.)

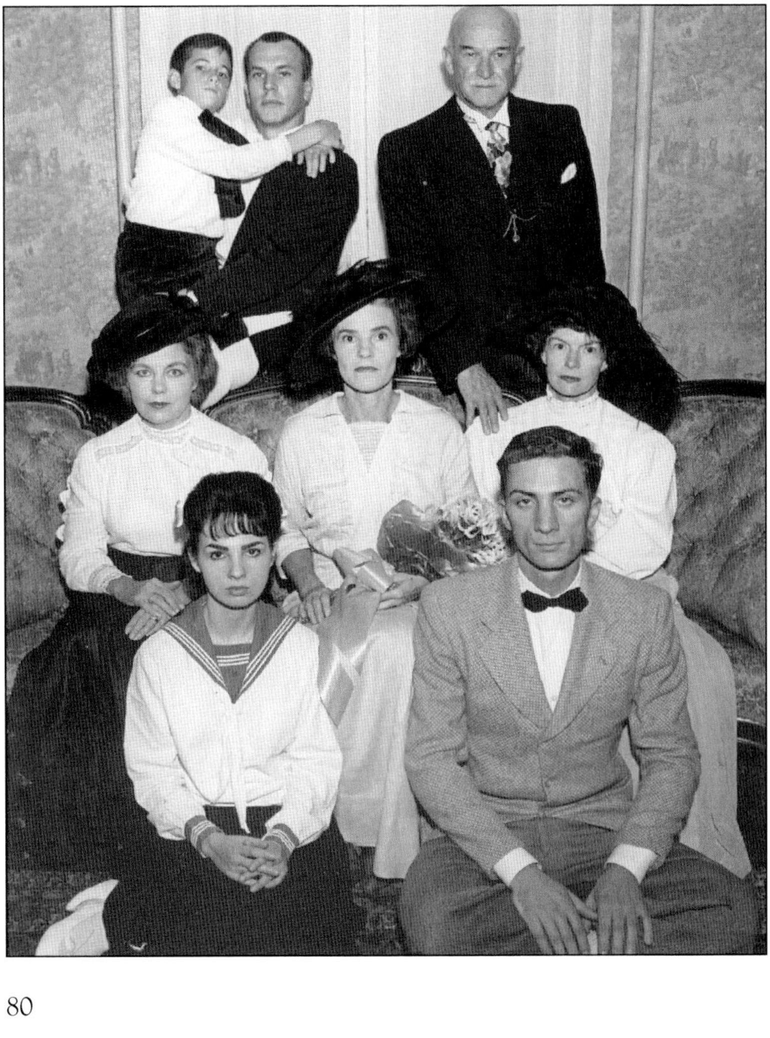

Strange Bedfellows, a comedy depicting the merry-go-round of women's suffrage set in 1896, had a cast of 19. Shown here are the cast members who played Senator Cromwell's family. They are, from left to right, (first row) Sue MacDonald and Greg Godwin; (second row) Pearl Wells, Jean Scott, and Mary Broadfoot; (third row) Billy Emerson, Wally Warr, and David Herney. (THCPA.)

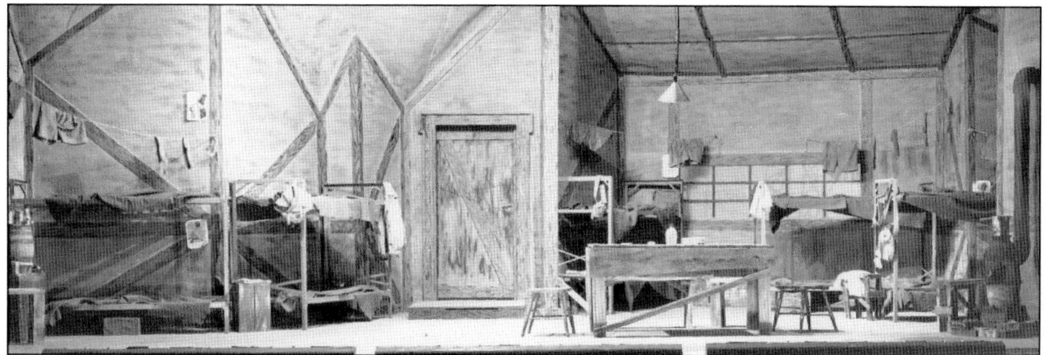

Stalag 17, directed by Doug Swink, featured an all-male cast of 23 members. It played for three nights in February 1964. The setting for *Stalag 17* is a Nazi prisoner-of-war camp in Germany at the end of World War II. (Swink Collection, THCPA.)

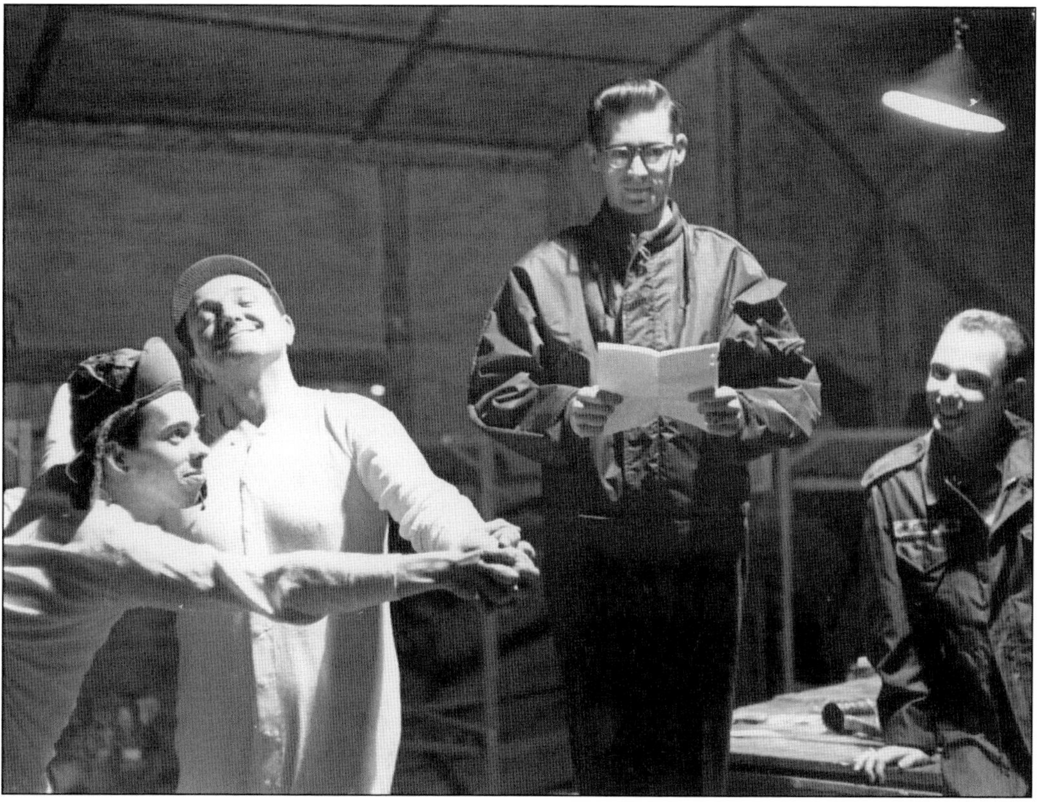

Paul Baninum (far left) and Moe Kotler (second from left) provide one of the lighter moments of *Stalag 17* for the benefit of Richard Cribb (second from right) and Richard Gerrish. The tension mounts when the Germans convict one of the prisoners of sabotage, and the members turn against one another from fear of an informant. (THCPA.)

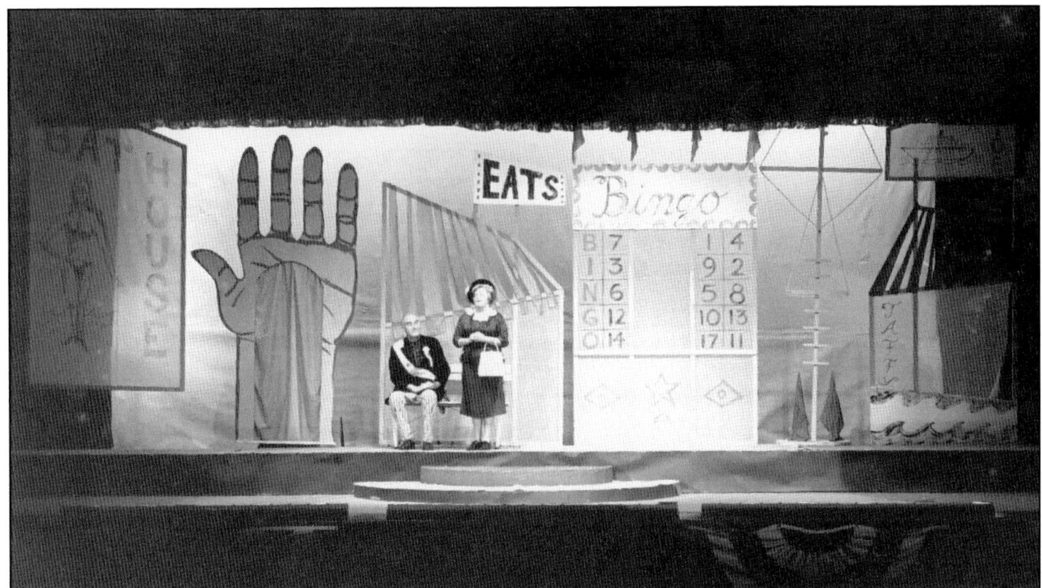

Tom Bradshaw and Mary Hodgin are seen in the 1964 production of *Skin of Our Teeth.* This is the set of act II, which takes place in Atlantic City. (THCPA.)

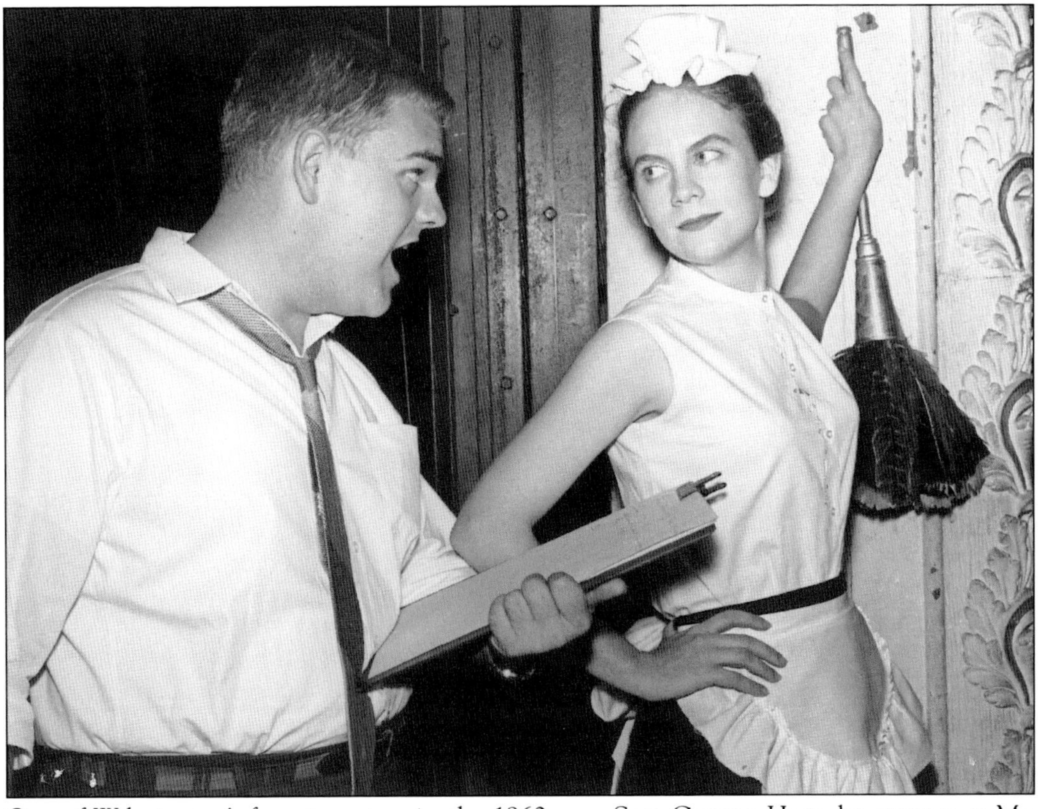

One of Wilmington's favorite actors in the 1960s was Sam Garner. Here, he appears as Mr. Fitzpatrick with Winnie Healy, playing the role of Sabina. In this promotional photograph, she is dusting the proscenium arch. (THCPA.)

For the 1965 production of *Look Homeward, Angel*, director Doug Swink brought in David March (center) to play the lead. March had trained at Wilmington College under Swink. Then, he moved to New York, where he appeared with Lauren Bacall in the television production of *Mr. Broadway* and played supporting roles on *The Edge of Night*. (THCPA.)

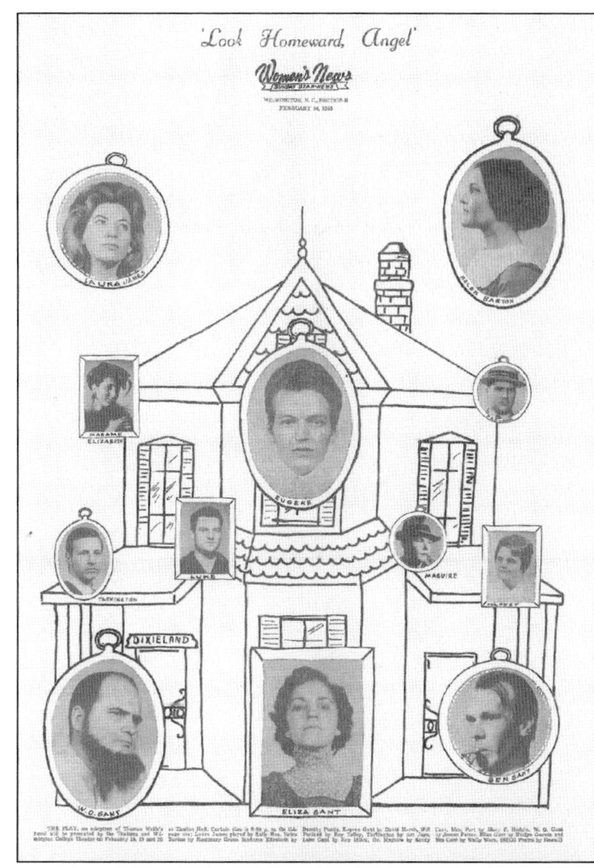

Many Wilmington favorites provided the supporting cast to *Look Homeward, Angel*, including Wally Warr, Mary Hodgin, Rosemary Green, Dorothy Pastis, Sally Rea, Jim Potter, and Sandy Carr. Doug Swink appeared himself, under his stage name, David Stone. In this photograph, Swink is seen sitting on the set with a cigarette. (Swink Collection, THCPA.)

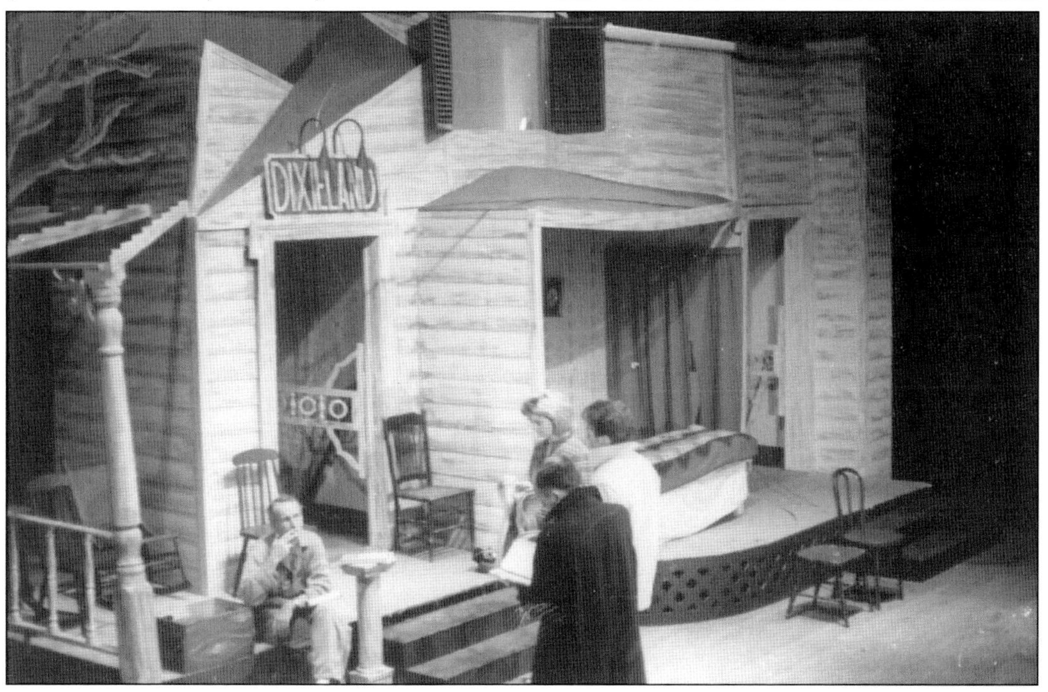

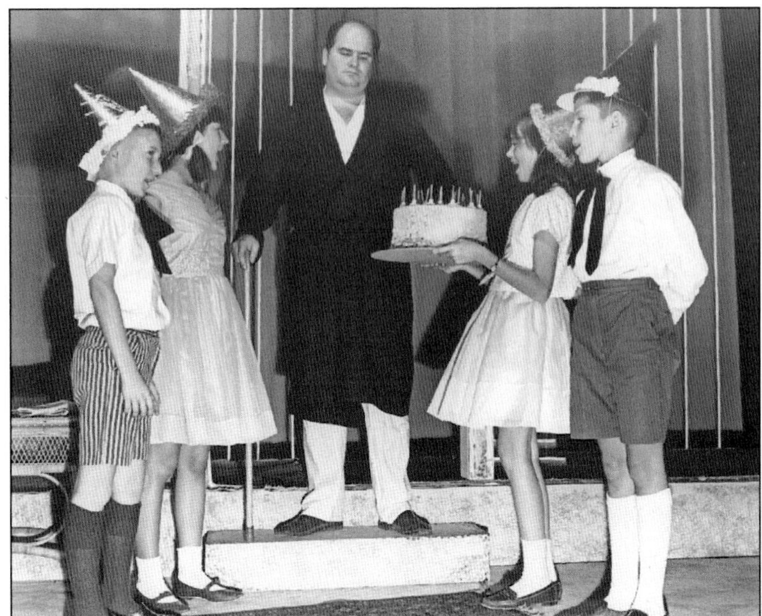

For the 1965 production of *Cat on a Hot Tin Roof*, Big Daddy was played by Jim Potter (center). Also shown are, from left to right, David Porter, Ellen Olsen, Deborah Rogers, and Alan Hill. (THCPA.)

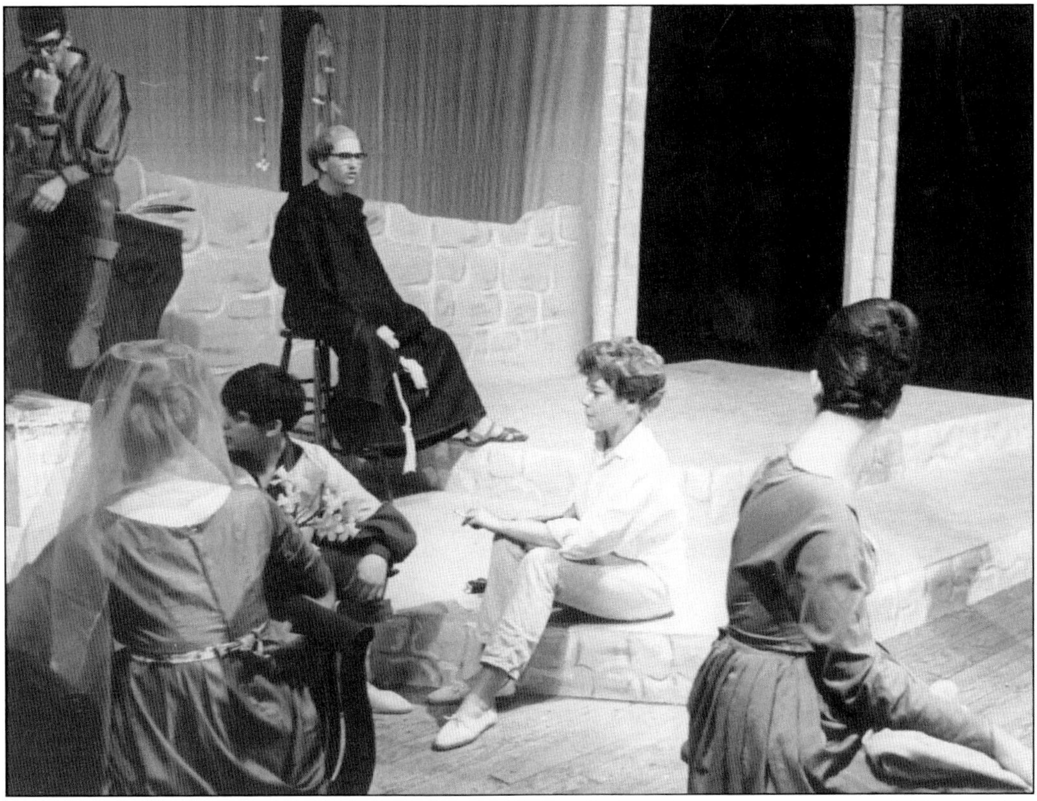

On March 25–26, 1966, Wilmington College and the Thalian Association presented Christopher Fry's *The Lady Not for Burning*. In this rehearsal photograph are, from left to right, Bill Weir, Rosemary Green, Robert Wood, Frank Hall, Anne Fitzgibbon, and Sharon Covert. The production was directed by Fitzgibbon, who joined the Department of Drama in 1965. (THCPA.)

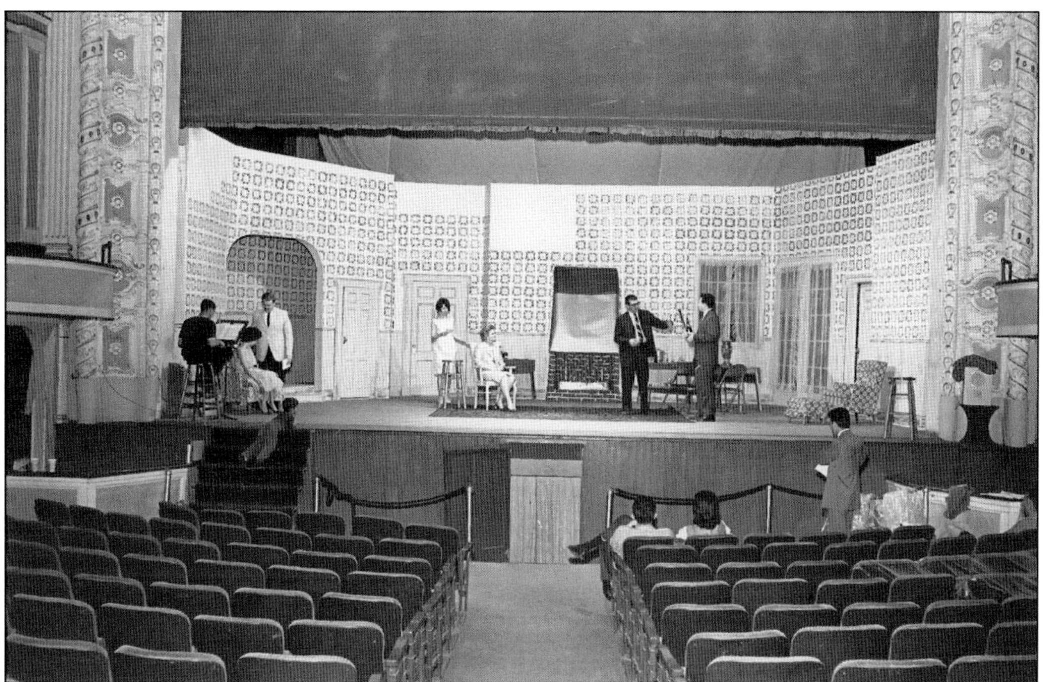

This 1966 photograph shows a rehearsal for *The Man in a Dog Suit*. The cast consisted of some of Wilmington's most popular community and college players, including George Deaton, Sam Garner, Sally Rea, Art Bannon, Jean Rogers, and Frank Hall. (THCPA.)

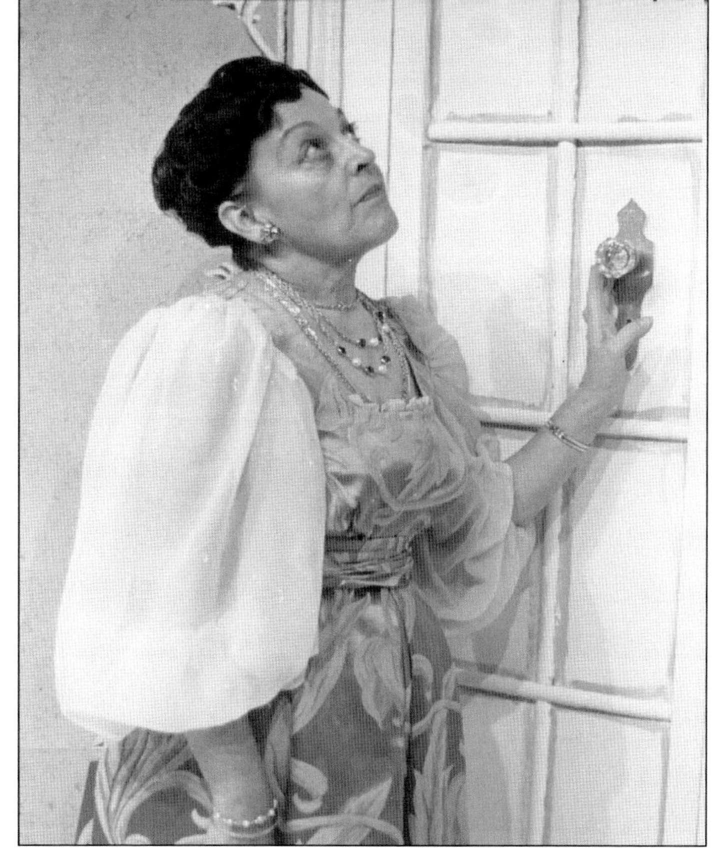

Tina Forrester was a great fan of Doug Swink and appeared in many shows he directed. Here, she is pictured on the stage of Thalian Hall in *Tartuffe*. The Tina Award, given each year by the Thalian Association, is named for her. (THCPA.)

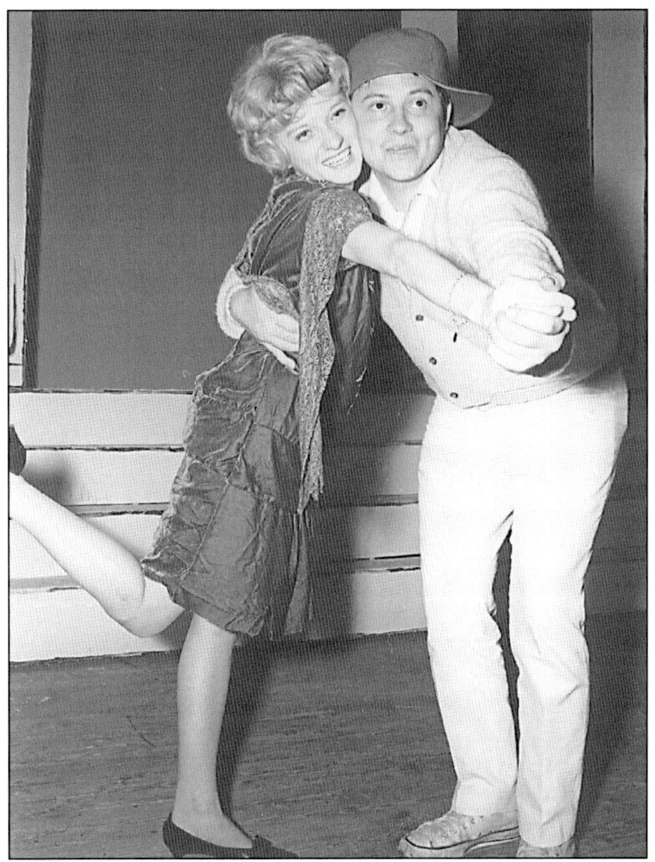

Though the Thalian Association had presented shows with music as a part of a performance, the 1966 production of *Good News* with Wilmington College was the first full-scale musical comedy for both groups. The show was set on a college campus in the Roaring Twenties. Seen here dancing are Carol Benton and George Deaton. (THCPA.)

Good News was a large show, with a cast of over 40 players. A working Ford roadster was driven across the stage in the opening number. Dancing in this 1966 production are, from left to right, Bill Walgren, Barbara Deaton, Michael Sampley, Tony Rivenbark, Chris Deasy, and Jere Hodgin. (THCPA.)

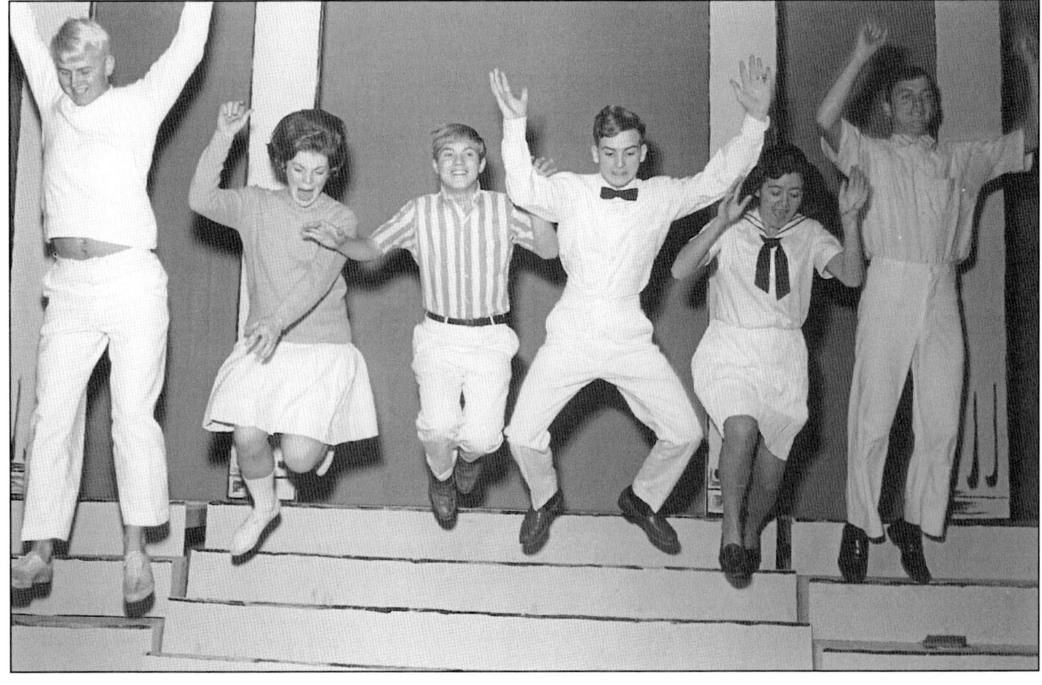

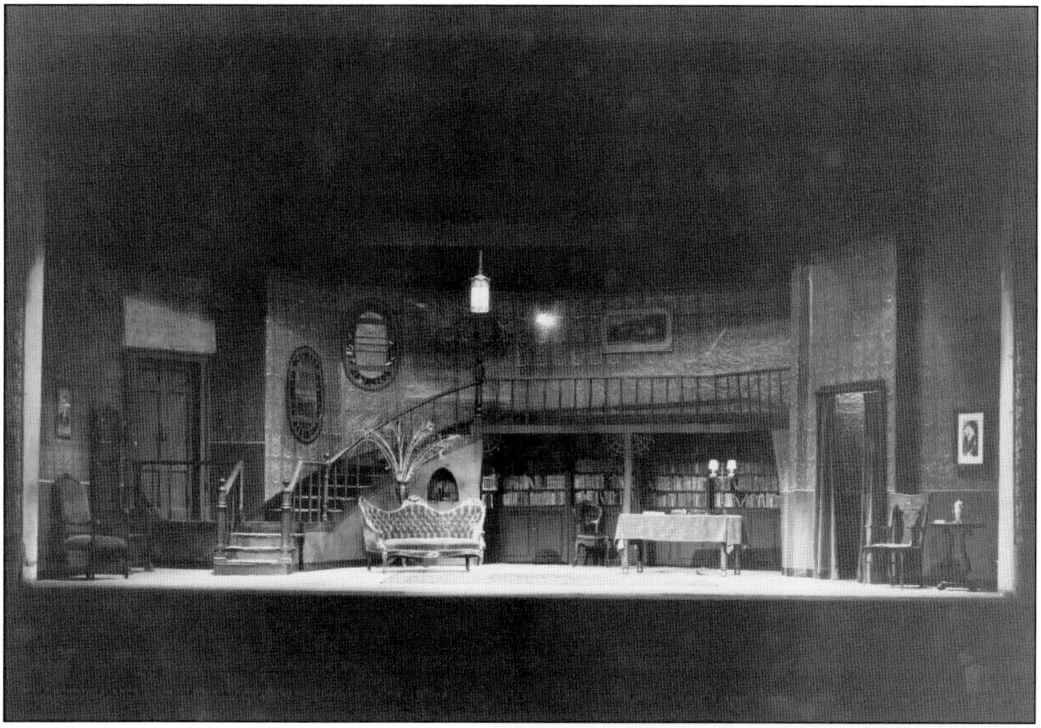

In 1967, Doug Swink revived *Cat and the Canary*, an old melodrama filled with surprising entrances followed by a series of murders. The opening act is set at the library at Glenclif Manor. Bookcases doubled as secret doors. (THCPA.)

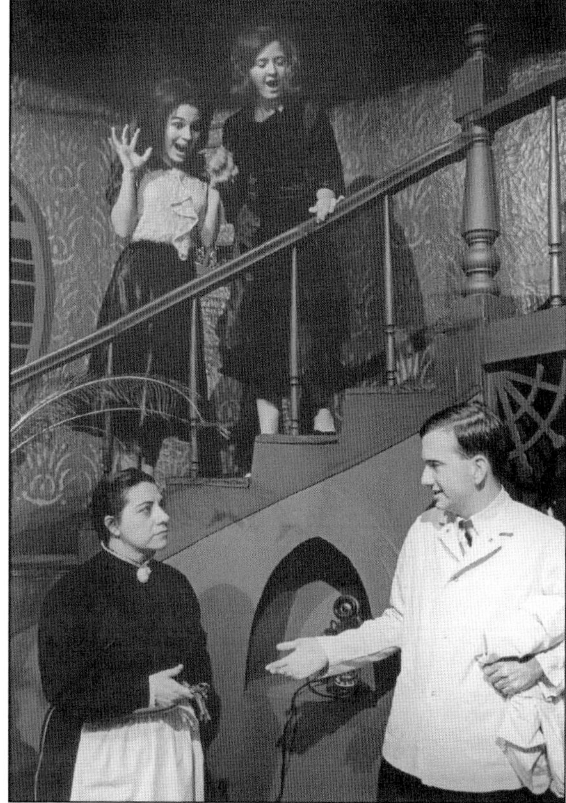

In this scene of the 1967 *Cat and the Canary*, Frank Hall (lower right), playing the butler, is demanding the keys from the housekeeper, Virginia Sonsky (lower left). This action clearly is upsetting Barbara Deaton (upper left) and Chris Deasy (upper right). (THCPA.)

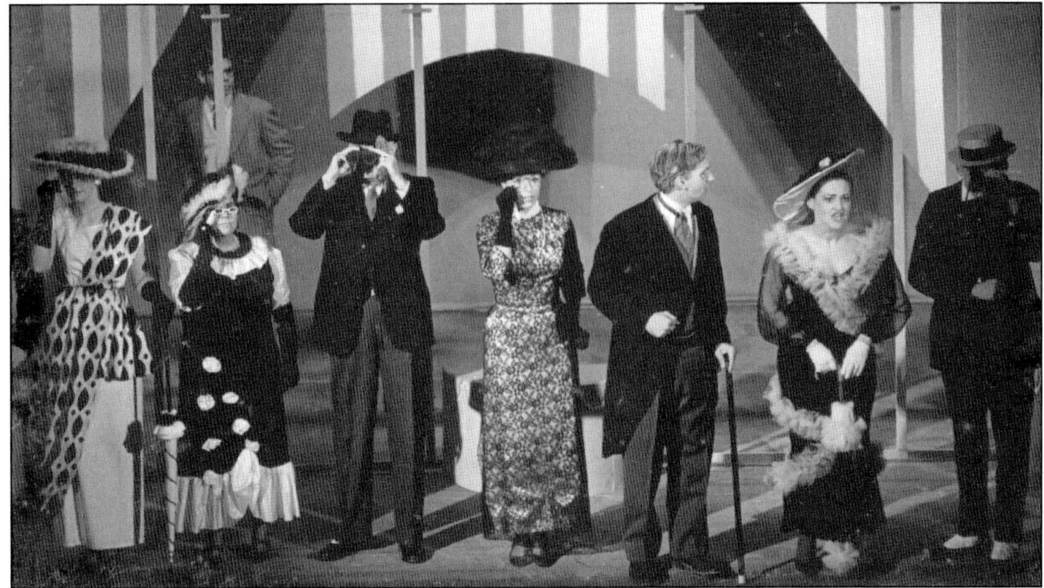

The 1966–1967 season ended with a production of *My Fair Lady*. This was a huge undertaking for a theatre that was ill equipped for flying scenery. This scene is the Ascot Opening Day. The costumes were black and white against a magenta set, which was Doug Swink's favorite color. (THCPA.)

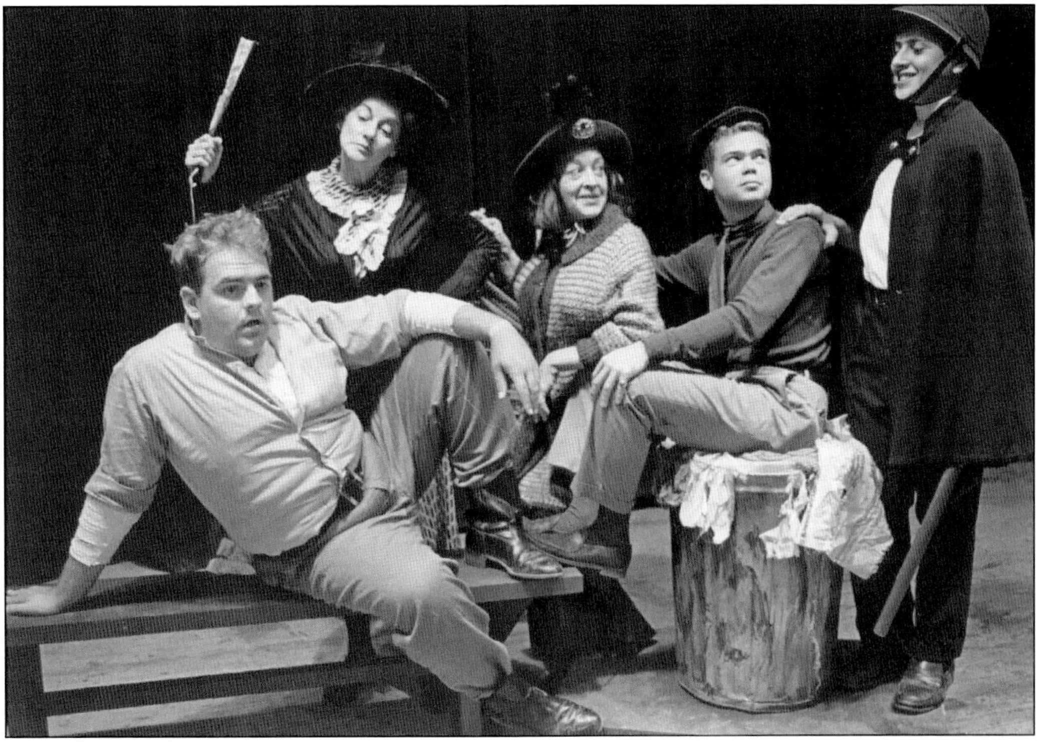

The cast of *My Fair Lady* included, from left to right, Sam Garner, Kay Swink, Tina Forester, Terry Wortley, and Steve Alper. Garner played Alfred P. Doolittle. Each night, he had to leap across the orchestra pit onto a ramp in the musical number "Get Me to the Church on Time." On more than one occasion, he stepped on the head of Bob Alexander, the conductor. (THCPA.)

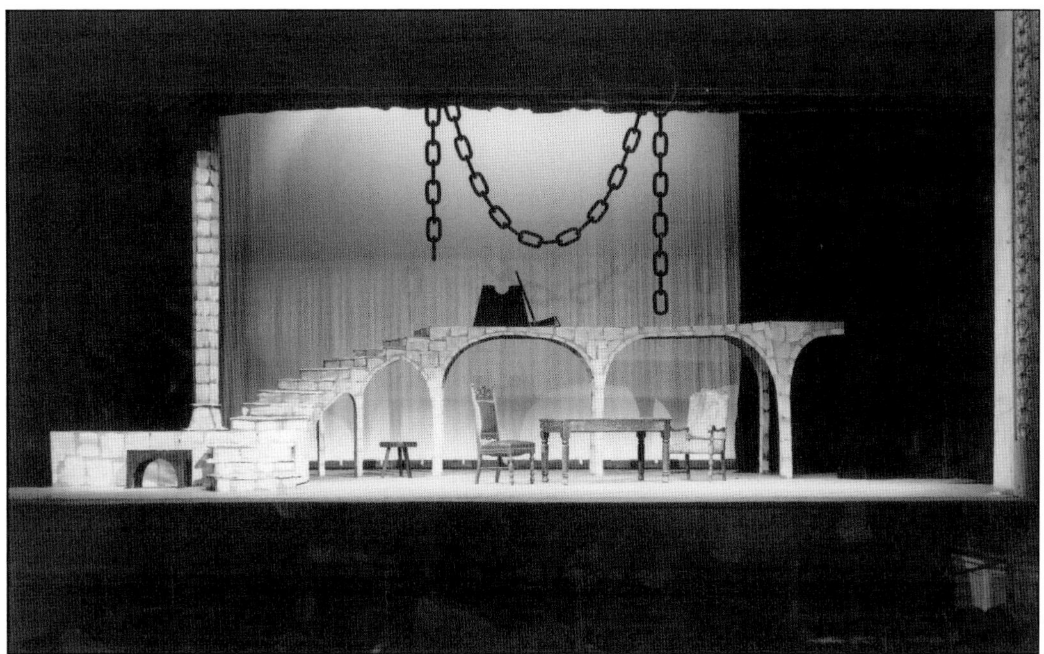

This photograph shows the striking set for *A Man for All Seasons*, which was directed by Anne Fitzgibbon. The curving staircase was taken out of an old house that was being demolished. It was recycled for three productions that season: *Cat and the Canary*, *The Recruiting Officer*, and this play. (THCPA.)

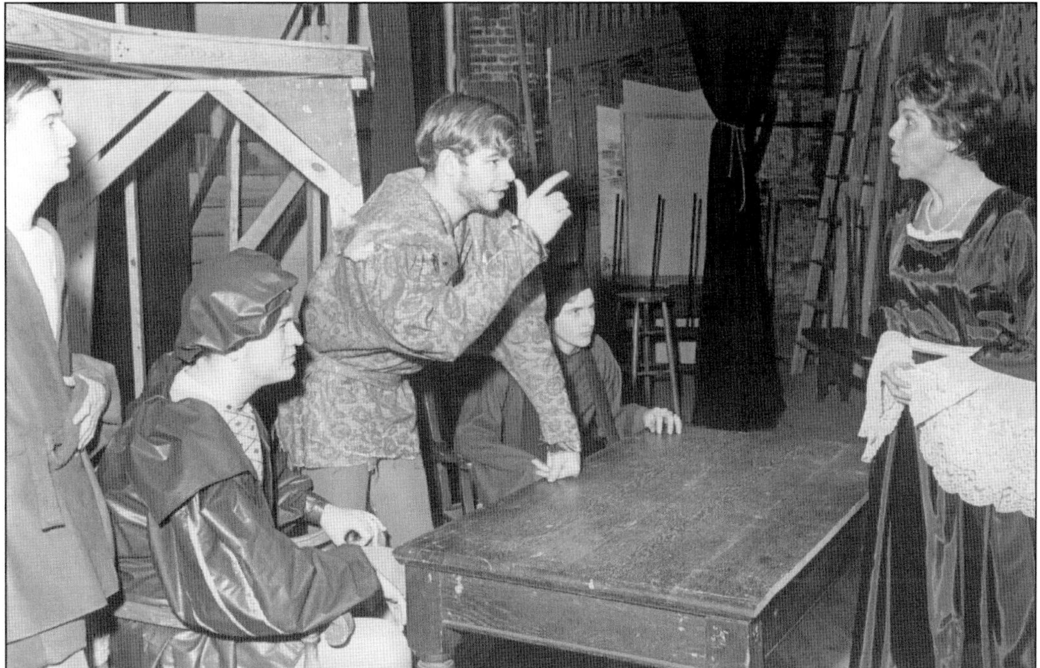

A Man for All Seasons dramatizes the downfall and execution of Sir Thomas More during the reign of Henry VIII. This rehearsal photograph shows, from left to right, Frank Hall, David Jones, Hank Blaustein, Tony Rivenbark, and Gerald Dowdy. (THCPA.)

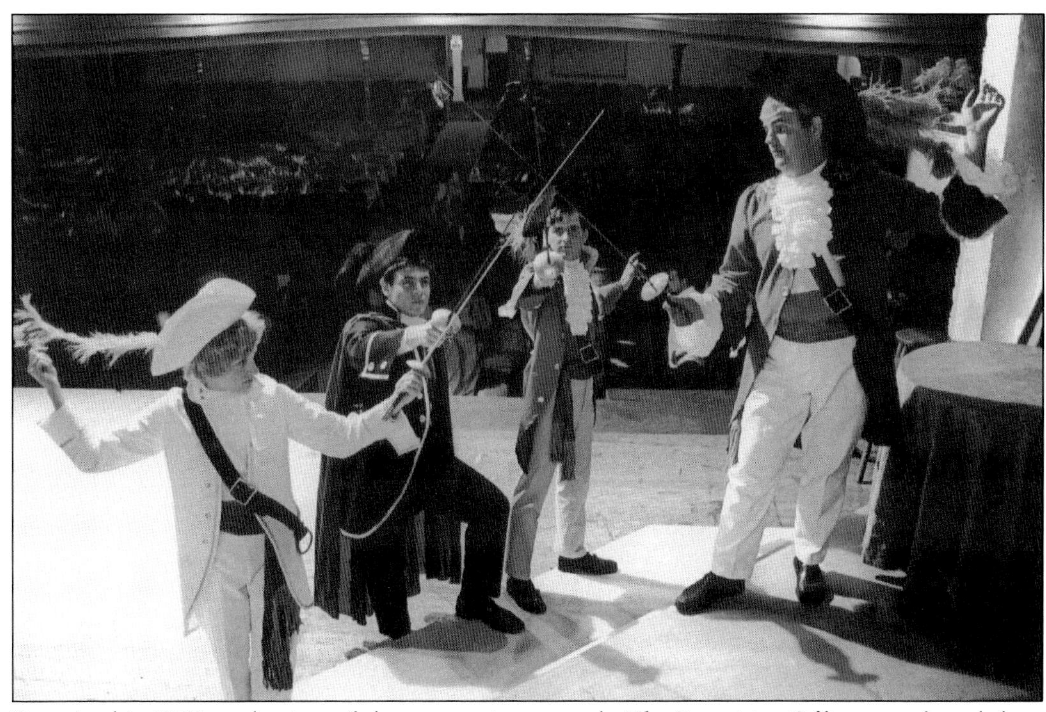

Seen in this 1967 production of the restoration comedy *The Recruiting Officer* are, from left to right, Carol Benton, Randolph Del Lago, Tony Rivenbark, and Sam Garner. (THCPA.)

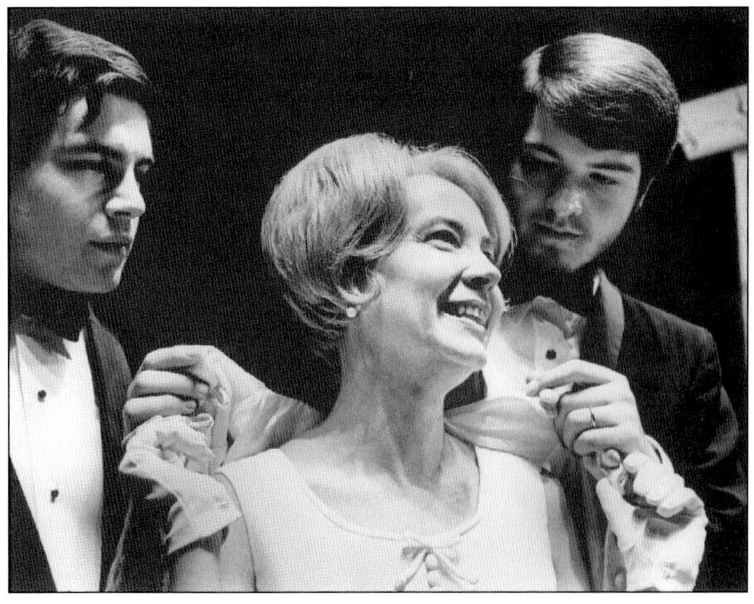

Prof. Anne Fitzgibbon directed the 1968 production of *Antigone*. From left to right are Randolph Del Lago, Berta Madely, and David James. This was the last show of the five-year series of coproductions between Wilmington College and the Thalian Association. (THCPA.)

In the 1960s, it became a rite of passage to explore Thalian Hall and look for the ghosts that many believe haunt the theatre. This photograph appeared in the *Star-News* in a story about ghosts. Tom Saks (left), Kent Raphael (center), and Bill Cameron climb the old staircase (now removed) to the first balcony. (The Star-News Collection, NHCPL.)

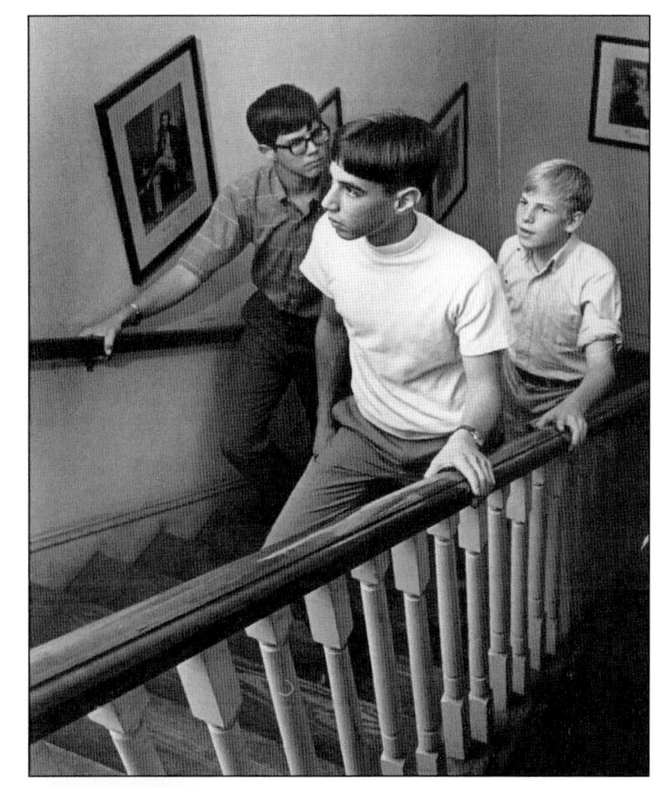

Ramona Warren (left) is demonstrating how to sew costumes for the Thalian Association's production of *Gypsy* in one of the dressing rooms under the stage. Warren was a veteran performer of many theatre productions at Thalian Hall and at UNCW. For this 1970 production, Warren played Electra, one of the strippers. (The Star-News Collection, NHCPL.)

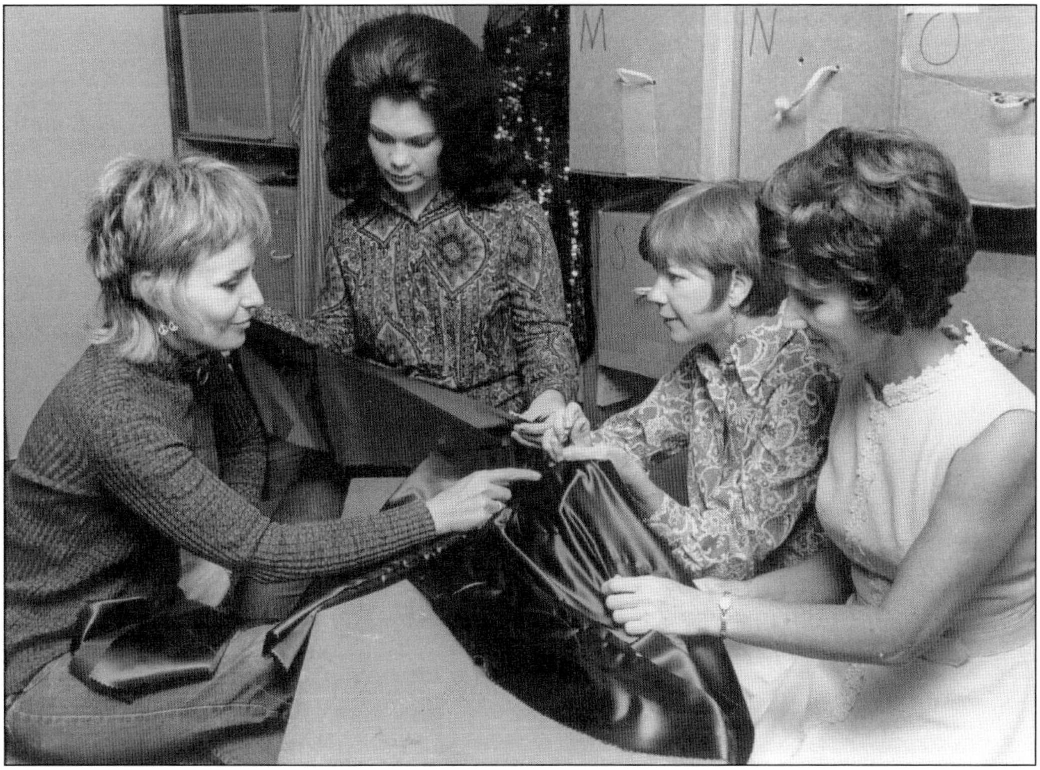

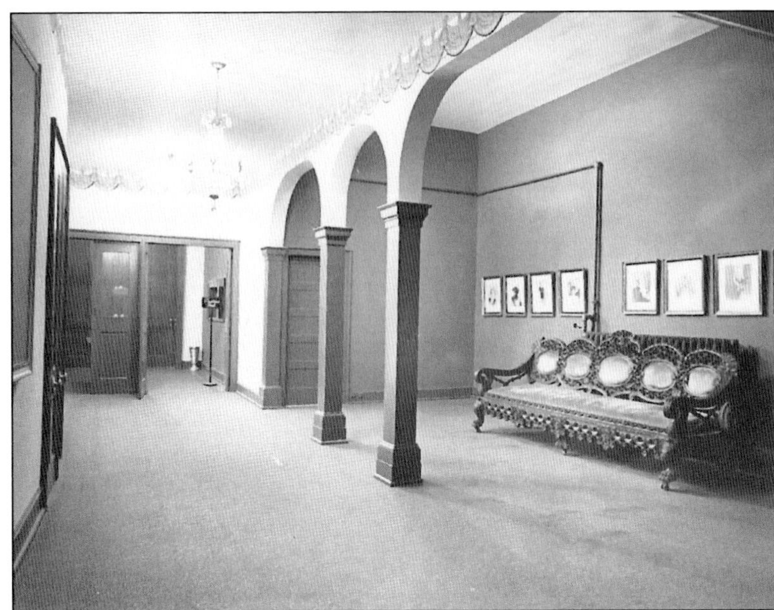

This 1970s photograph of the original Thalian Hall lobby looks south toward Princess Street. The auditorium is to the left, and the public entrance was through the doors at the end of the lobby. (The Star-News Collection, NHCPL.)

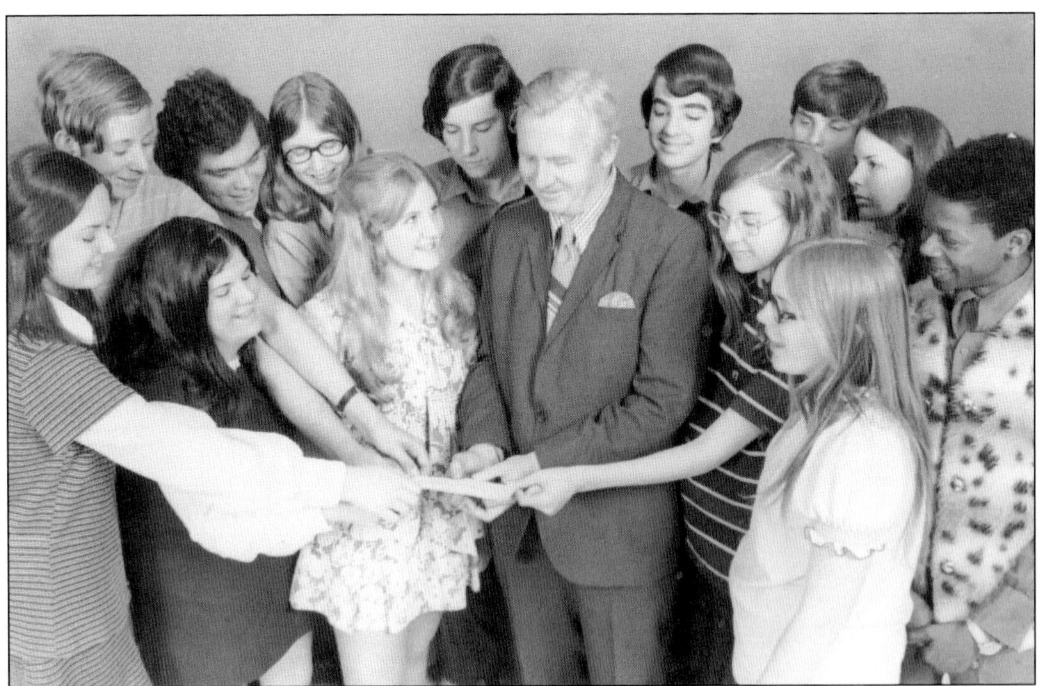

This 1973 photograph shows a group of young thespians presenting a contribution to Jim Pridemore, a longtime board member of the Thalian Association. Shown here are, from left to right, (first row) Sara Barnhill, Dorgene Gurganus, Barbara McDaniels, Barbara Johnston, Paula Gravih, and George Boynton; (second row), David Crockett, Carson Benson, Betsy Cobb, Alan Hill, Ben Liles, Bruce Sullivan, and Leslie Jordan. (The Star-News Collection, NHCPL.)

Eight

FIRE AND REBIRTH 1973–1982

On the afternoon of Saturday, February 3, 1973, a fire broke out in the historic theatre. The blaze was probably caused by electrical wiring, much of which dated from the turn of the century. The Thalian Hall Commission had two options. The first was to limit the necessary repairs so that the theatre could reopen, postponing the restoration until adequate funds could be raised. The second option was to proceed with the restoration plan while public concern was high. The commission decided that there would never be a time when the project would have as much public support, and it decided to move forward.

A new lease agreement was created between the Thalian Hall Commission and the city, giving them the authority to proceed with the restoration. The firm of Boney Architects was retained, and the project proceeded with the removal of the floor and repairs to the structure. New theatre seats, period carpet, the first air-conditioning system, and a repainted auditorium were all a part of the project. The commission raised $300,000 from the city, foundations, and private sources.

On October 17, 1975, the theatre reopened with a gala reception at the Governor Dudley Mansion, followed by a production of the musical *1776*, presented by the Thalian Association. Following the restoration, the Thalian Hall Commission took over management of the facility. In conjunction with the chamber of commerce, the Historic Wilmington Tour was developed, with the hall as the starting point. The commission also began the development of a plan for the renovation of the back stage. The Thalian Association, which had been using the Community Arts Center, returned its productions to Thalian Hall. It was joined by many events presented by the newly formed Arts Council.

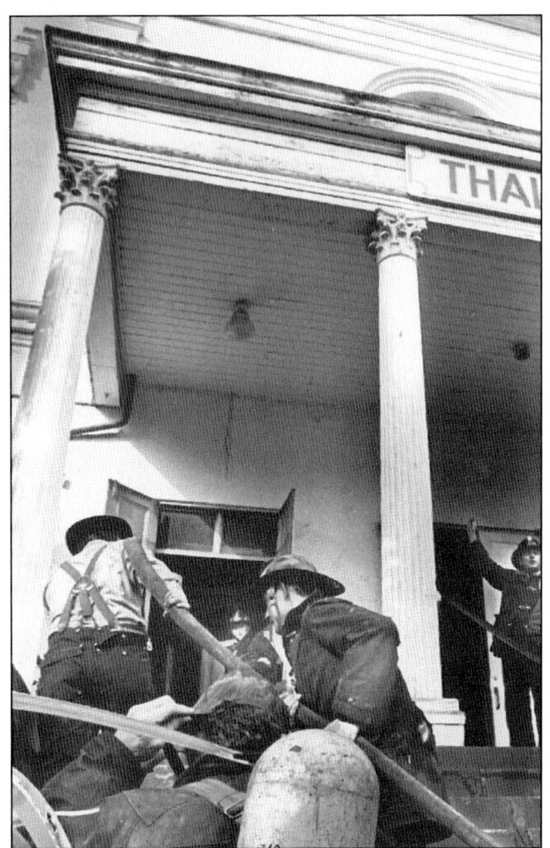

On February 3, 1973, smoke was seen coming under the exit doors as the stage crew was arriving to work on an upcoming production. Ironically, the next show was *The Last of the Red Hot Lovers*. Answering the call were 30 firemen from five companies. They fought heat and smoke for two hours before the blaze was finally extinguished. The cause was never determined, but it is thought old wiring was the reason. (The Star-News Collection, NHCPL.)

The damage was mainly confined to the area near the stage-left boxes and in the area underneath the wooden floor. Though studies had been undertaken by the Thalian Hall Commission, Inc. for the theatre's restoration, the projected cost had forestalled an active campaign for the project. However, as is often the case, the near escape led to a renewed effort to restore the 113-year-old theatre. (The Star-News Collection, NHCPL.)

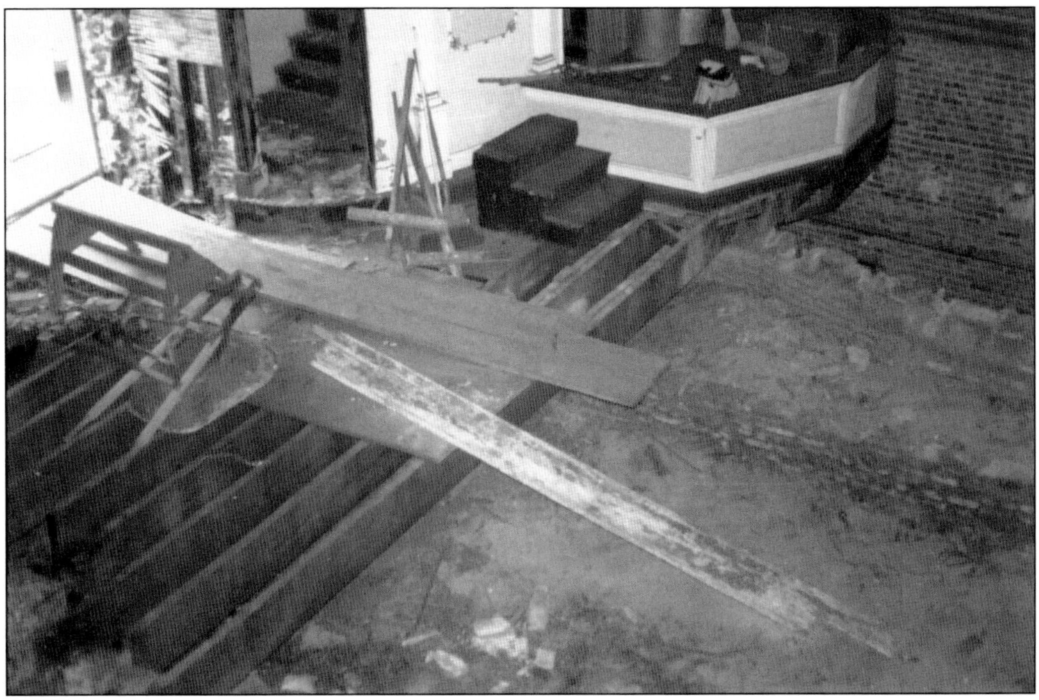

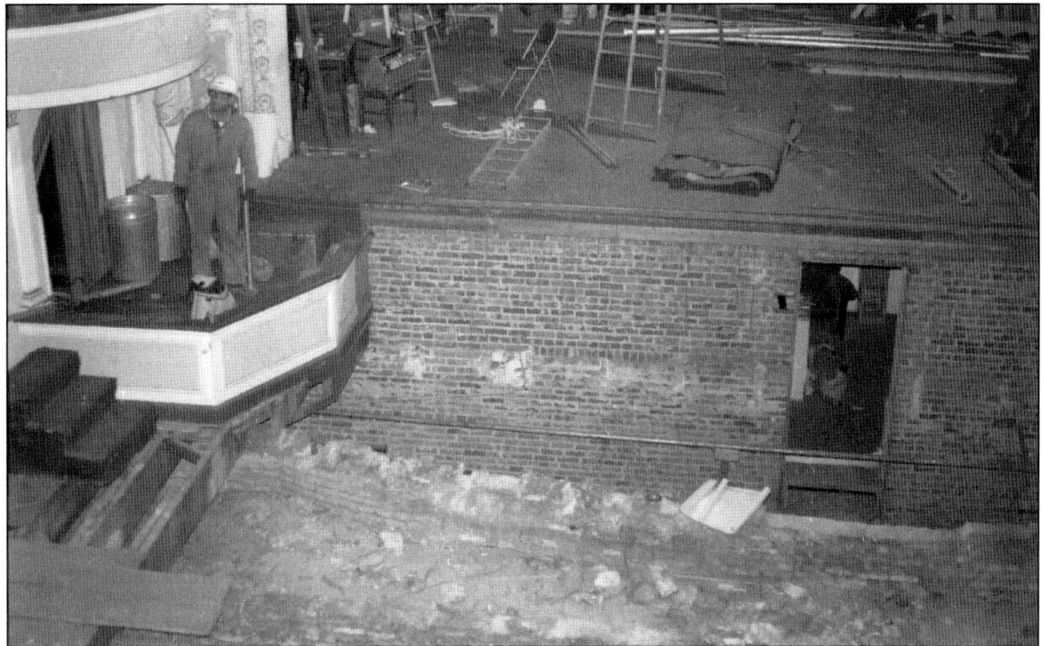

Following the 1973 fire, work began on the restoration of the auditorium in 1974. The removal of the floor revealed many details about the original arrangement of Thalian Hall, including the foundations for the forestage, which is the curving wall in front of the stage. The 1909 orchestra pit was constructed over those foundations and followed that curve. (THCPA.)

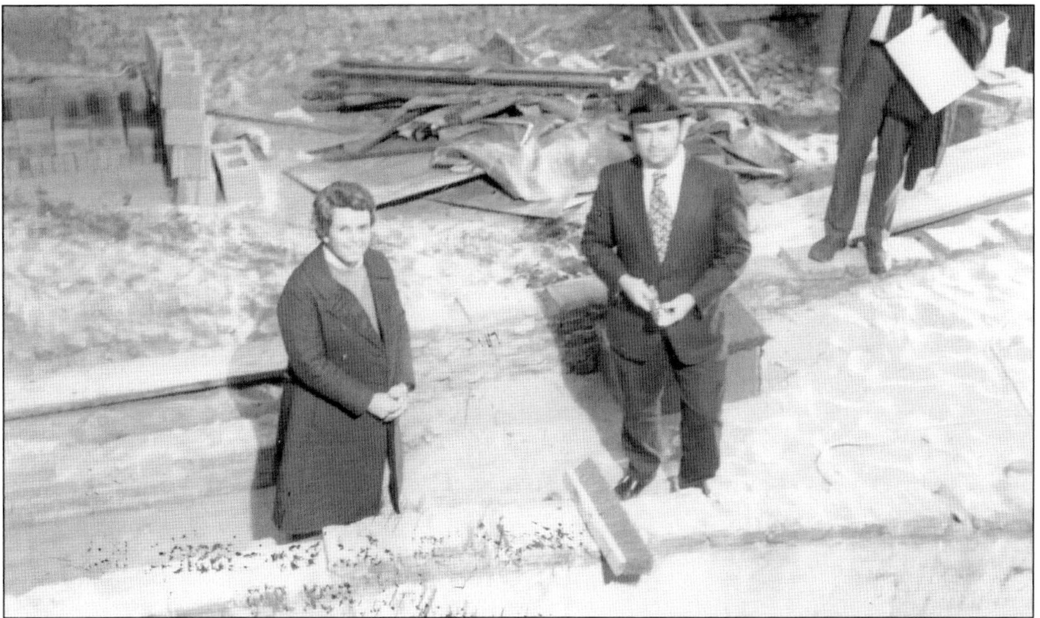

In this 1974 photograph, Elizabeth Wright, a member of the Thalian Hall Commission, Inc. and A.L. Huneycutt with the North Carolina Department of Archives and History stand on the sandy ground that lies under the floor of Thalian Hall. Wright was instrumental in the decision to replace the floor with wood rather than concrete, which had been recommended as a cost savings. (THCPA.)

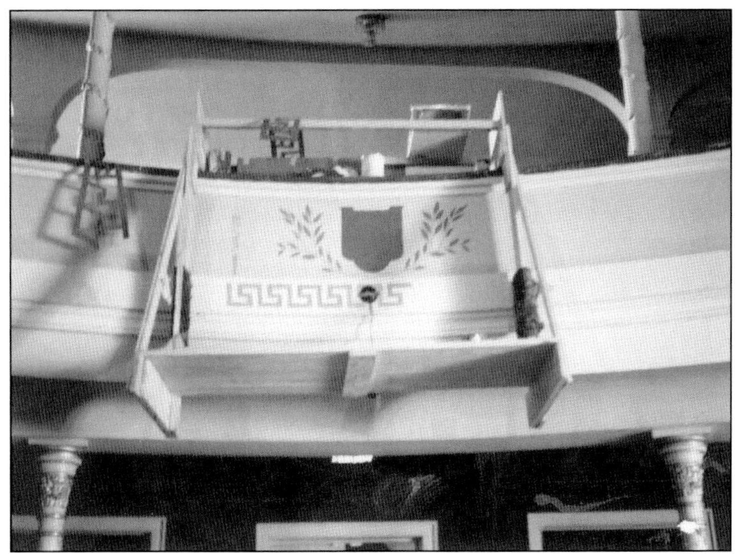

This 1975 photograph shows the re-creation of the 1909 stenciling decoration. Claude Howell tells the story in his journal: "When I was in my teens and the Hall was being painted, I went down and made drawings of the decorations before they were covered over. For some unknown reason the drawings were still in my desk." Howell made full-scale drawings, which were made into stencils for the repainting. (THCPA.)

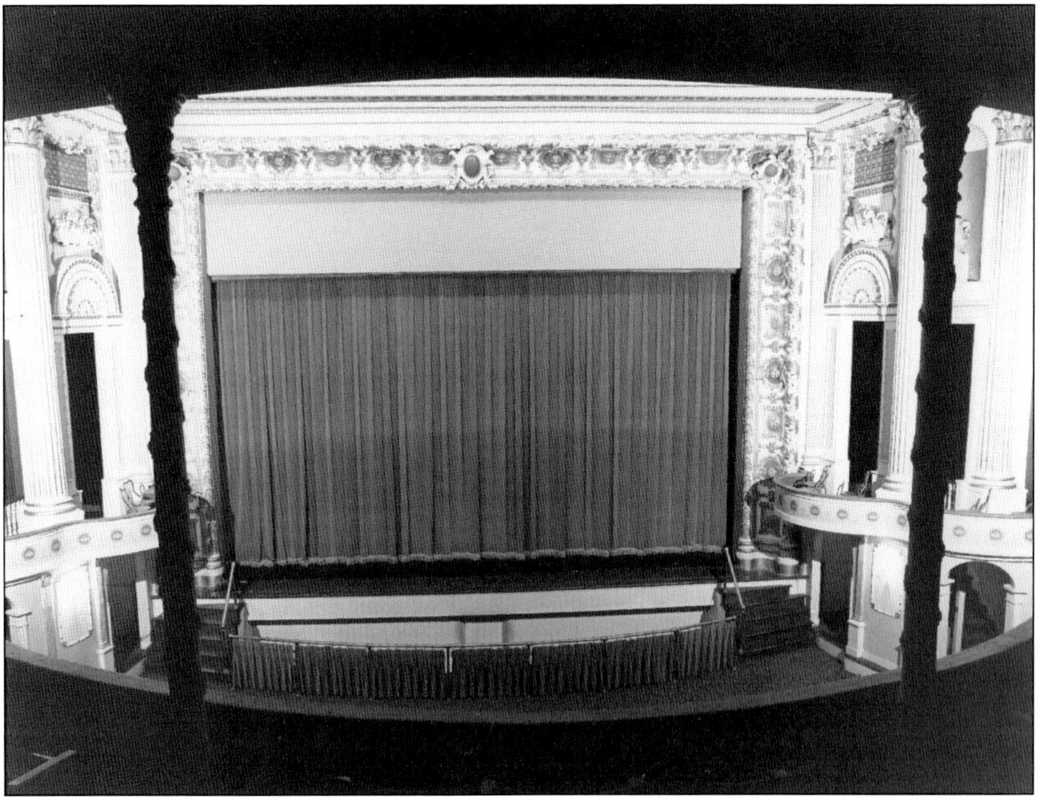

Thalian Hall is seen here as it appeared upon completion of the 1975 restoration. The curtain was reused; the line seen running across it was caused by the smoke damage. The large plaster rectangle beneath the top of the proscenium was installed in 1952 to allow the fire curtain to be flown out. (THCPA.)

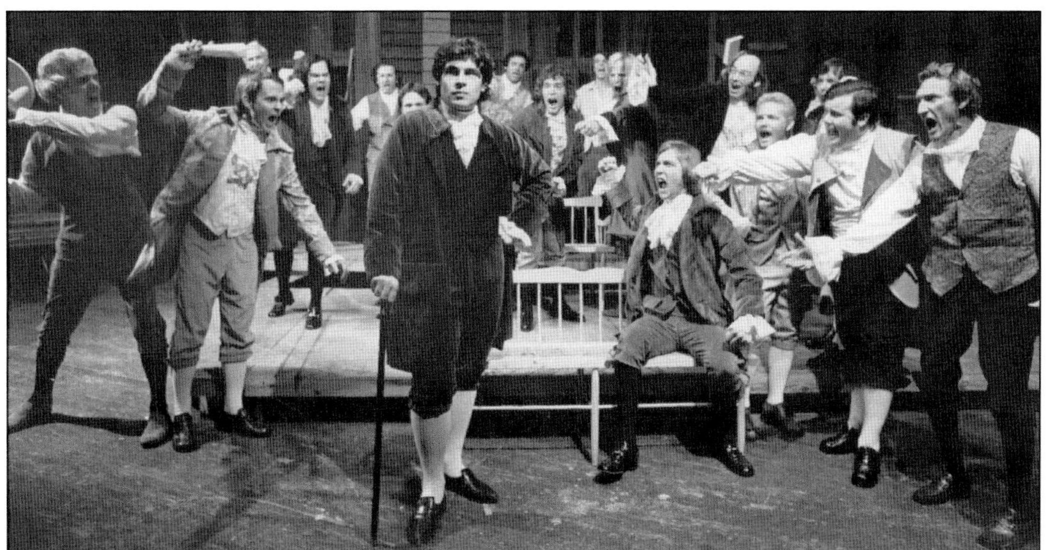

Thalian Hall reopened in 1975 with a gala performance of *1776*, with the governor in attendance. Randolph Del Lago (standing, center) played John Adams, and the cast also included Frank McNeil, Bill Conner, Floyd North, Mark Kavanaugh, Graig Rivenbark, Thom Clemmons, Leslie Boney, James MeGivern, Donn Ansell, Gilbert Tillet, Tony Rivenbark, Pat Adams, Bob Daum, Jack Blackman, Wayne Boyd, Allen McDowell, Jim Lockamy, Michael Sampley, Kelly Jewell, Richard Tomes, John Hardison, Bruce Steimer, Beth Bell, and Debbie Poirier. (THCPA.)

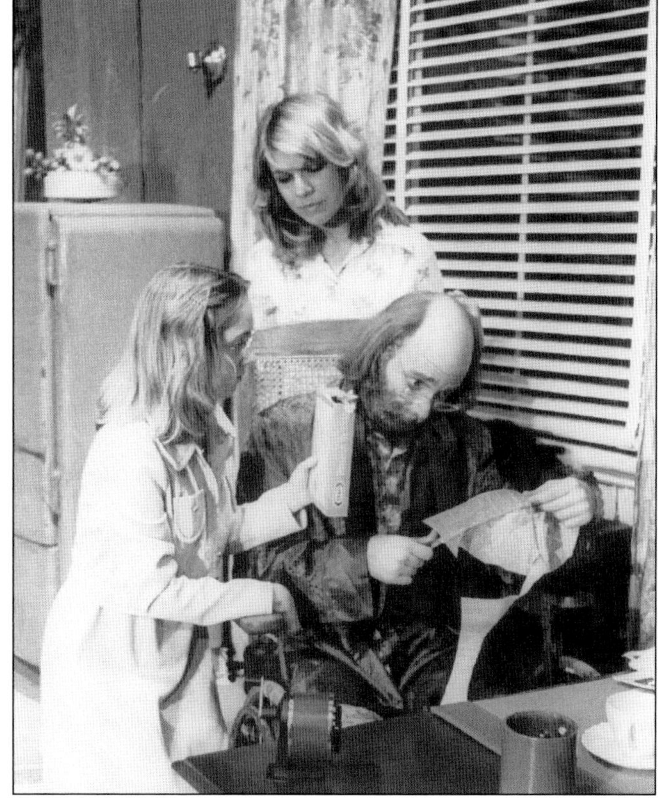

The next play in the restored theatre was the thriller *We Have Always Lived in a Castle*, seen in this publicity photograph. Pictured are Jean Connor (left), Debra Arsten (center), and Donn Ansell in the lead. Ansell would become very active in the Wilmington theatre community. The director for the 1975–1976 season, Peter Smith, had worked professionally as an actor before moving to Wilmington. (THCPA.)

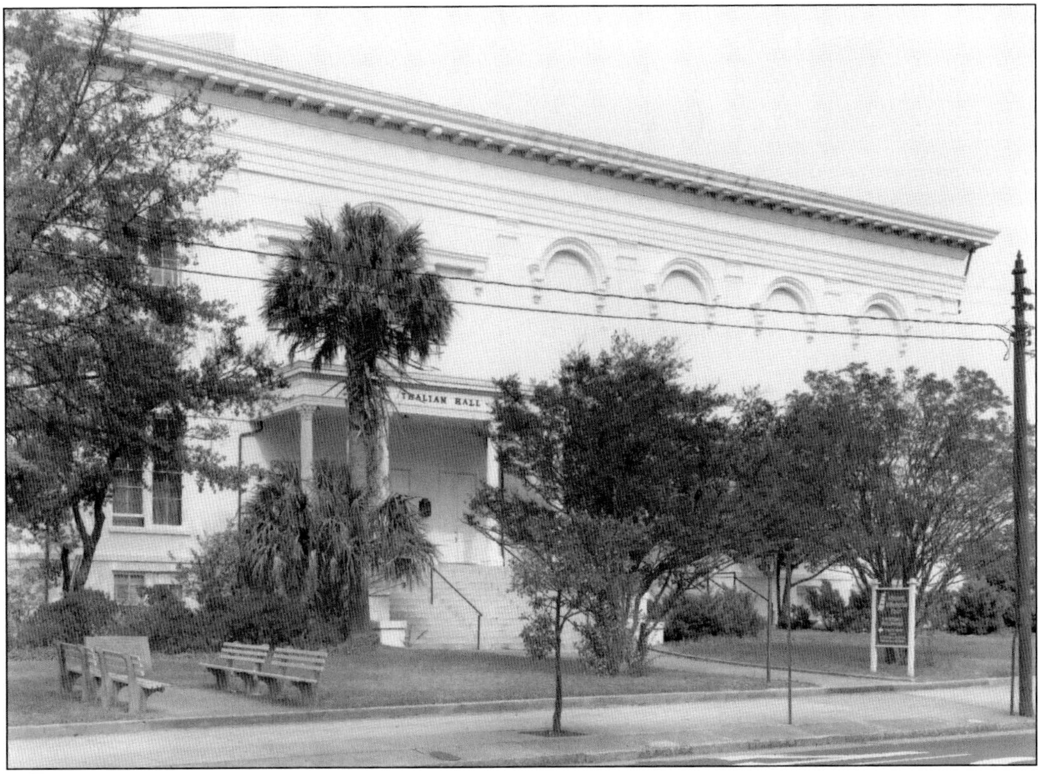

Following the 1975 restoration, the Thalian Hall Commission, Inc. (THCPA) worked with the chamber of commerce to establish the Historic Wilmington Walking Tour, which began operation in 1977. The tour originally included Thalian Hall, the Burgwin-Wright House, the Latimer House, St. John's Museum of Art, and the Governor Dudley Mansion. Tickets were purchased at Thalian Hall, and visitors were seated in the auditorium for an audio-visual presentation on the Lower Cape Fear area, narrated by Wilmington native David Brinkley. (THCPA.)

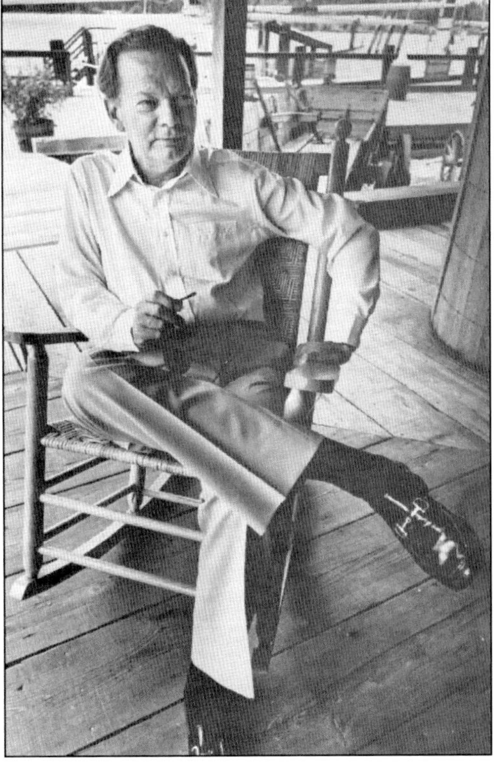

During the 10-year existence of the Historic Wilmington Walking Tour, thousands of visitors heard the voice of David Brinkley. He was born in Wilmington in 1920. In high school, he got his start in journalism, writing for the *Wilmington Star-News*. In 1943, he became a reporter for NBC. He died in 2003 and is buried in Wilmington's Oakdale Cemetery. This photograph of Brinkley was taken at Chandlers Wharf in 1976. (NHCPL.)

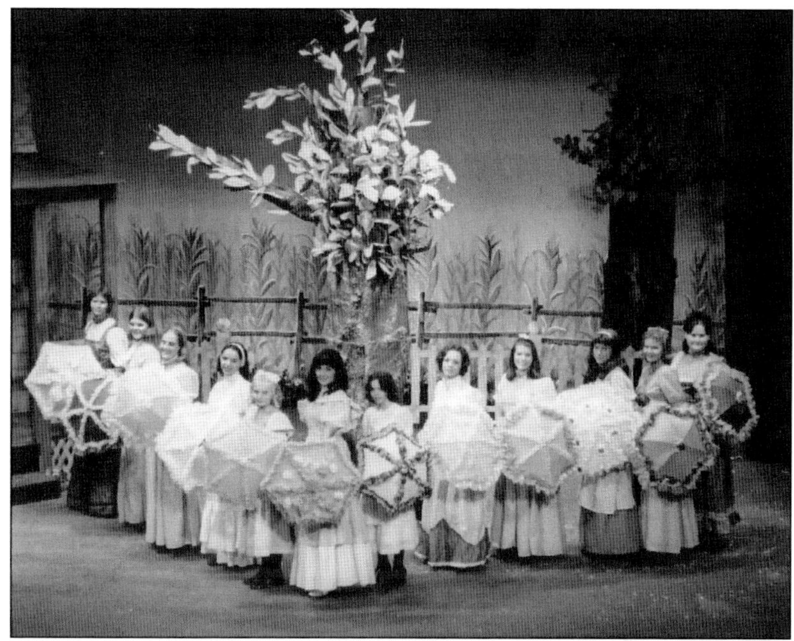

Oklahoma! closed the 1975–1976 season in the restored Thalian Hall, with Peter Smith directing. The season also included *My Three Angels* and Smith's own adaptation of *The Taming of the Shrew*, entitled *The Tamer Tamed*. (Thom Clemmons.)

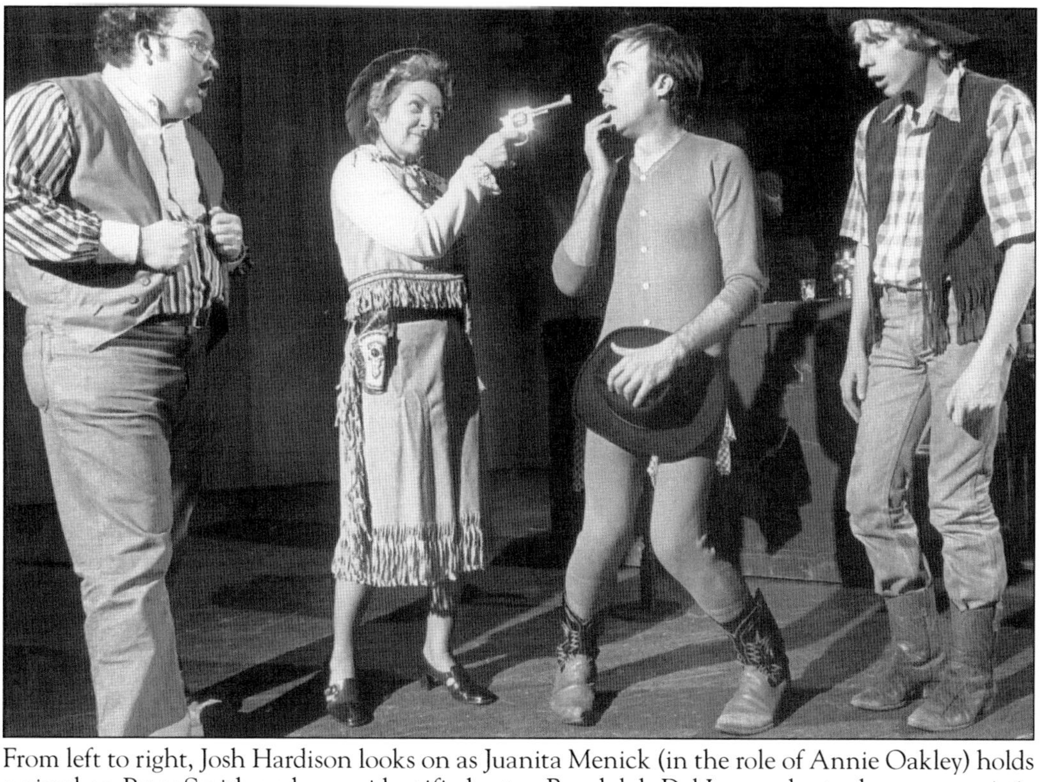

From left to right, Josh Hardison looks on as Juanita Menick (in the role of Annie Oakley) holds a pistol on Peter Smith and an unidentified actor. Randolph Del Lago, who took over as artistic director from Smith, directed this Thalian Association production of *Annie Get Your Gun* in 1976. (The Star-News Collection, NHCPL.)

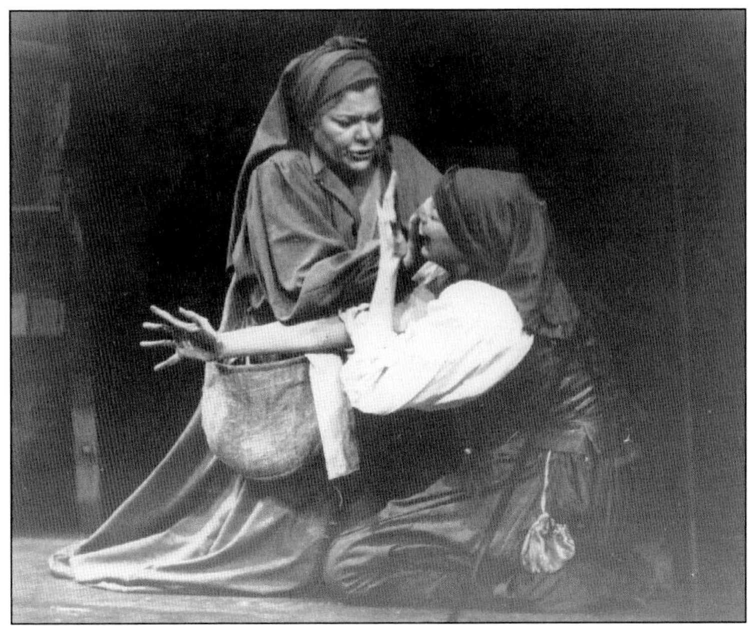

For the 1977–1978 season, Randolph Del Lago took the reins of the Thalian Association production and brought Bertolt Brecht's *Mother Courage and Her Children* to the Thalian Hall stage. He cast UNCW professor Anne Fitzgibbon in the title role. In this scene, Mother Courage is trying to comfort her wounded daughter Kattrin, played by Kathleen Fitzgibbon, Anne's daughter in real life. (Kathleen Fitzgibbon.)

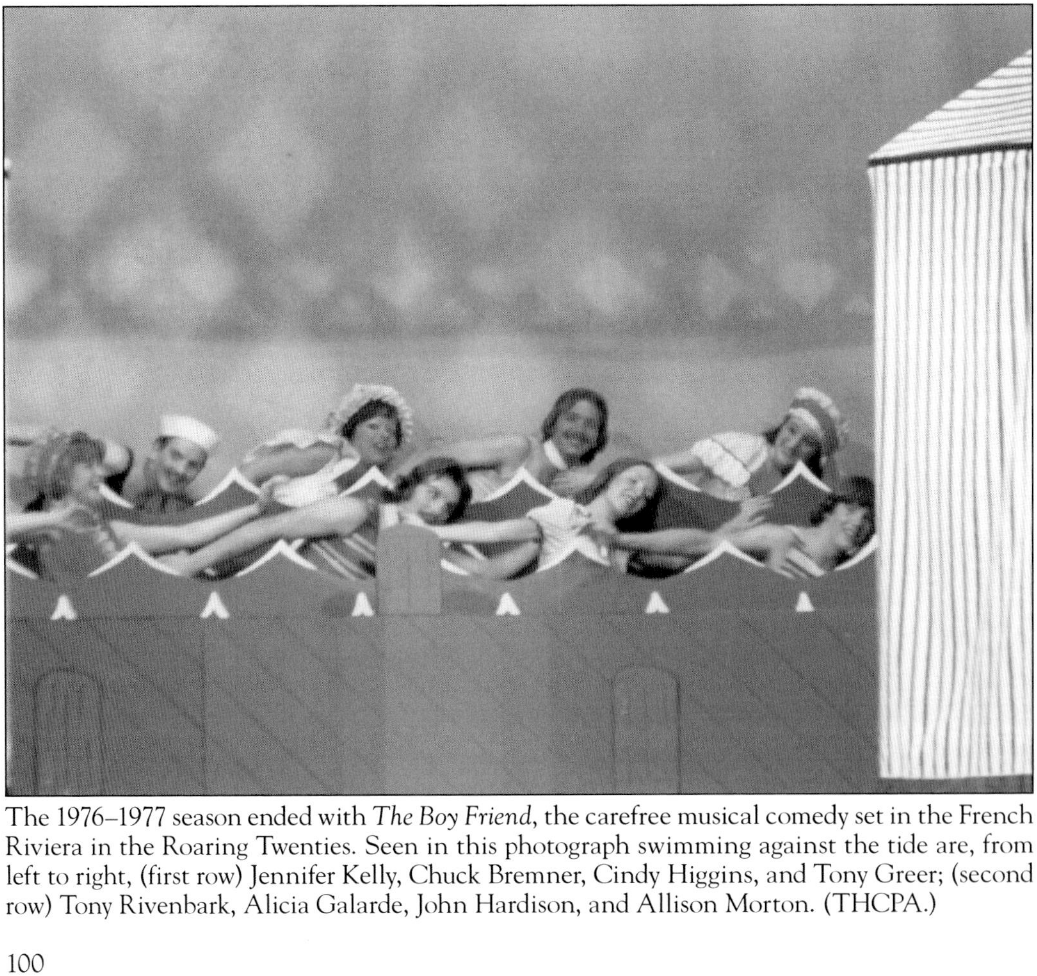

The 1976–1977 season ended with *The Boy Friend*, the carefree musical comedy set in the French Riviera in the Roaring Twenties. Seen in this photograph swimming against the tide are, from left to right, (first row) Jennifer Kelly, Chuck Bremner, Cindy Higgins, and Tony Greer; (second row) Tony Rivenbark, Alicia Galarde, John Hardison, and Allison Morton. (THCPA.)

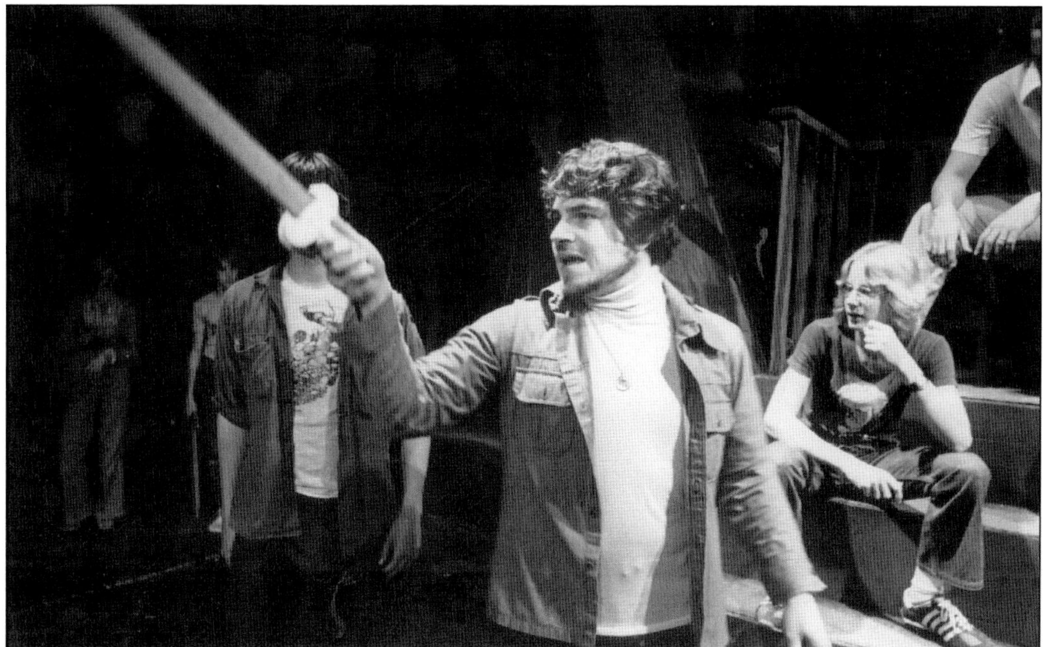

This *Star-News* photograph captures Randolph Del Lago directing *Pippin*, which ran for three nights as the closing show for the 1978–1979 season. Other shows that season were *Berlin to Broadway with Kurt Weill*; *The Bacchae*, by Euripides; and *Visit to a Small Planet*, by Gore Vidal. (The Star-News Collection, NHCPL.)

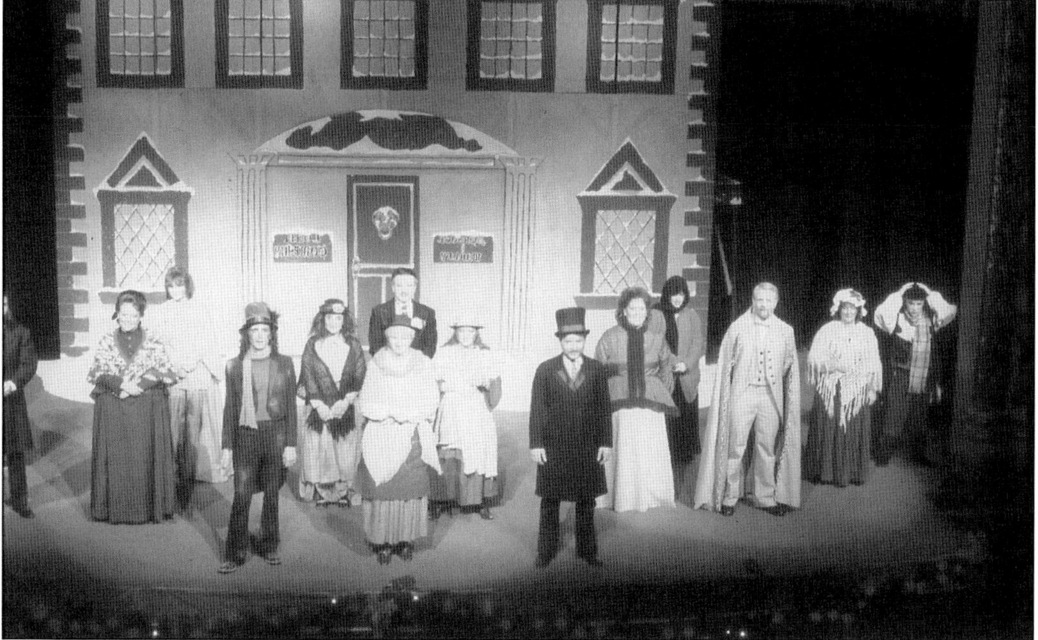

In 1979, the Thalian Association began mounting an annual production of *A Christmas Carol*, which continued into the mid-1980s. The first version was called *Scrooge*, then for several seasons the association used Ira David Wood's adaptation. This production is a version written by local playwright Steve Cooper. (THCPA.)

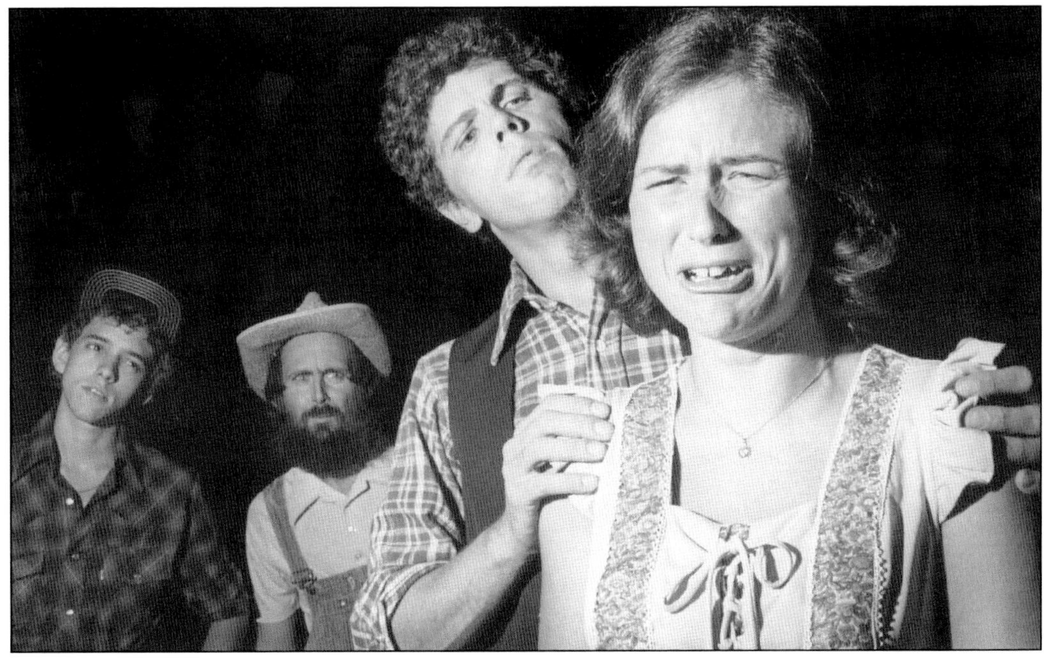

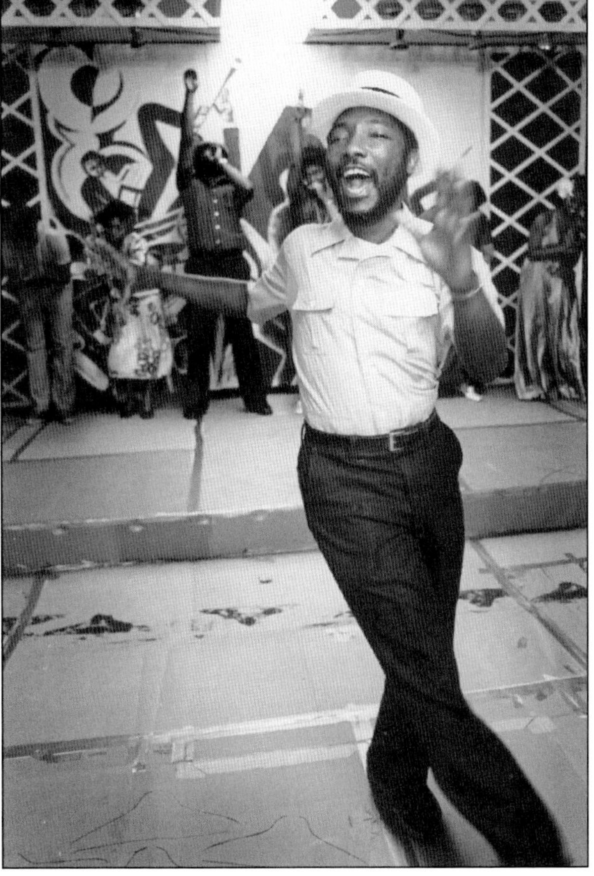

The Tugboat Players and the Arts Council produced a musical based on *A Midsummer Night's Dream*. The original script was written by a young playwright named Steve Cooper. He wrote many musicals while in Wilmington. Pictured here are, from left to right, Cooper, C.W. Casey, Billy Smith, and Terry Casey. They were all active in the Wilmington theatre scene in the 1980s. (The Star-News Collection, NHCPL.)

The Willis Richardson Players, organized in 1974, was named for the first African American playwright to be produced on the Broadway stage. In addition, Richardson was born in Wilmington. Here is a scene from *Jive Jazz and Blues*, with Anthony Ginwright performing. (The Star-News Collection, NHCPL.)

Nine

Celebrating the Arts 1982–1987

The 1980s witnessed increased activity in all arts disciplines in Wilmington. The Thalian Hall Commission, Inc. hired its first executive director, and the focus was changed from restoration and tourism to the development of a program of improvements that would make the theatre more efficient for performances. The management actively participated in the creation of the St. Thomas Celebration of the Arts, and for the first time in many years major performing artists appeared on the Thalian Hall stage to full houses.

In 1983, the commission retained the services of Theatre Projects of London to develop a master plan to address the needs of the theatre and the public. In order to focus public attention on the plan, a month-long celebration was developed for the 125th anniversary of the theatre. The centerpiece was an original musical comedy, *Remembered Nights*, by Randolph Umberger and Benjamin Keaton. The production was produced by the Thalian Hall Commission, Inc., the Arts Council, and the Thalian Association, with additional support from Walter and Lynn Pancoe.

Appearing in the production was New York actor Lou Criscuolo, who later formed a theatre group called Opera House. He mounted his first summer season in 1985, and Thalian Hall began to host performances on a year-round basis. That same year, a $2.4 million bond issue passed for the expansion of Thalian Hall.

To better reflect the mission, the Thalian Hall Commission, Inc. became the Thalian Hall Center for the Performing Arts, Inc. in 1986. The city retained the services of Paul Hanbury of Norfolk and Ligon Flynn of Wilmington as the architects. The scope of the project was expanded to include the reopening of the second floor of Wilmington City Hall for public use.

By 1987, usage of Thalian Hall had reached record proportions. In addition to the Thalian Association and Opera House, there were other significant users, including the Wilmington Civic Ballet and the Thalian Hall Concert Series. The facility was operating seven days a week with 110 public events and attracting 40,000 people annually.

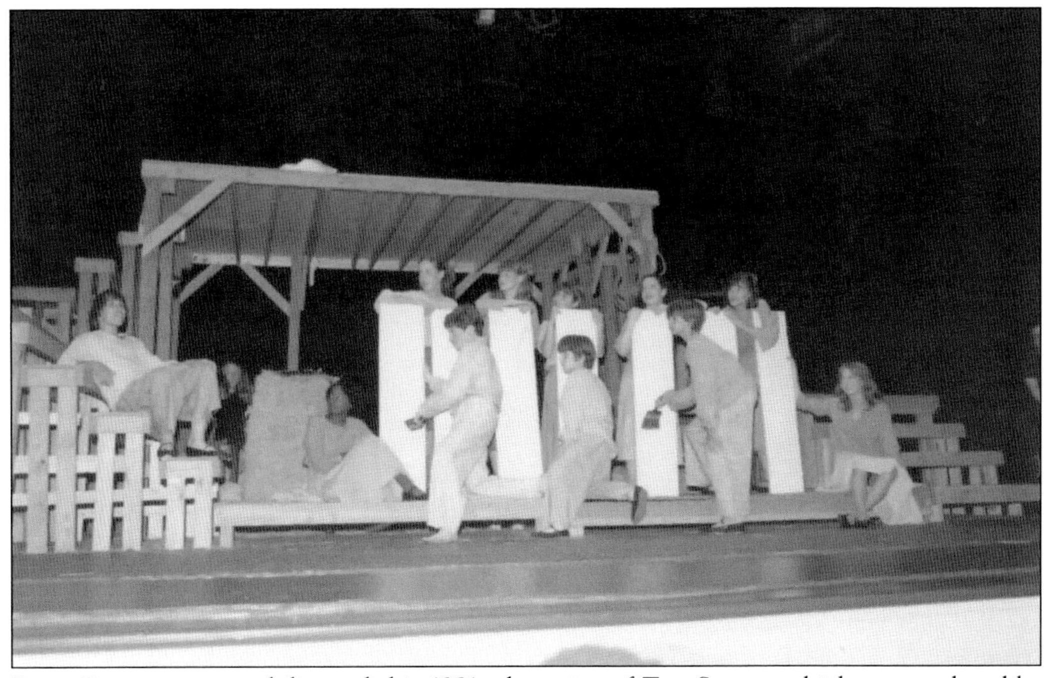

Steve Cooper wrote and directed this 1981 adaptation of *Tom Sawyer*, which was produced by the City of Wilmington Parks and Recreation. In this "white-washing" scene, Latty Bost is Tom and Marianne Kunz is at the piano. Also shown here are, from left to right, April Jordan, Nicoa Clemmons, Chris Highsmith, Kellie Lee, Shelia Lorek, Mathew Levy, Rachel Levy, Richard Kunz, Kim Heinberg, and M.K. Leete. (Steve Cooper.)

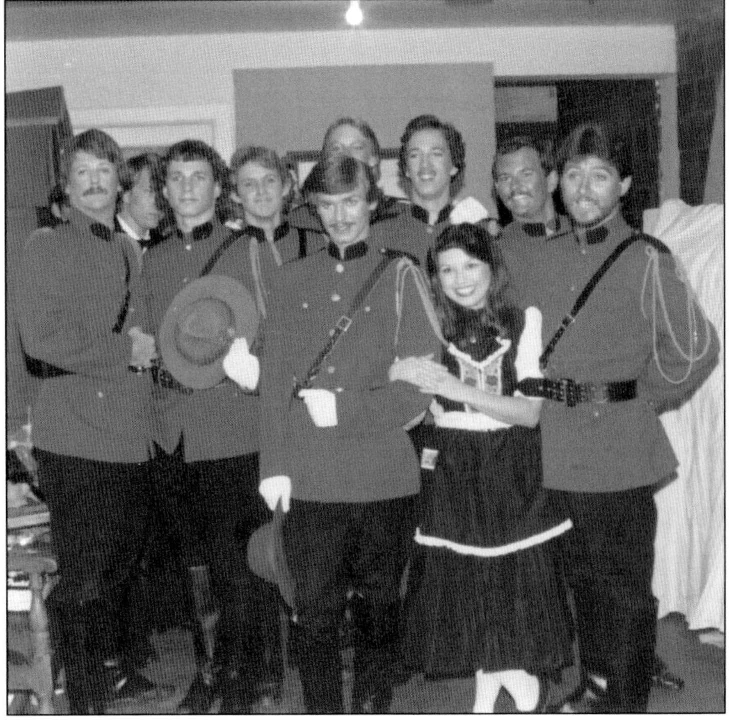

This photograph was taken outside the basement dressing rooms for the 1981 production of *Little Mary Sunshine*. From left to right are (first row) Henry Rehder Jr., Don Payne, Peter Phillips, Yolanda Evans, and Curt Hursey; (second row) Bobby Sheffield, Todd Weeks, Ben Butler, Rick House, and Bob Daum. Weeks went on to appear in the Broadway productions of *The Last Night of Ballyhoo* and *The Full Monty*. Payne was an award-winning writer and producer of *The Simpsons* and an inductee to the Wilmington Walk of Fame. (THCPA.)

This is a publicity photograph for the 1982 production of *The Lion in Winter*, which deals with a dysfunctional family in the 12th century. It features, from left to right, Virginia Callaway as Eleanor of Aquitaine, Richard Tomes as Henry II, and Victoria Daum as Princess Alais. (The Star-News Collection, NHCPL.)

Kay Swink directed the 1981 production of *Over Here!*. During dress rehearsal, members of the cast and crew of the World War II musical pose at the loading dock. They are, from left to right, (first row) Ron Smith, Audrey Tolar, Betsy Cobb, Lisa Cobb, Karen Smith, Gary Winley, and Marianne Kunz; (second row) Dawn Manning, Anne Lowe, Sid Crowley, and Steve Cooper. Standing at the stage door is Juanita Menick. (THCPA.)

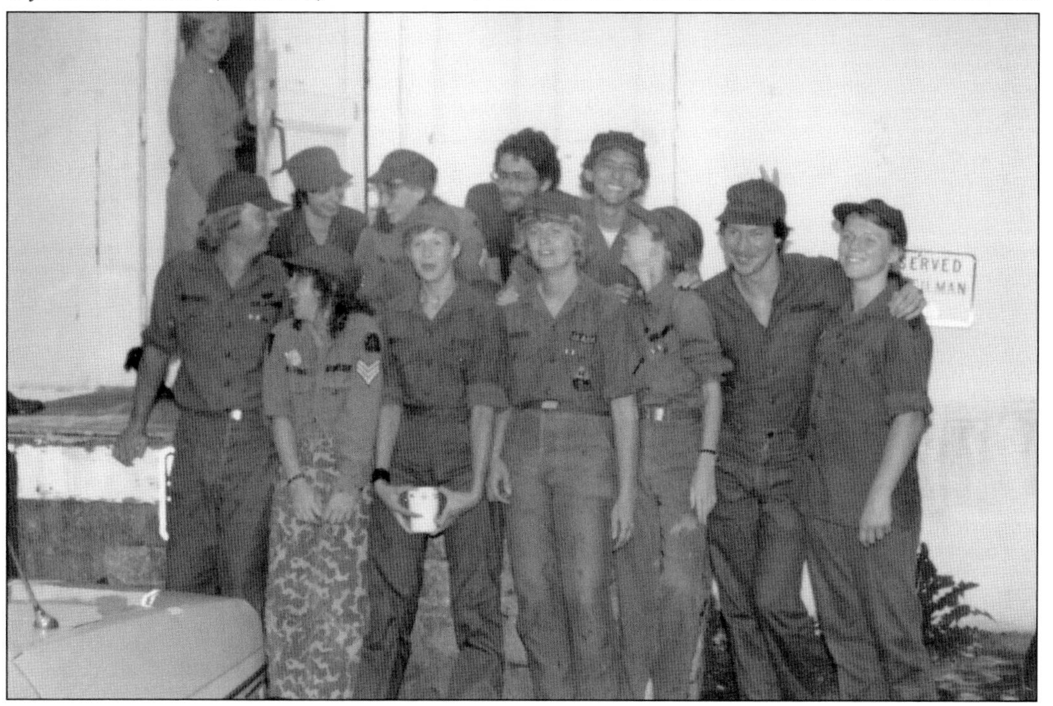

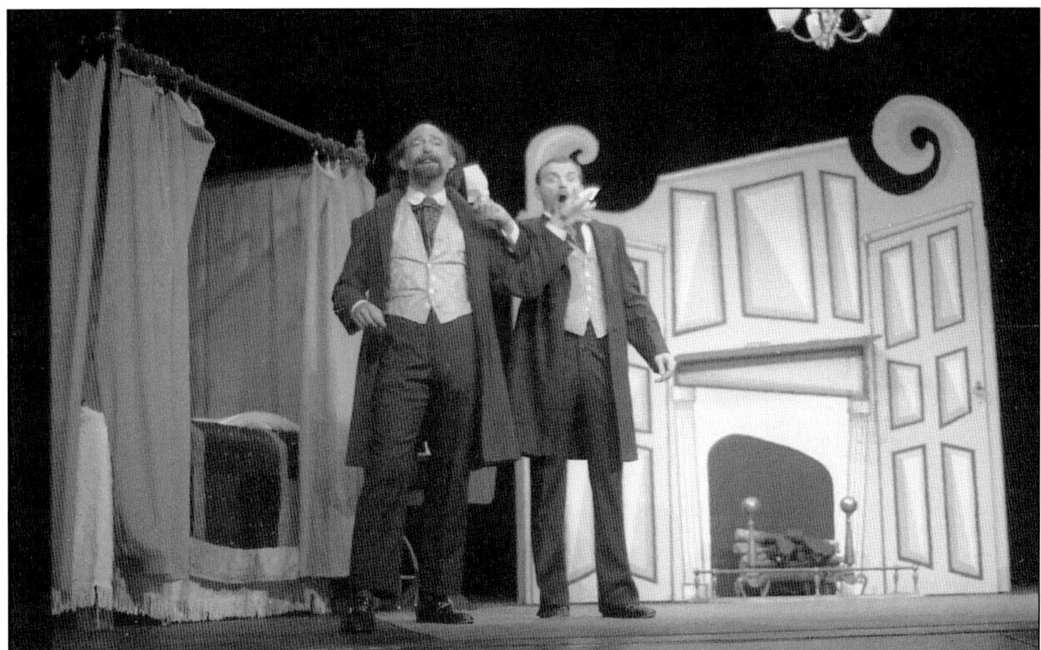

The Thalian Hall Commission, Inc. did not regularly stage local theatrical productions. However, for the 1982 annual meeting of the North Carolina Press Association, it produced the classic farce *Box and Cox*, with Donn Ansell (left) and Tony Rivenbark (right) in the title roles. The effort paid off when many daily newspapers across the state ran full-page articles when the theatre celebrated its 125th anniversary. (THCPA.)

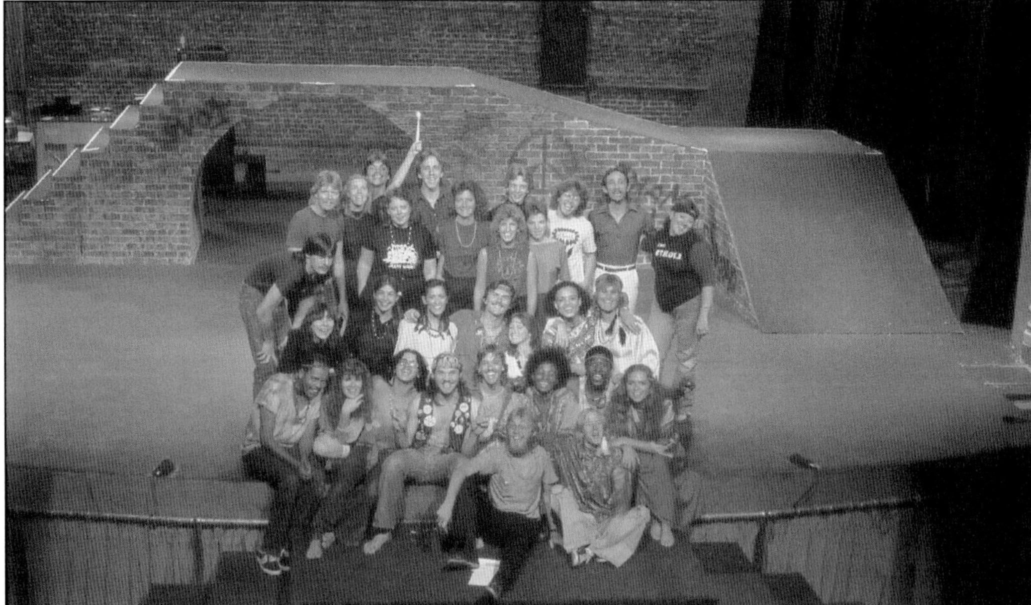

In 1982, the Thalian Association presented a very popular production of *Hair*. The cast of over 20 performers featured some of most active members of the Wilmington theatre community. The production, directed by Scott Davis and Donn Ansell, featured the first nudity on the Thalian Hall stage, even though it was heavily veiled by theatrical fog. (THCPA.)

Thalian Hall has always been a popular venue for classical and folk concerts. Local and touring artists have praised the hall's acoustics and intimacy. Local musician and balladeer John Golden is seen standing in one of the Thalian Hall's boxes with classical guitarist Rob Nathanson, a music teacher at UNCW. (THCPA.)

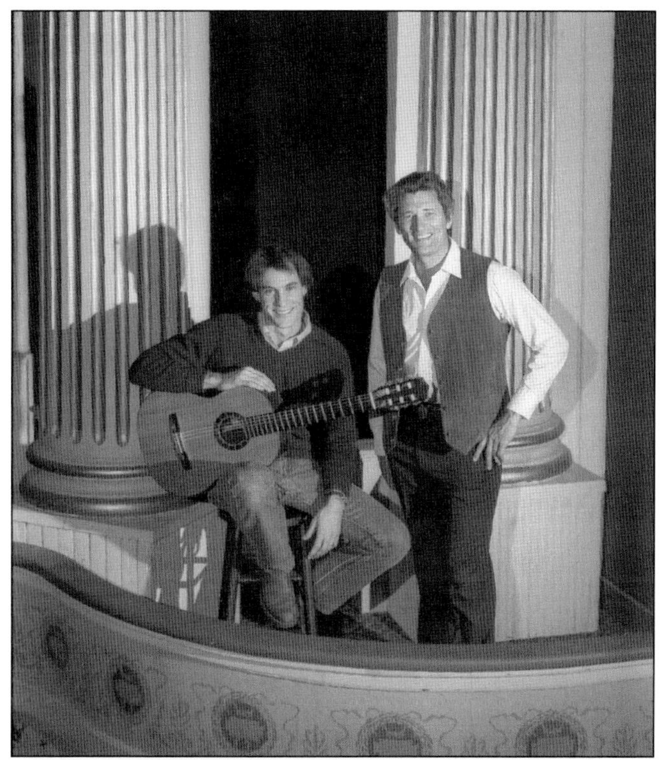

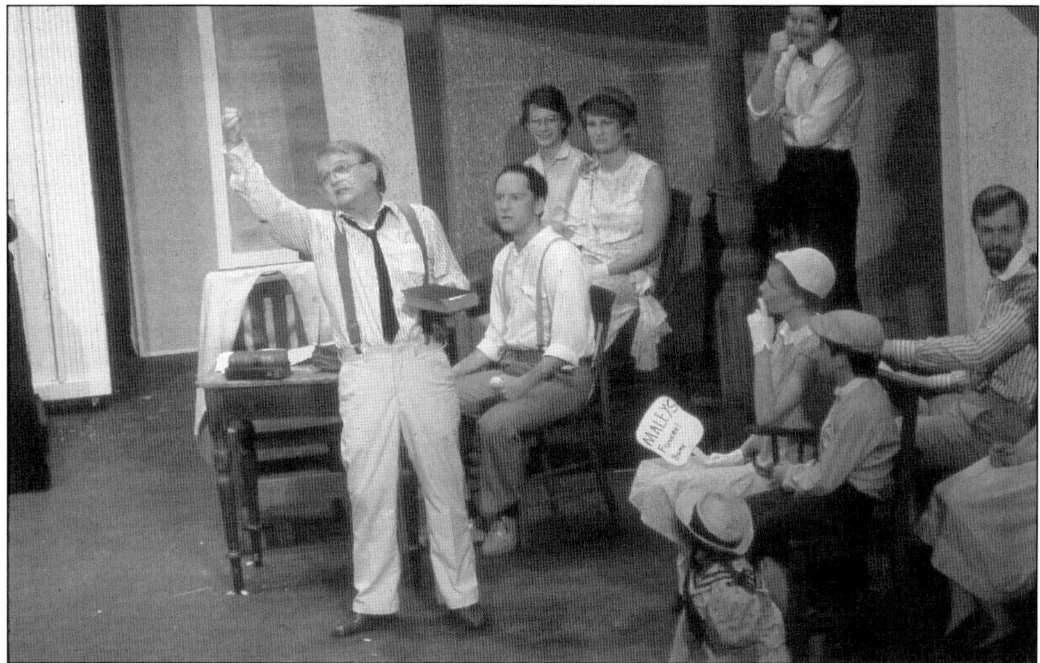

In the 1983 production of *Inherit the Wind*, Richard K. Olsen (left) played Henry Drummond, whose character was based on the famous trial lawyer Clarence Darrow. The play is based on the famous 1925 "Scopes monkey trial," which pitted Darrow against William Jennings Bryan. In 1912, Bryan gave a lecture in Thalian Hall. (THCPA.)

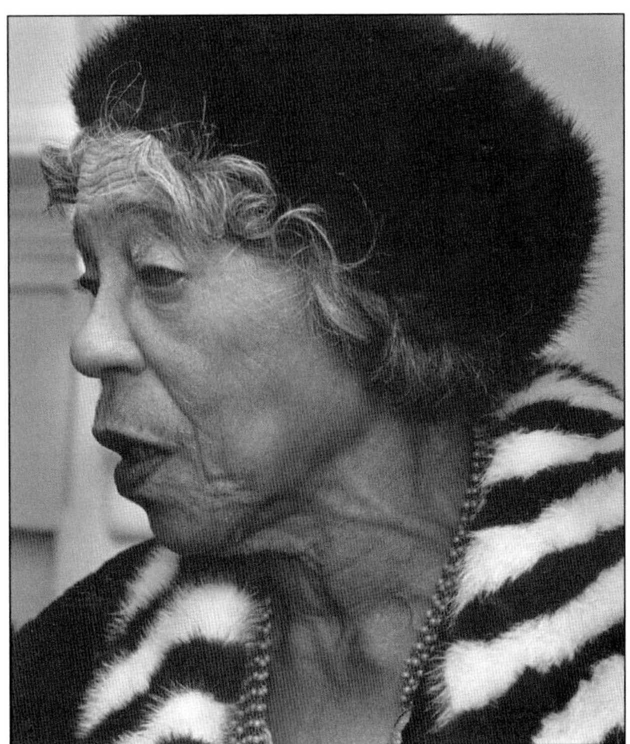

In 1982, the Arts Council brought the arts community together for a weeklong festival and a series of performances, most of which took place in Thalian Hall. The honored guest for the first festival was Wilmington native Caterina Jarboro, who was instrumental in breaking the color barrier in classical music in America (see page 50). She performed in Thalian Hall in 1933. (Author's collection.)

Thanks to the St. Thomas Celebration of the Arts, Thalian Hall once again took its place as a major concert venue for Wilmington and helped to focus the need for expansion and renovation. This 1984 photograph shows Joan Mondale with members of the St. Thomas Celebration Committee. (THCPA.)

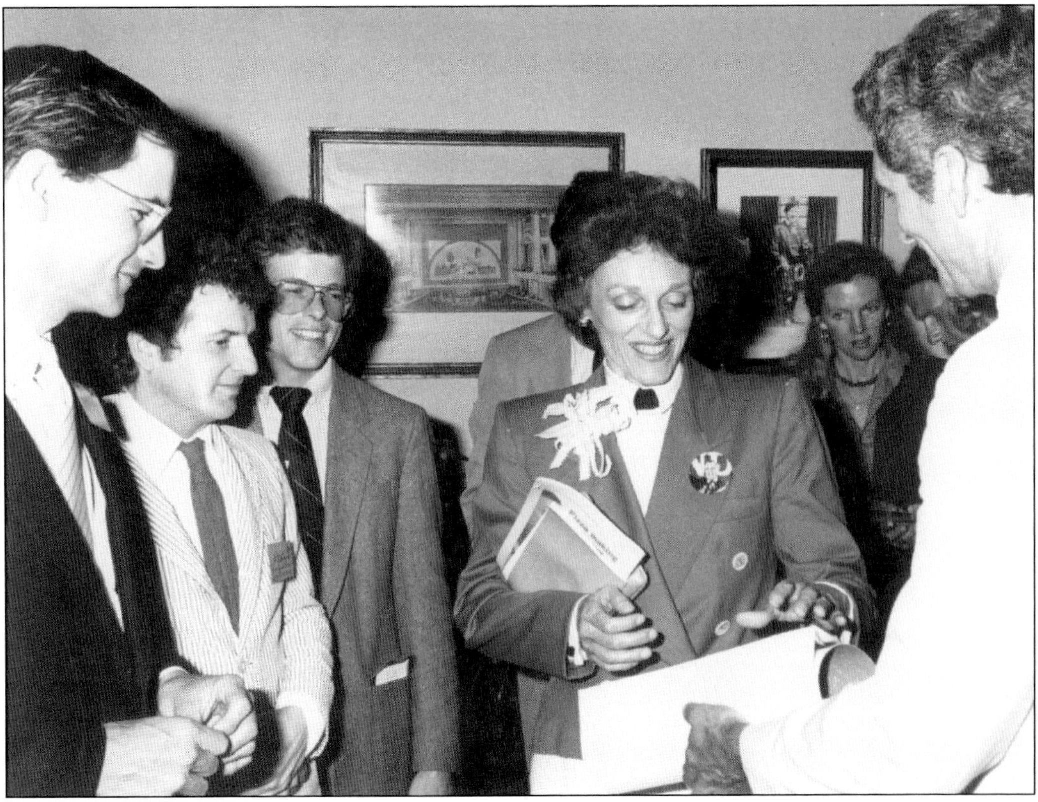

Herbie Mann, seen here in the box at Thalian Hall, was one of the many performers who appeared in the annual St. Thomas Celebration of the Arts. Other artists and groups who appeared in Thalian Hall for the celebration in the 1980s included Billy Taylor, the North Carolina Shakespeare Festival, McCoy Tyner, the National Opera Company, Teddy Wilson, and the New York Baroque Dance Company. (THCPA.)

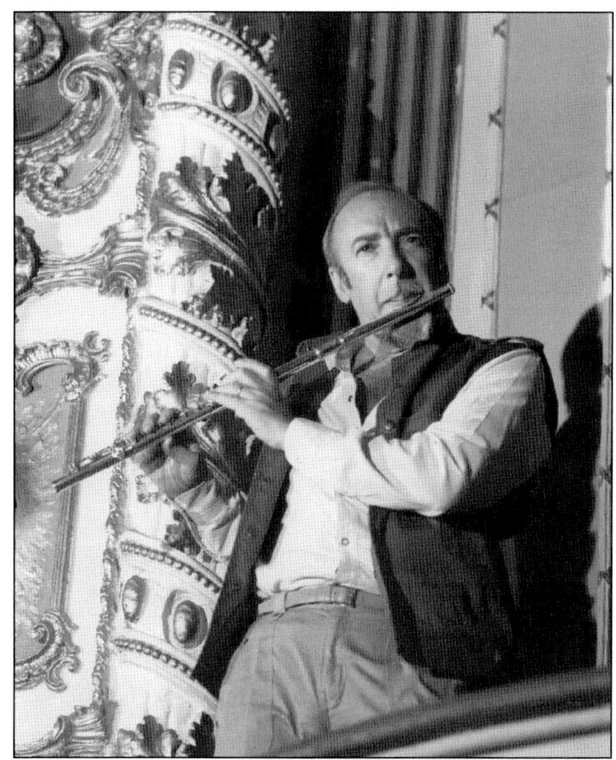

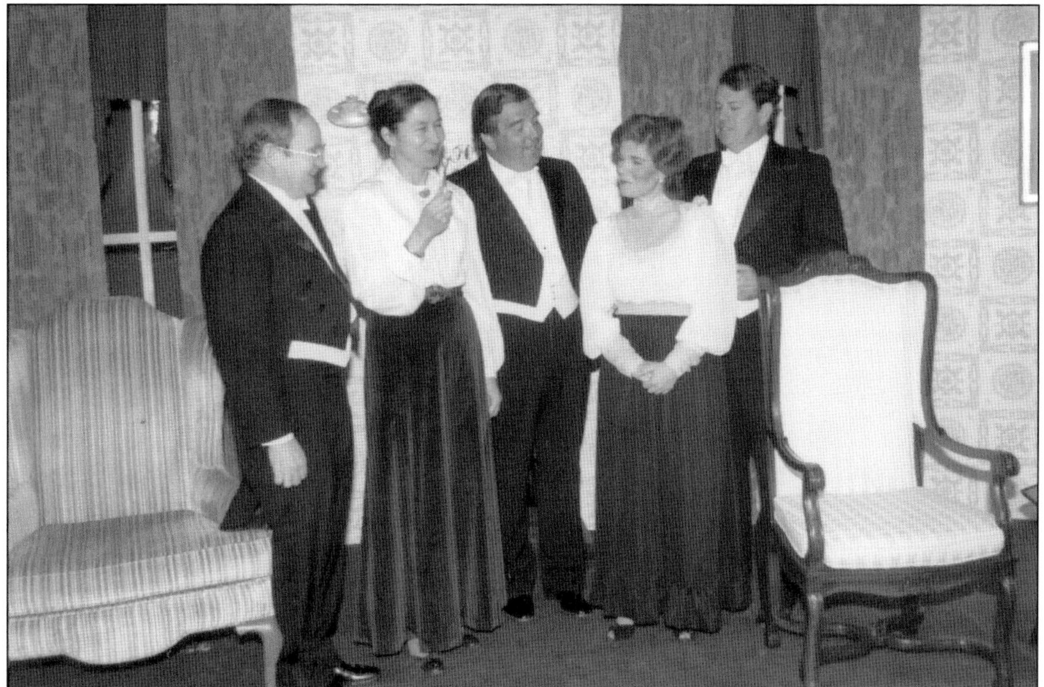

As a part of the second St. Thomas Celebration of the Arts in 1983, Lynn Pancoe produced an original play, *The Secret Lives of the Barrymores*. The cast included, from left to right, David Barefoot, Diane Cashman, Lucien Wilkins, Rhesa Stone, and Douglas Miller. (Walter Pancoe.)

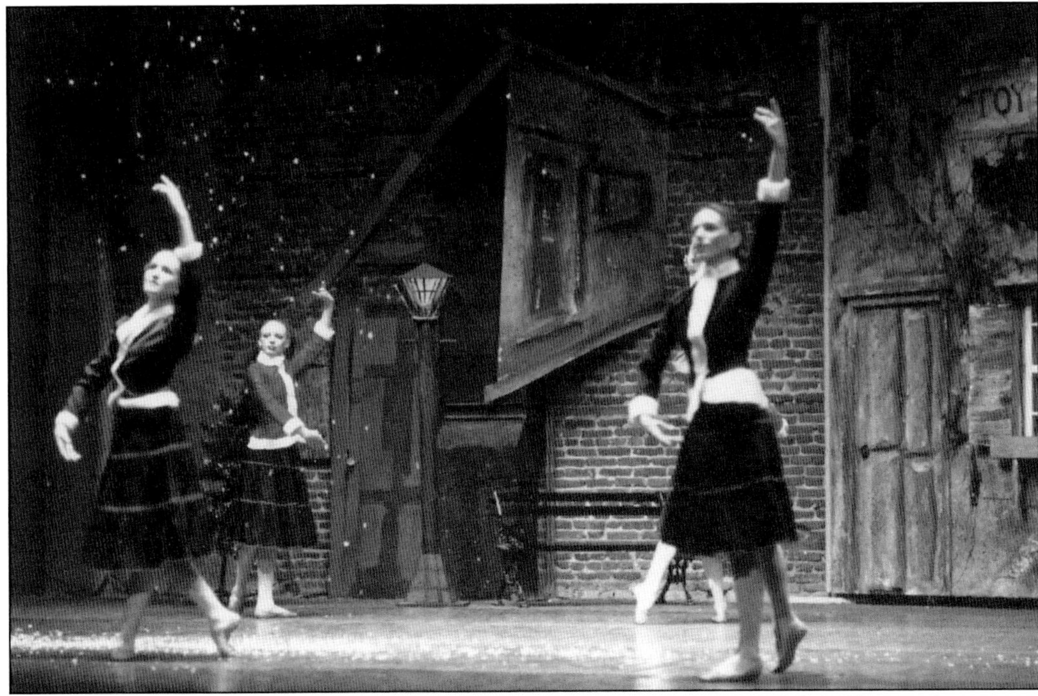

The Wilmington Civic Ballet, organized in the late 1970s, mounted full ballet performances on the stage at Thalian Hall for a number of years. Here, the stage of Thalian Hall hosts *The Enchanted Toy Shop*. In December 1987, the ballet group gave the last public performance in the theatre before the renovation. (THCPA.)

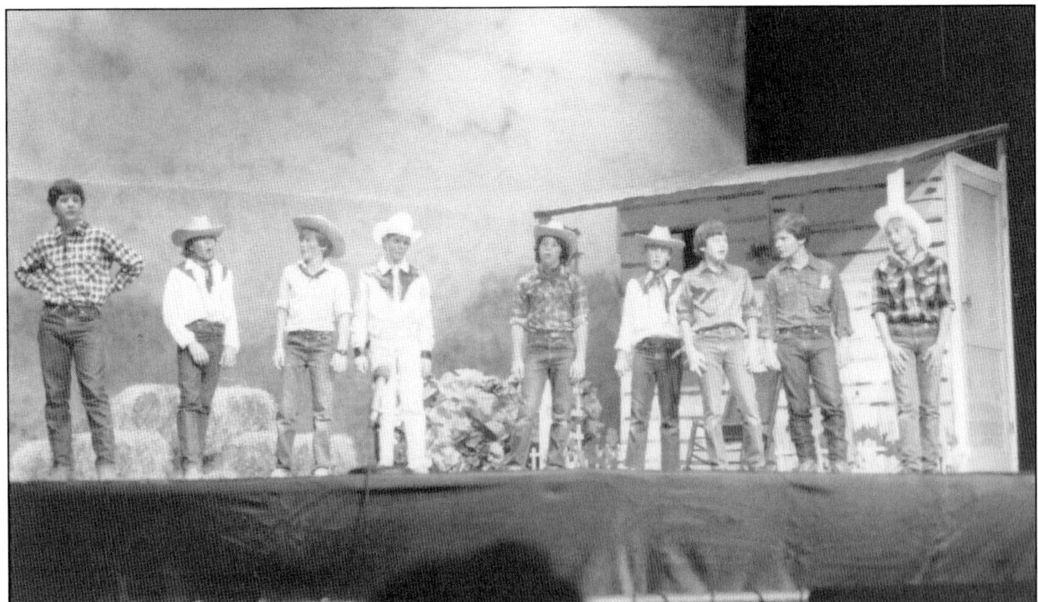

In 1979, Lynn Pancoe established a creative-arts program for young people called Kicks and Company. It lasted for a number of years. Featured in this scene from her 1983 production of *Oklahoma OK* are, from left to right, Nicholas Butts, Edwin Toone, Donnie Reid, Cary Carlberg, Sandy Wilkins, David Getz, Ben McCoy, Carl McKoy, and Harry Tebay. (Walter Pancoe.)

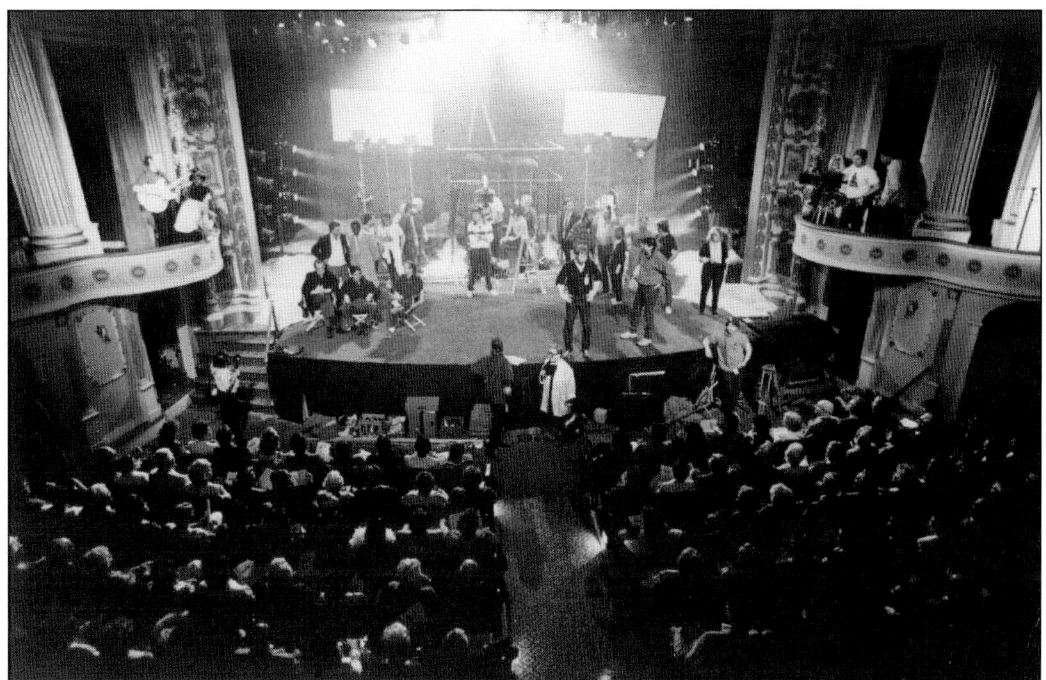

In 1983, with the filming of *Firestarter,* Wilmington became a filmmaking center. Thalian Hall, along with hundreds of sites throughout the area, became the setting for movie and television productions. Thalian Hall was used for sequences in *Sleeping with the Enemy, Young Indiana Jones Chronicles, Matlock,* and *Dream a Little Dream.* Thalian Hall was a stand-in as a Broadway theatre in the *Divine Secrets of the Ya-Ya Sisterhood* and as the movie house in *Dawson's Creek.* (THCPA.)

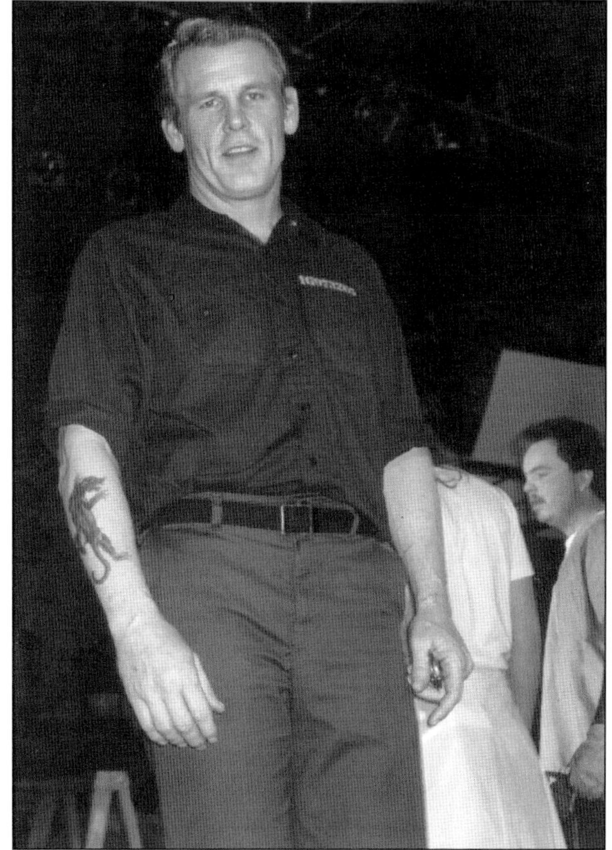

Nick Nolte poses backstage at Thalian Hall, which was used as a New York theatre for the 1987 film *Weeds.* The movie is about a prison acting company that makes it to Broadway. Nolte was the first star to appear in a movie shot in Thalian Hall. Other stars that have appeared in film and television scenes shot on the stage include Andy Griffith, Sandra Bullock, Jason Robards, and Julia Roberts. (THCPA.)

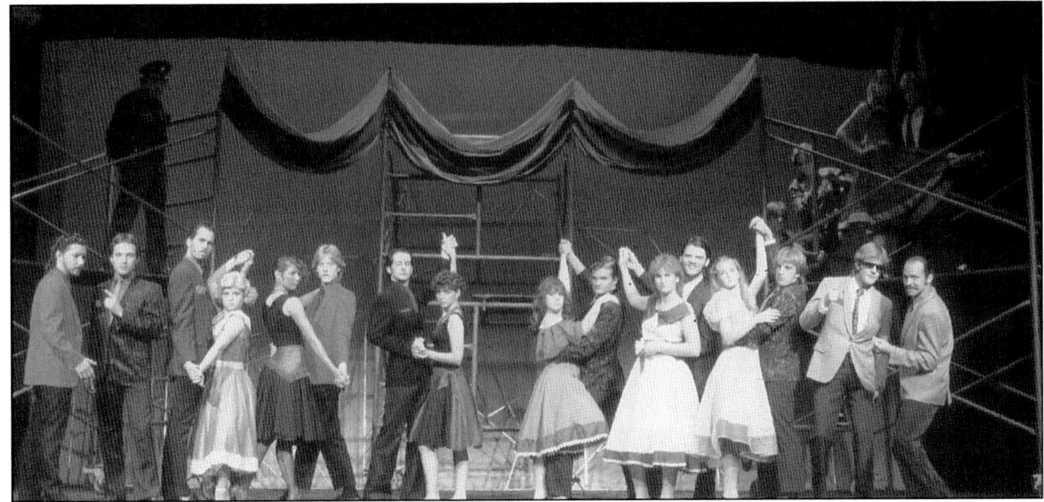

Pictured here is the Thalian Association's production of *West Side Story*. The production was directed by Donn Ansell. It featured Alexander Miller, Thom Clemmons, Chet Spear, Aurelia Huff, Denise Bass, Frank Williams, Cary Worthy, and Joan Preston. (THCPA.)

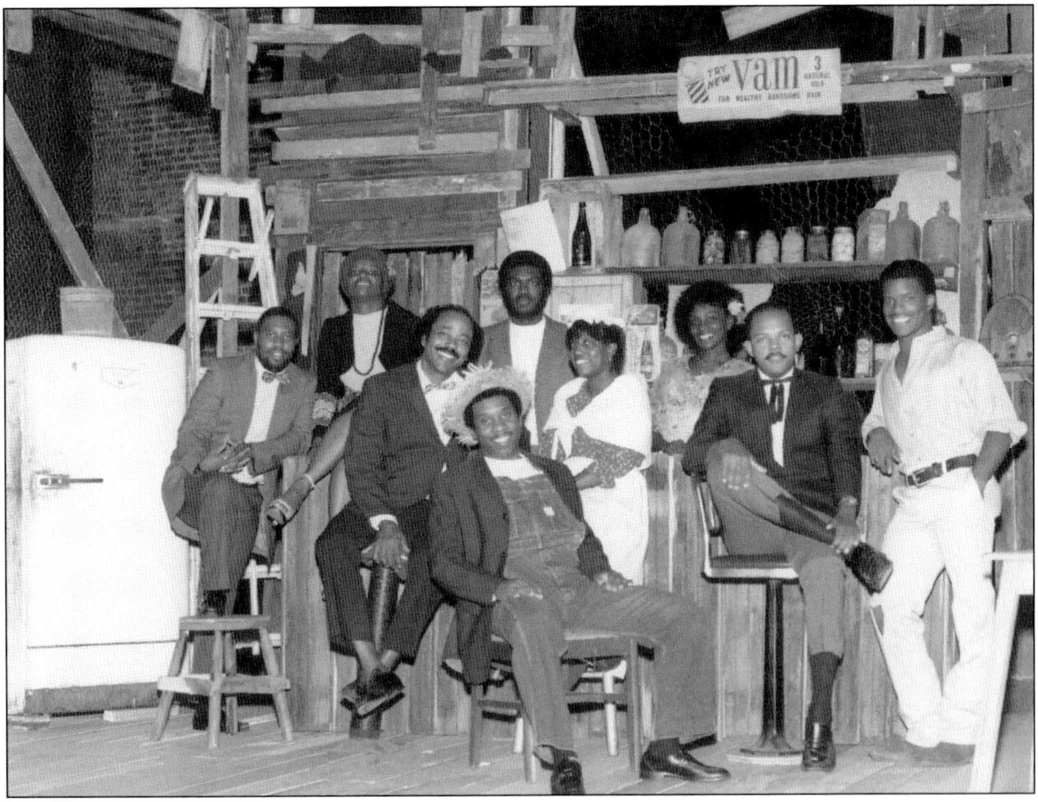

The Fascination Man, an original play by Randolph Umberger based on the *Playboy of the Western World*, premiered at Thalian Hall in a joint production by the Willis Richardson Players and the Opera House Theatre Company. The cast included C. Ward Freeman, Vince McCoy, William Vereen, John Bellamy, Michael Thompson, Charles Denson, Dale Wright, Vercelli Blanding, and Bert Freeman. (THCPA.)

With increased use of the facility in the 1980s, it became increasingly evident that major upgrades were needed for the stage and its infrastructure. This photograph of the lighting booth on a platform on stage right shows the problems with the lighting system. (THCPA.)

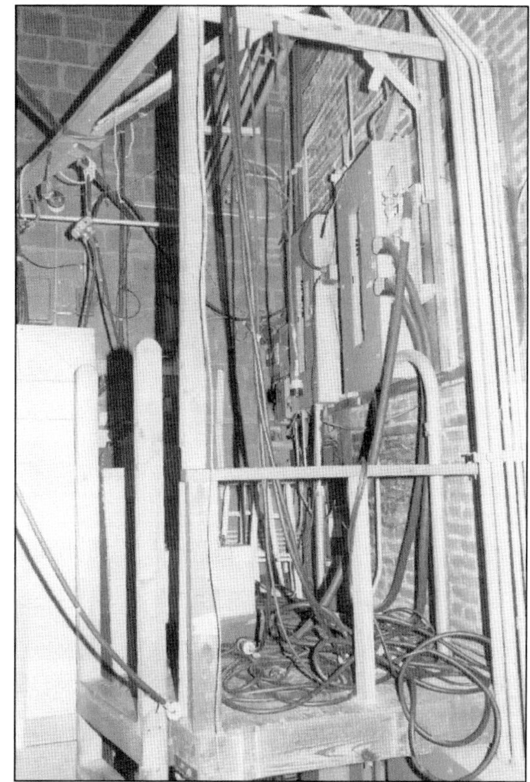

An issue that had been apparent for some time was the need for improved dressing-room space. Underneath the stage were only two dressing rooms, one hand sink, one paint sink, and two toilets, which could not be flushed during quiet scenes on stage. (THCPA.)

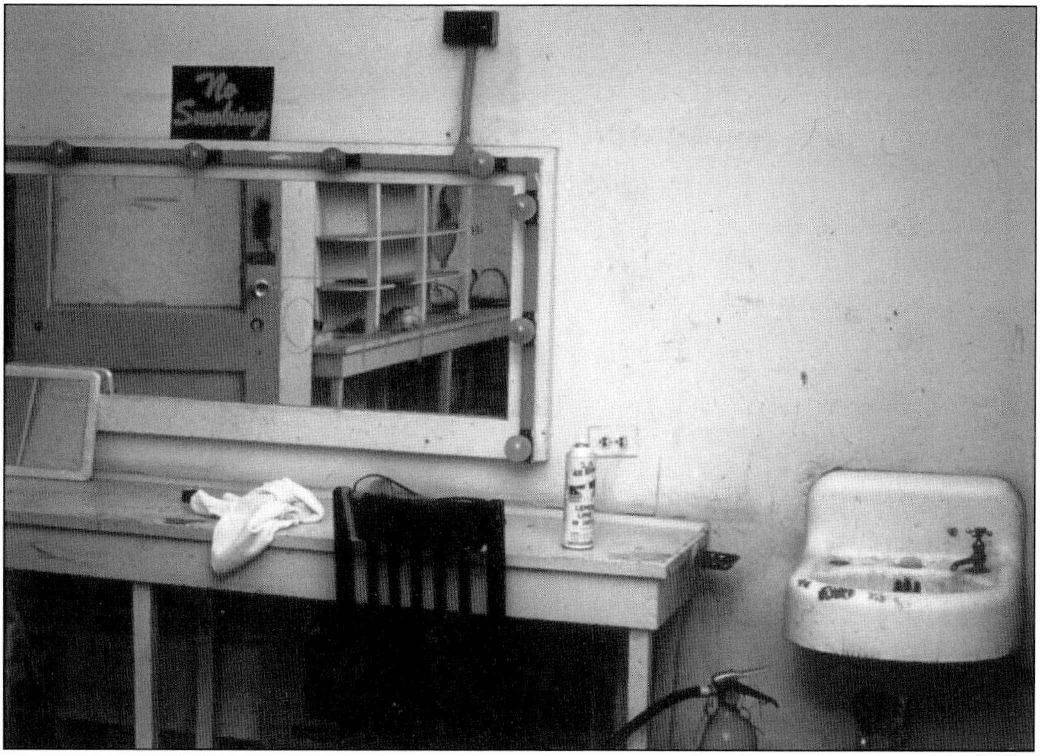

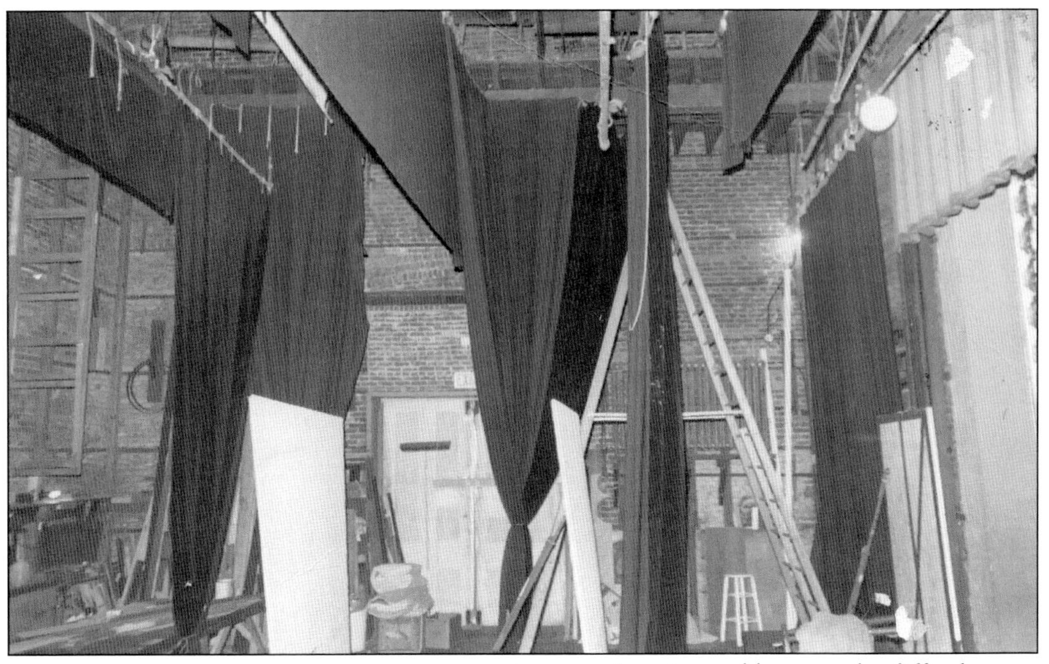

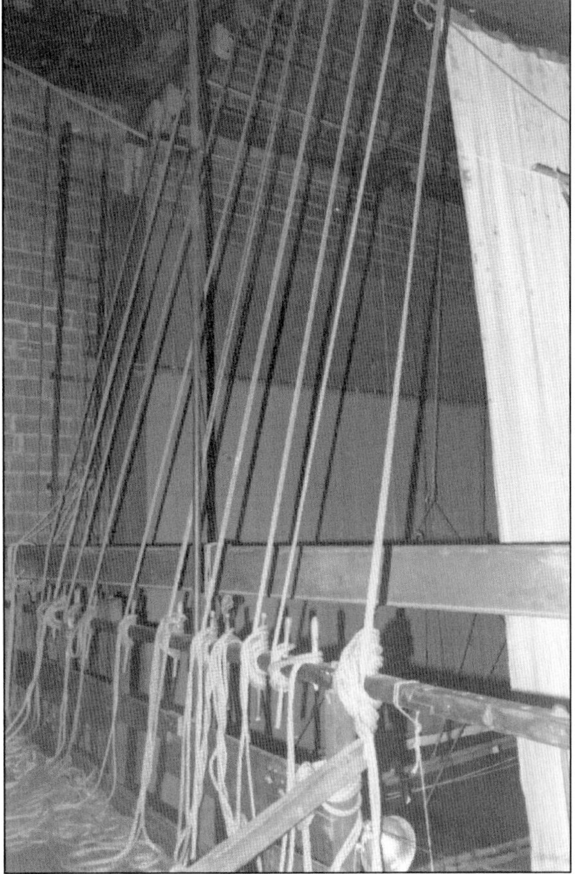

A major problem was the difficulty in flying (the raising and lowering of scenery), as there was very little wing space or storage. All adjustments to the lighting equipment had to be done by tall ladders, which became very problematic when the stage was filled with scenery. This photograph shows the congested state of the stage, which severely taxed the efforts of the stage crew. (THCPA.)

For the 1939 renovation, the original wooden grid-and-fly system for the stage was removed, which caused strain on the outside brick walls. To address the issue, a steel frame was installed. Due to its design, however, the steel beams prevented the proper operation of raising scenery. This 1982 photograph shows the jerry-rigged system of ropes and pulleys used for flying of scenery. (THCPA.)

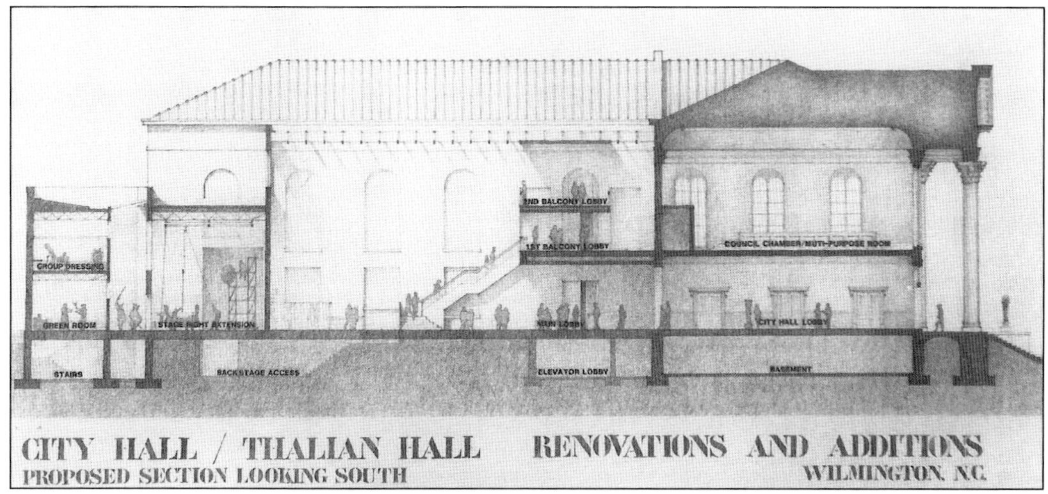

In 1983, the Thalian Hall Commission, Inc., which was to change its name to the Thalian Hall Center for the Performing Arts, Inc., embarked on an ambitious plan to renovate the stage house and expand the building. The master plan called for the renovation of the stage house, new support space, and a new entrance lobby on the north side of the building. To focus attention on the presentation of the plan, a celebration was held in honor of Thalian Hall's 125th anniversary. (THCPA.)

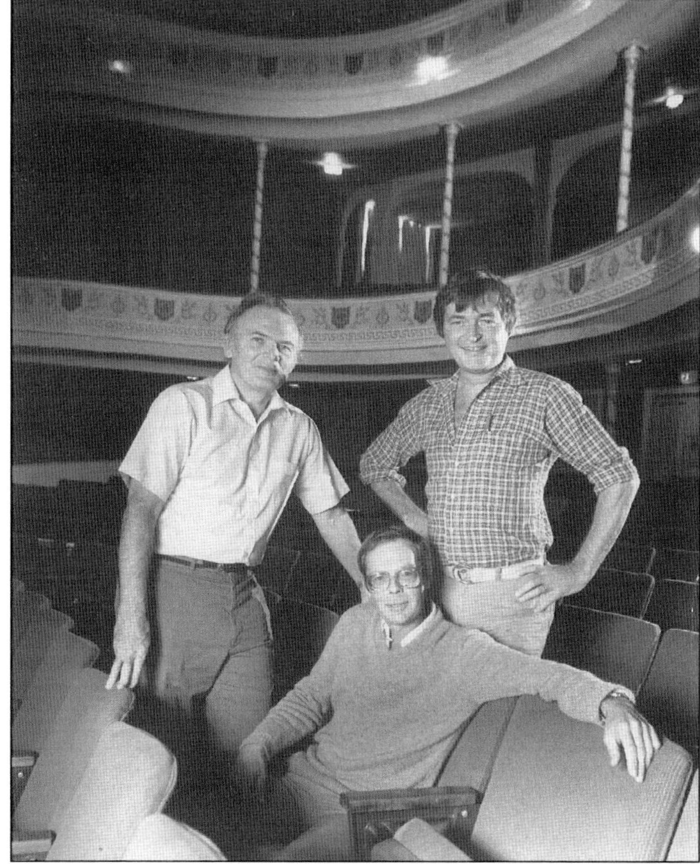

To celebrate the anniversary, the Thalian Hall Commission, Inc. engaged Randolph Umberger and Benjamin Keaton to write an original musical based on the theatre's rich history. The show was entitled *Remembered Nights*. Shown here are Fort Bragg Theatre director Lee Yopp (left), composer Benjamin Keaton (center), and playwright Randolph Umberger. (The Star-News Collection, NHCPL.)

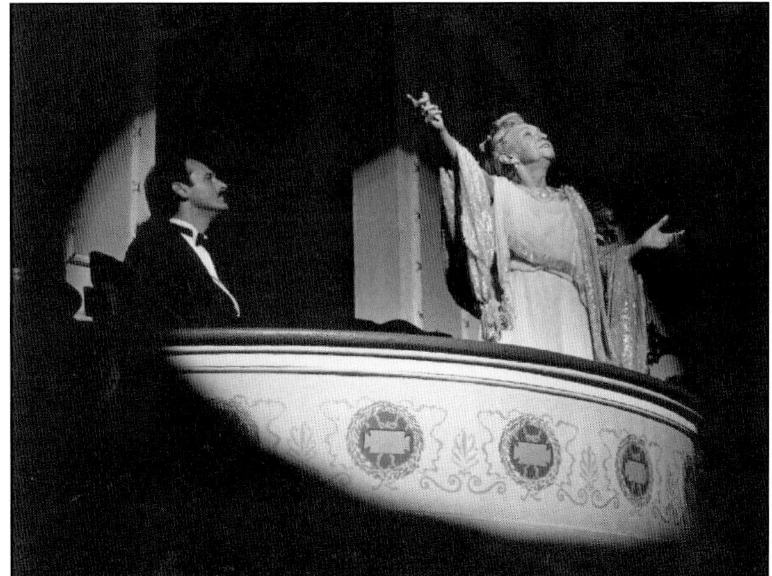

Remembered Nights depicts the final night of a historic theatre like Thalian Hall. The stage manager turns off the ghost light, and the spirits of the great stars of the past return to give a final performance of a comic parody written by the muse Thalia. Playing that role was Minerva Davenport, seen here in the box with Michael Little, playing the role of John T. Ford. (THCPA.)

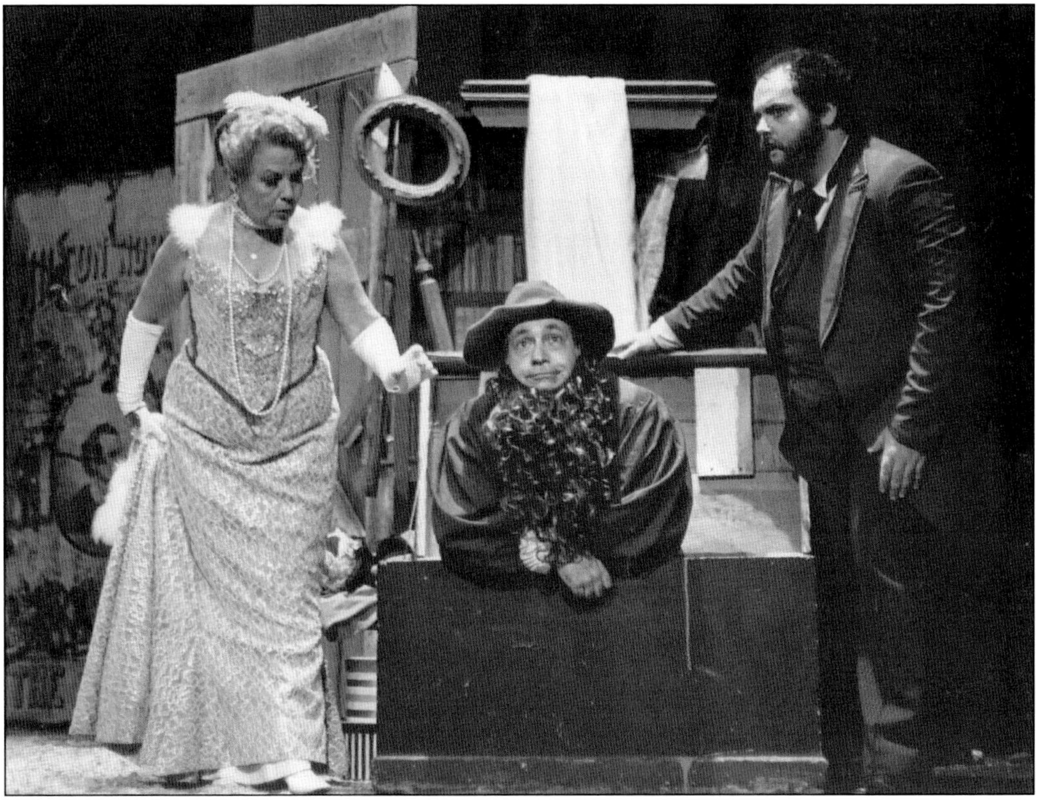

The 125th anniversary show was produced by the Thalian Hall Commission, Inc. and the Thalian Association. It brought Broadway actor Lou Criscuolo (center) to Wilmington. Here, he is seen in the role of Joseph Jefferson, discovered by the great stage legends Helena Modjeska (played by Betsy Setzer), who performed in Thalian Hall in 1896, and Edwin Forrest (Randy Brayant), who played King Lear in 1870. (THCPA.)

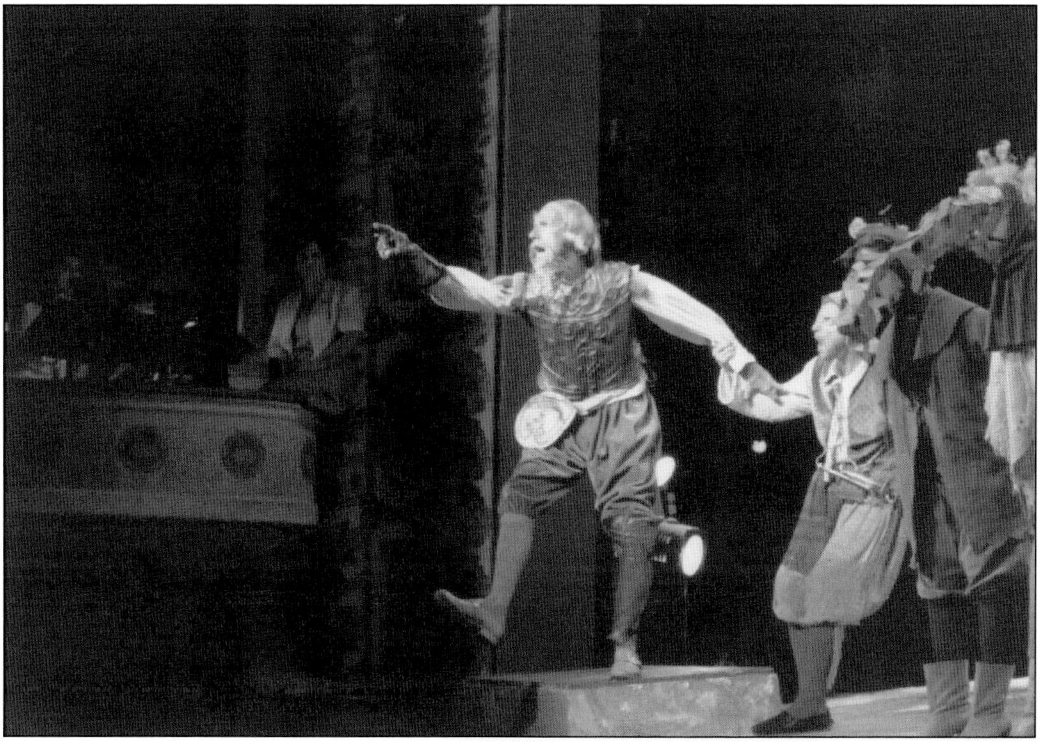

A special production of *Man of La Mancha* was produced by the Thalian Hall Commission, Inc. and the Thalian Association in 1984. The play was directed by Broadway and television actor Lou Criscuolo, who had appeared in the New York production. In this scene, Quixote, played by Terry Horton, is held from walking off a cliff by his faithful servant, Sancho (played by Tony Rivenbark). (THCPA.)

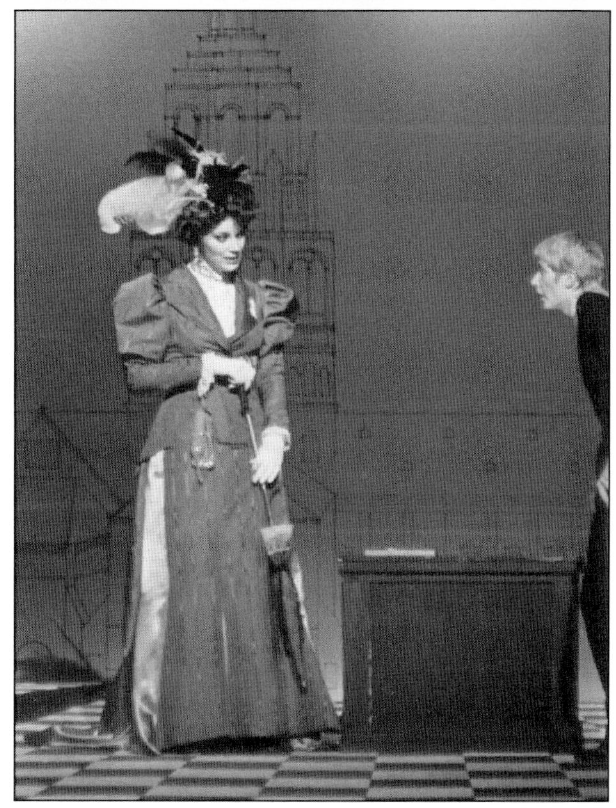

Also in 1984, the Thalian Association mounted a production of the drama *The Elephant Man*, with Steve Coley in the challenging title role. The part is notable because no prosthetic makeup is used in the portrayal of the character. Only through the actor's physicality is the deformity displayed to the audience. Here, he is seen meeting the sympathetic actress Mrs. Kendal, played by Kathleen Fitzgibbon. (Kathleen Fitzgibbon.)

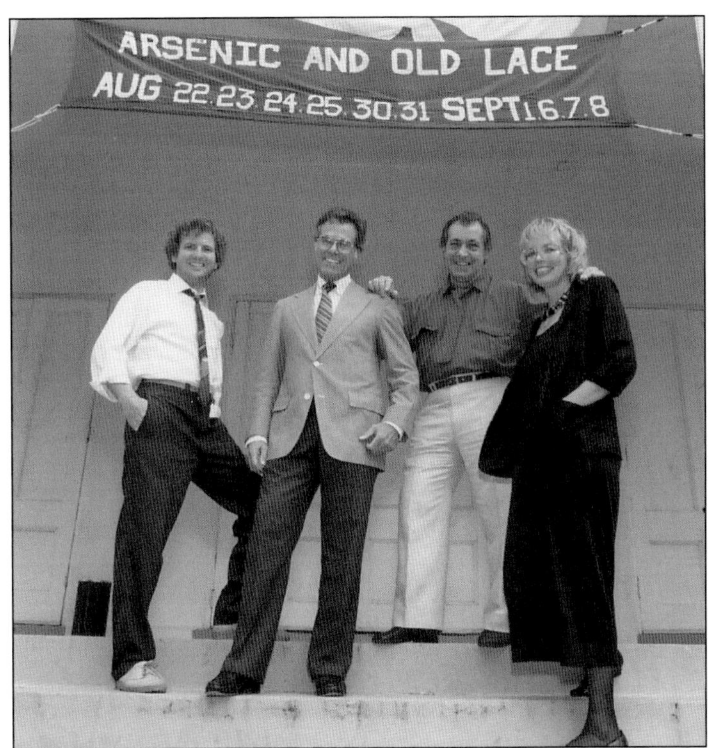

Frank Capra Jr. was instrumental in bringing the film industry to Wilmington. He also directed several productions at Thalian Hall, including *Arsenic and Old Lace* and *You Can't Take It with You*, starring local resident and film actor, Pat Hingle. From left to right, Tony Rivenbark (director of Thalian Hall), Capra (head of Screen Gems Studio), and Lou Criscuolo and Mary James Morgan (founders of Opera House Theatre Company) pose on the Thalian Hall steps for Opera House's first summer season. (THCPA.)

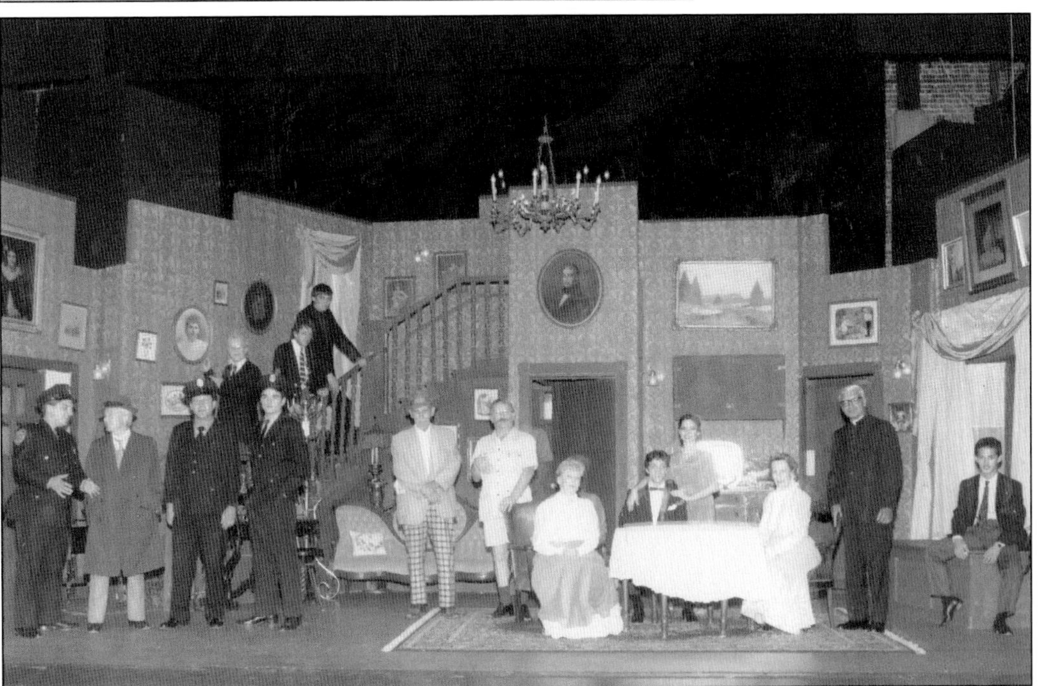

Arsenic and Old Lace, directed by Frank Capra Jr., was also the famous film directed by Capra's father. The large cast is shown here, including Michael Titterton at the top of the stairs. He was instrumental in establishing WHQR public radio. Seated at the table is Clifton Daniels, an actor and author who appeared in many productions at Thalian Hall. (THCPA.)

Ten

A Performing Arts Center 1987–1990

By 1987, the design for the new facility had been completed. When the State of North Carolina made a $1 million appropriation, the final funding for the $5 million project had been secured. On September 1, 1988, the official ground-breaking ceremony was held in Innes Park. As work began, the renovation was constantly in the news. At one point, human bones were discovered underneath the floor of the auditorium. It was determined that the large sand hill on which the original Innes Academy was built was a burial site of pre-Columbian inhabitants before the colonization of the area.

The renovation and expansion of Thalian Hall took 18 months. On March 2, 1990, Thalian Hall reopened with a performance by Peter Nero and members of the North Carolina Symphony. The master of ceremonies was Dr. William C. Friday, president of the University of North Carolina. Honored guests included poet Maya Angelou, artist Dorothy Gillespie, and Mary Regan, director of the NC State Arts Council. Over 600 Wilmingtonians turned out for the black-tie opening, followed by a ball and reception in the new city council chamber, called the Thalian Hall Ballroom. The following night, there was another gala, with a touring performance of *Kismet*, which highlighted the technical improvements and fly system. The weekend's events were completed by a public dedication and open house.

Over the next two weeks, over 20 other events were presented in the complex. They included a Victorian Fashion Show by the Lower Cape Historical Society and musical revues presented by the Thalian Association and the Opera House Theatre Company. The Cape Fear Museum presented a program on the Civil War. Theatre productions were given by Tapestry, Playwrights Producing Company, and the Willis Richardson Players. Touring productions included *A Celtic Evening* with Fiona Ritchie, sponsored by WHQR, and the Tulsa Ballet, sponsored by the Arts Council. Musical performances were presented by Larry Price, the Wilmington Choral Society, The Cape Fear Chordsmen, and the Wilmington Symphony. The new Thalian Hall had truly become a center for the performing arts.

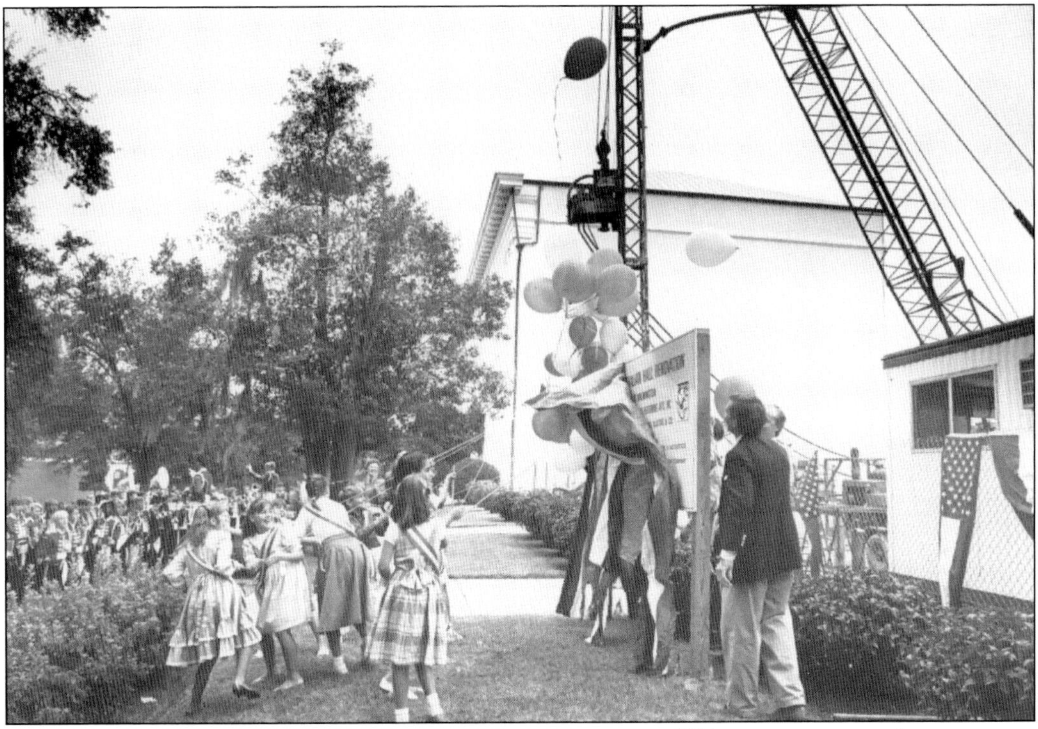

Wilmingtonians gather as schoolchildren release balloons as part of the ground-breaking ceremonies for the new addition to Thalian Hall in 1988. This was 185 years after work began on the construction of the first theatre on the site. (THCPA.)

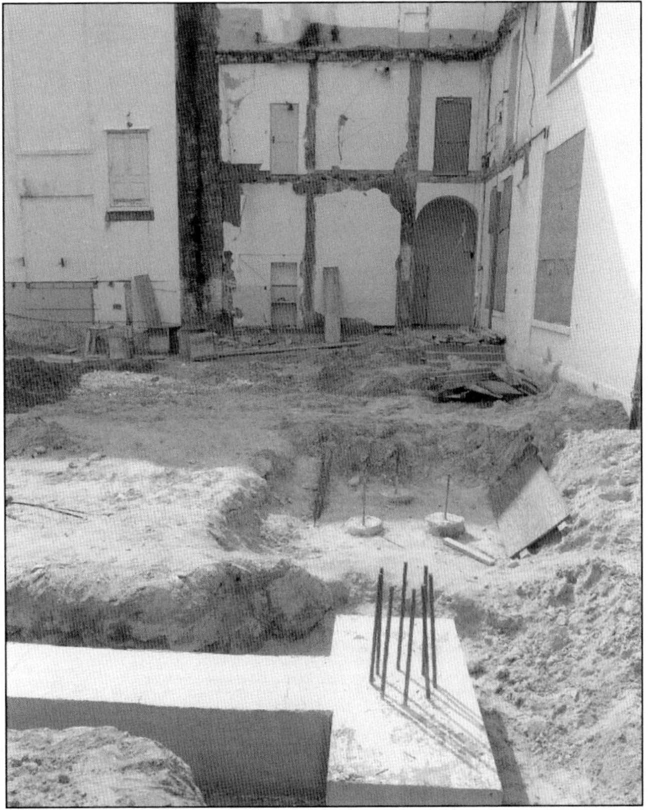

This 1988 photograph shows the area of new construction following the demolition of the 1939 restroom wing. The circular arch was an outdoor vestibule that provided a back entrance to the old lobby of Thalian Hall on the left. An entrance to Wilmington City Hall was through a doorway on the right. Prior to 1990, the main entrance to Thalian Hall was located on the Princess Street side of the building. (THCPA.)

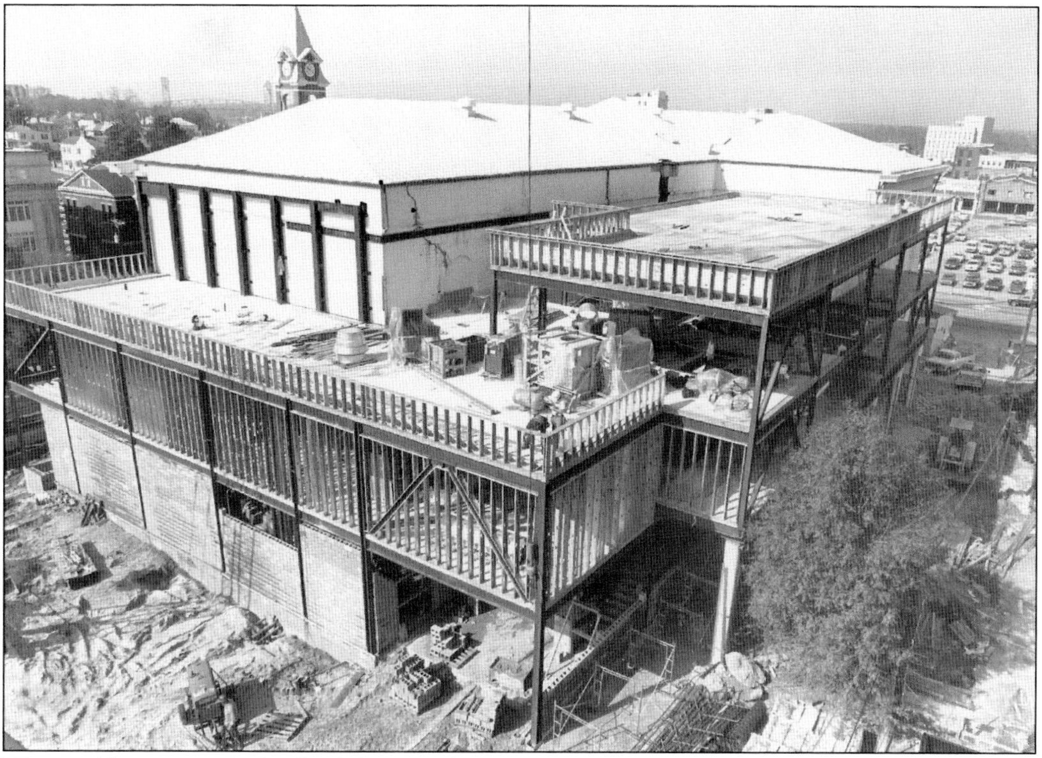

The steel beams on the back of the stage house were designed to support the new steel structure of the flying system for scenery. This photograph shows the two floors of dressing rooms and the loading-dock area. The three-story section contained the new entrance lobby and Studio Theatre. (The Star-News Collection, NHCPL.)

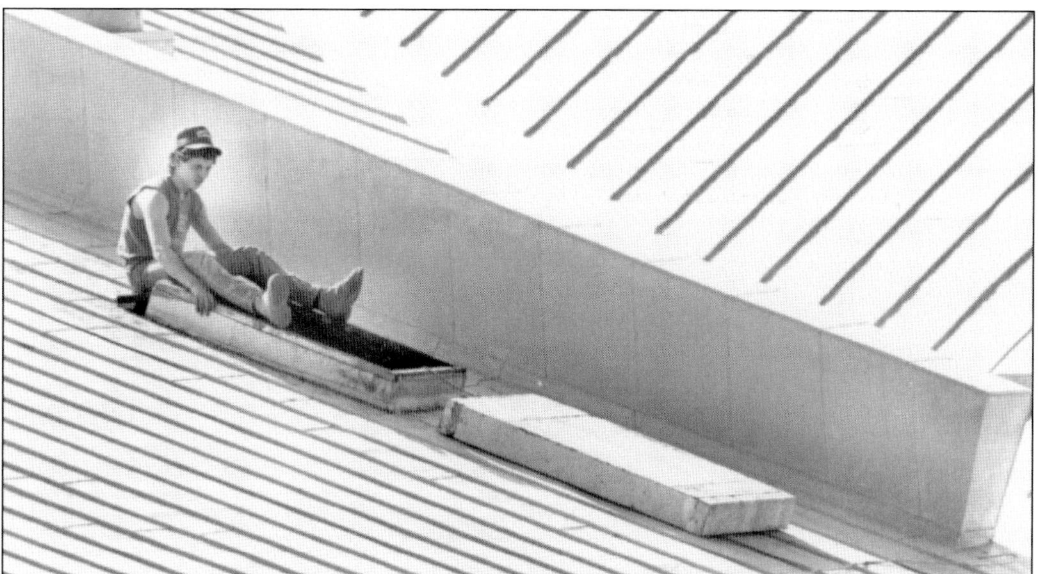

According to the caption for this photograph in the *Wilmington Star-News* in 1989, "Clancy and Theys worker, Kenny Wilkerson, is seen catching some of the afternoon breeze on top of Thalian Hall as the sun pelted the metal roof of the building." (Star-News Collection, NHCPL.)

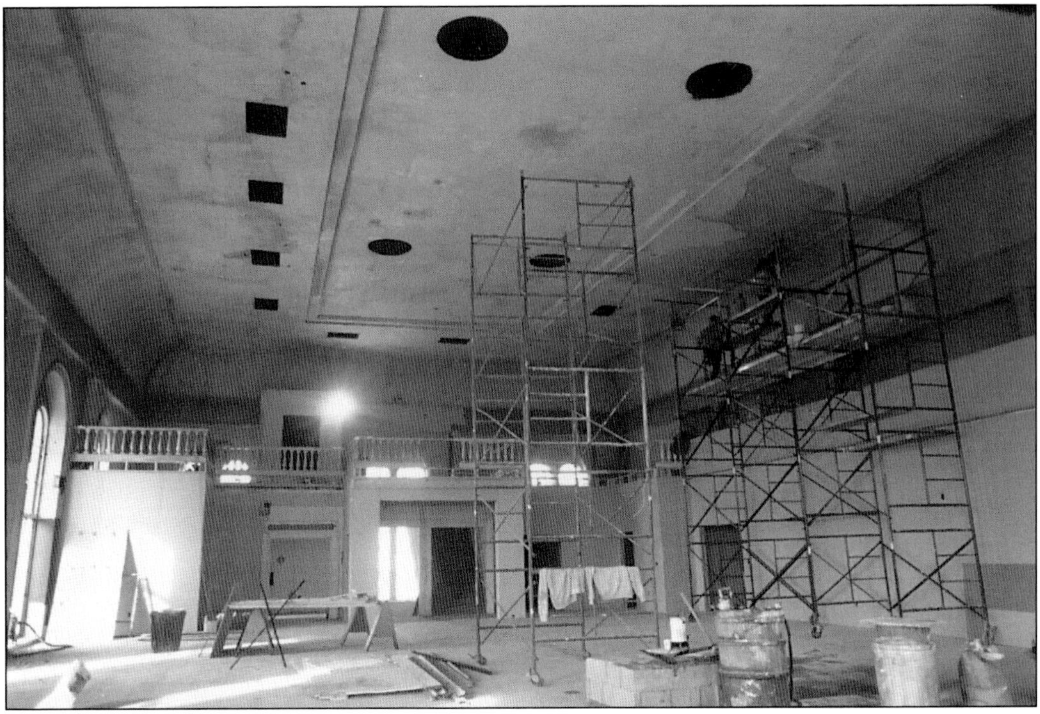

After the Wilmington Public Library moved out in 1956, the second floor of Wilmington City Hall was divided into offices. In order to provide access from city hall to the new lobby without going through Thalian Hall, it was decided to renovate the second floor for public meetings and create a new entrance into city hall through the old council meeting room. The new assembly room was designed also to serve as a reception room and concert space. (THCPA.)

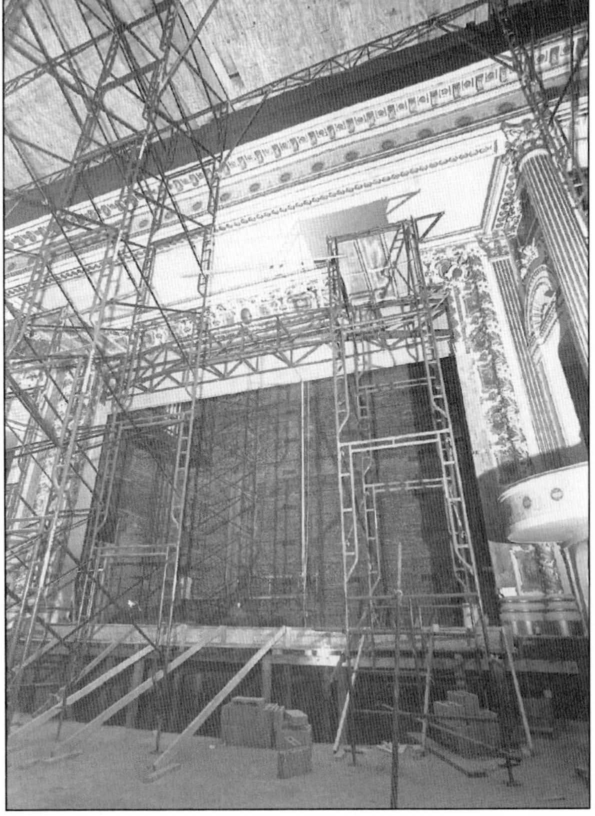

A new steel structure was installed in the stage house to support a new counterweight system for the flying of scenery. The orchestra pit was extended under the stage, making the pit large enough for 30 musicians. New sound and lighting systems were installed, and a new sprung floor was laid on the stage. (THCPA.)

By the end of March 1990, completion had been achieved on the stage house renovation, the new fly system, the equipment installation, the new dressing-room wing, the stage-right extension, the new box office, the theatre interior, and the new lobby expansion. Thalian Hall was ready to become a center for the performing arts. (THCPA.)

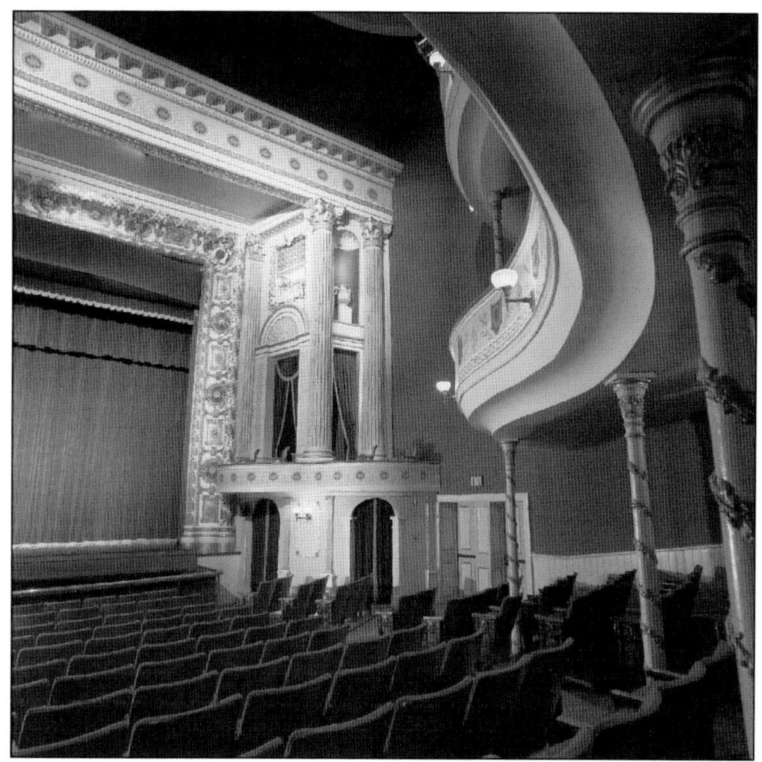

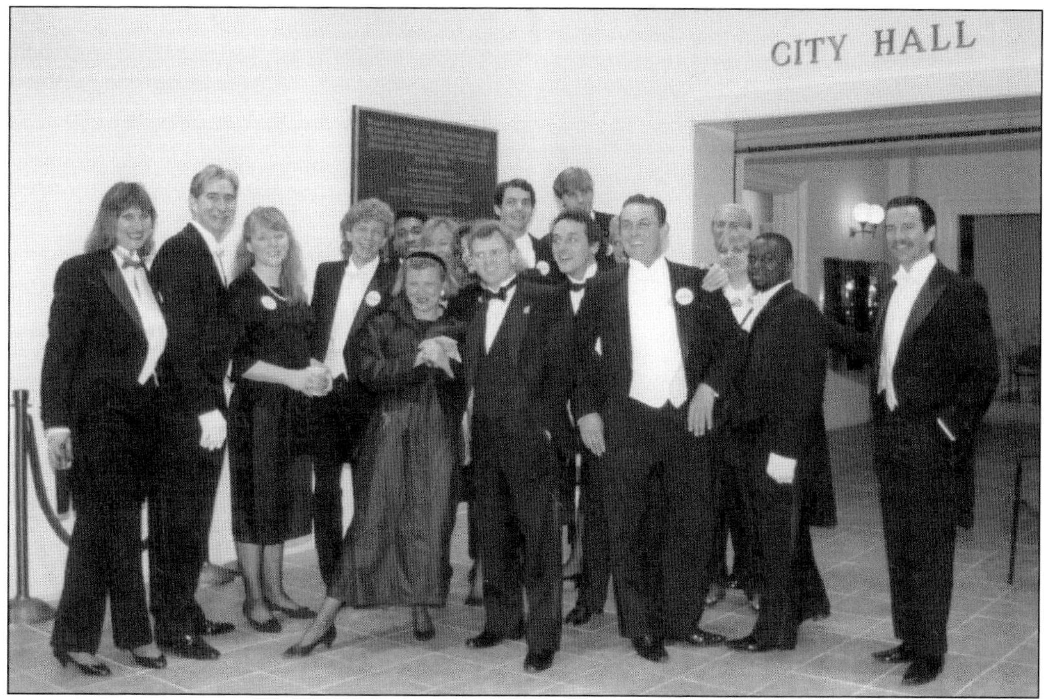

A host of local actors and artists wait in the new lobby to greet the audience on opening night. Included here are Francine DeCoursey, Don Squires, Marianne Nubel, Tony Pender, Tommy Hull, Phil Locke, Robin Dale Robinson, and Doug Campbell. (THCPA.)

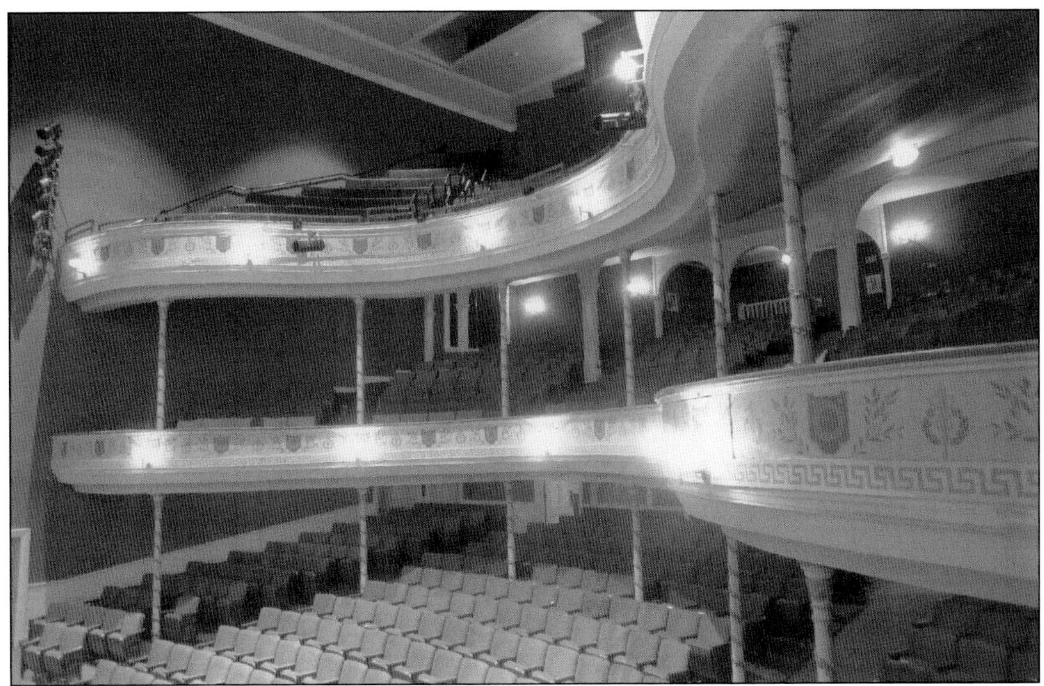

Every seat was sold for the reopening evening on March 2, 1990. The new facility hosted 23 events over the following two weeks. This provided an opportunity for the entire community to enjoy the revitalized performing arts center. (THCPA.)

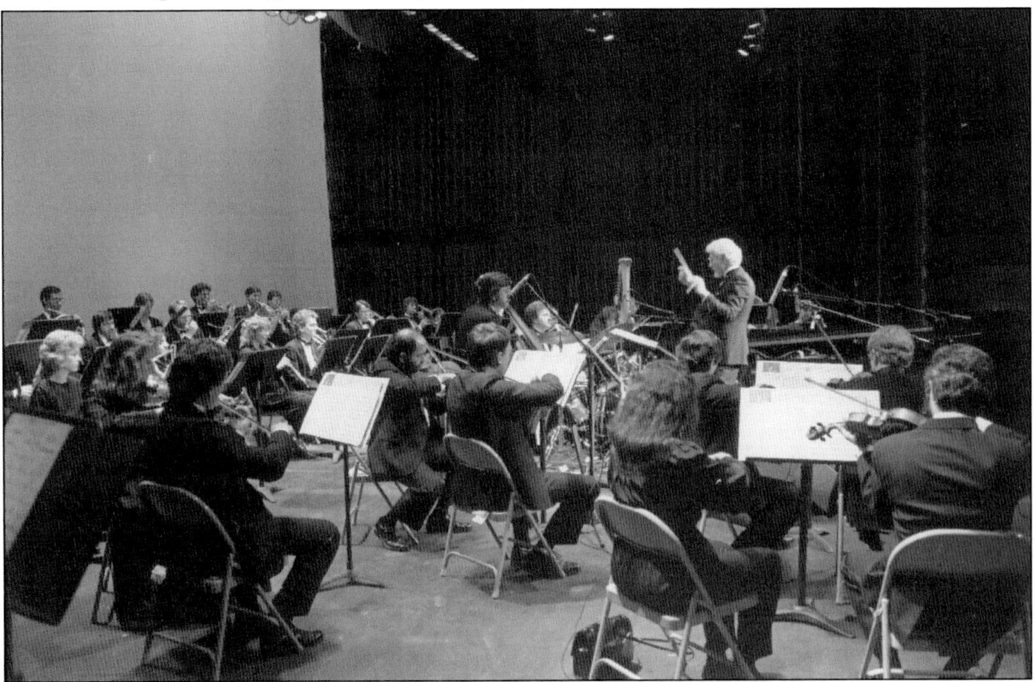

Peter Nero and the members of the North Carolina Symphony perform on the renovated stage of Thalian Hall. The evening was hosted Dr. William Friday, president of the University of North Carolina. Special guests included poet Maya Angelou and artist Dorothy Gillespie. (THCPA.)

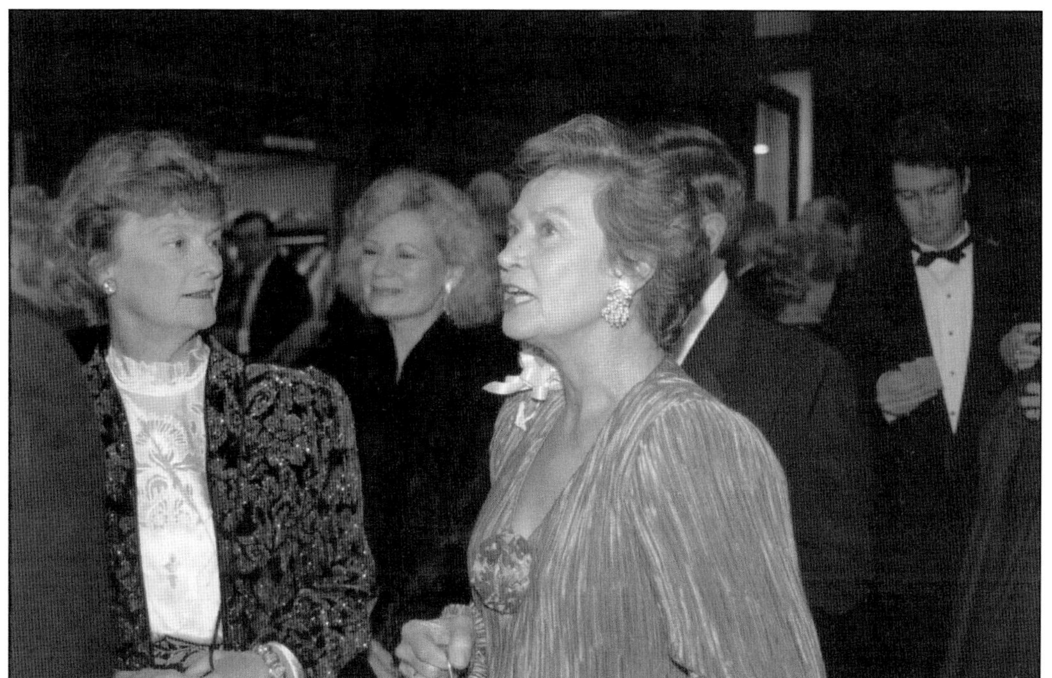

Standing in the lobby at the reopening gala are, from left to right, Georgia Joyner, Sherry Andrews, and Jean Anne Sutton, the longest-serving president of the Thalian Hall Center for the Performing Arts, Inc. Sutton and Wendy Block served as the cochairs for the Capital Campaign. For the Curtains Up! celebration, Sutton, Block, and Helen Willets chaired the reopening event. (THCPA.)

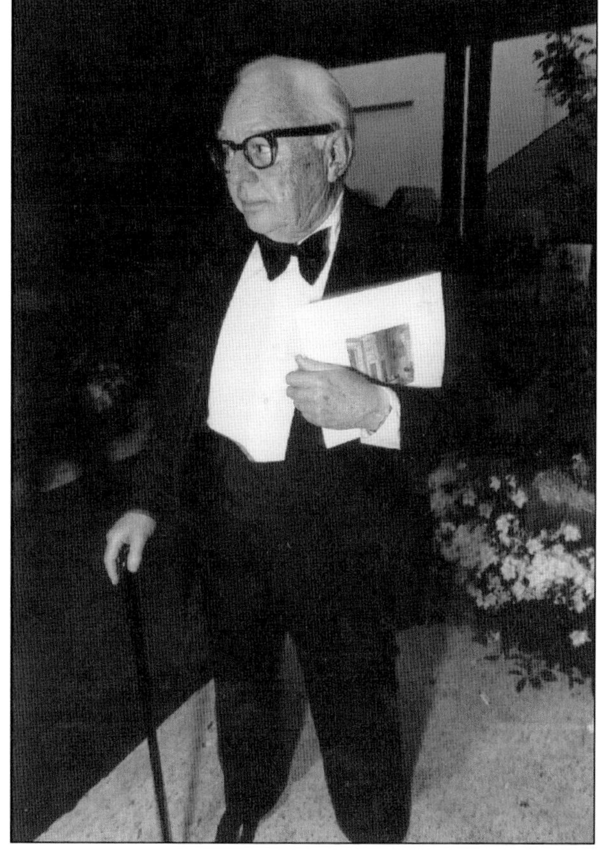

Henry MacMillan is seen at the gala reopening, holding the souvenir program created for the Curtains Up! celebration. On the cover of the program is an image of the 1938 watercolor he painted over 50 years before to stimulate interest in the preservation of the theatre that has become the most enduring symbol of Wilmington's cultural heritage. (THCPA.)

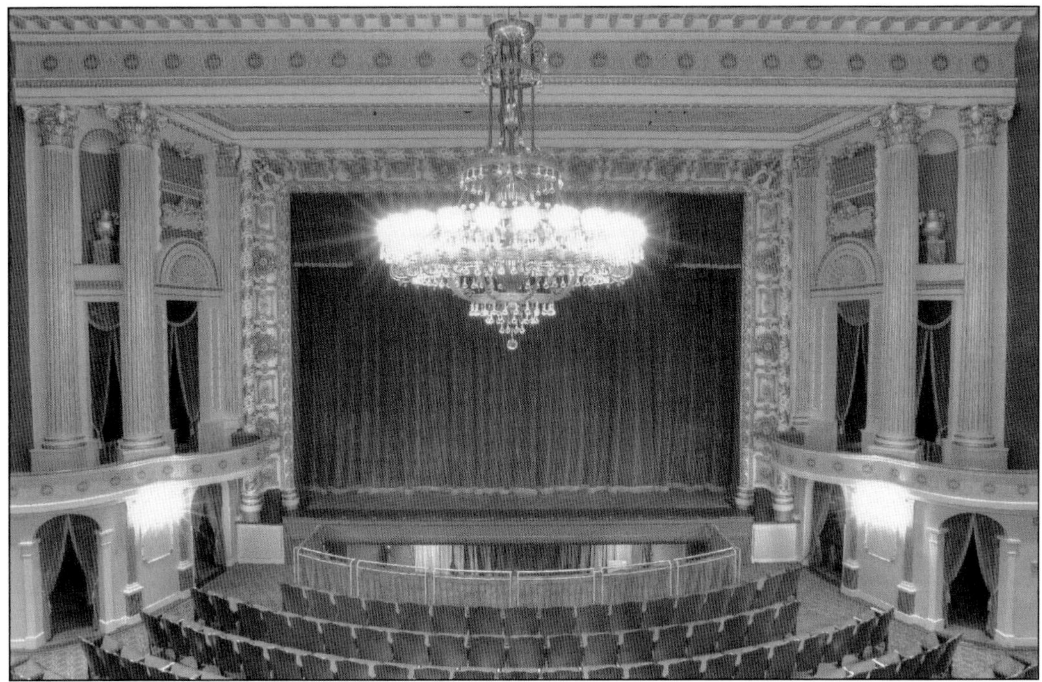

This is Thalian Hall as it appeared following the last renovation and restoration, completed in 2010. New floors and new theatre seats were installed, along with a complete repainting of the interior's decorative stenciling. There were major upgrades to the sound and lighting equipment. A new orchestra pit and lift was installed, and an 1871-style chandelier now rises before each performance. (THCPA.)

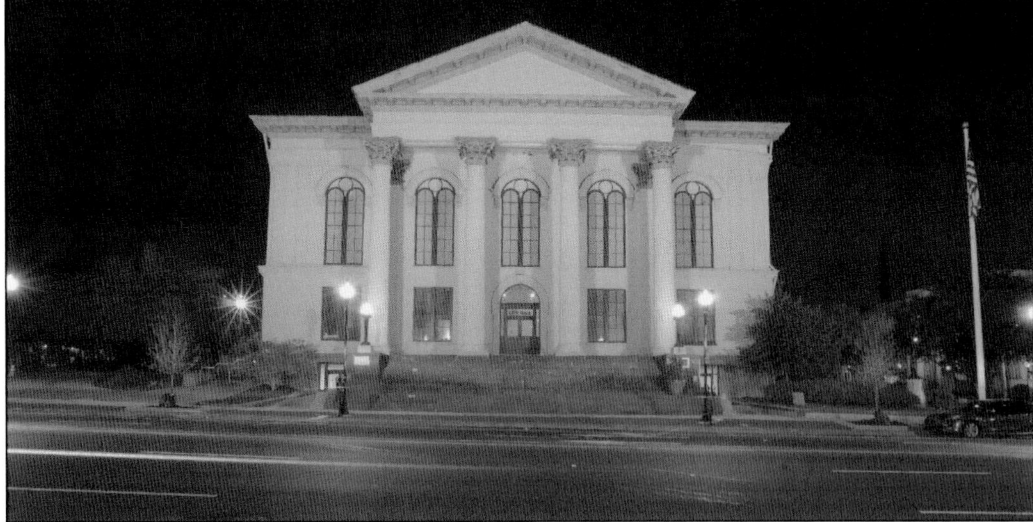

In 2013, a new system of LED architectural lighting was installed through a cooperative effort between Thalian Hall Center for the Performing Arts, Inc. and Musco Lighting. The Iowa-based firm has designed lighting for many historic monuments, including the Statue of Liberty and the Washington Monument. Over 85,000 people a year are attracted to the many performances and events at the theatre. To learn more about Thalian Hall and its many activities, visit www.ThalianHall.org. (THCPA.)

Bibliography

Allen, Nancy Winborne. *A Record of Thalian Hall from 1861–1865.* Master's Thesis, University of North Carolina at Chapel Hill, 1972.

Burr, J.G. *The Thalian Association of Wilmington, N.C. with Sketches of Many of its Members.* Wilmington, NC: J.A. Englehard, 1871.

Jefferson, Joseph. *Rip Van Winkle: The Autobiography of Joseph Jefferson.* London: Reinhardt & Evans, Ltd., 1890.

Johnson, Odai. *The Colonial Stage in America, 1665–1774.* Hackensack, NJ: Fairleigh Dickinson University Press, 2001.

Reaves, William M. *Strength through Struggle, 1865–1950.* Wilmington, NC: New Hanover County Public Library, 1998.

Rulfs, Donald J. "The Professional Theatre in Wilmington, 1858–1930." *North Carolina Historical Review* XXXVIII, Nos. 2, 3, 4, (April, July, October 1951).

Seapker, Janet, ed. *Time, Talent, Tradition: Five Essays on the Cultural History of the Lower Cape Fear Region.* Wilmington, NC: Cape Fear Museum, 1995.

Spearman, Walter. *The Carolina Playmakers.* Chapel Hill: University of North Carolina Press, 1970.

Sprunt, James. *Chronicles of the Cape Fear River 1660–1916.* Wilmington, NC: Broadfoot Publishing Company, 1992.

Storm, W.W. *Wilmington, Where the Cape Fear Rolls to the Sea.* Wilmington, NC: 1933.

Weeks, Stephen B. *Libraries and Literature in North Carolina in the Eighteenth Century.* Washington, DC: American Historical Association, 1896.

Williams, Isabel M. *History of Thalian Hall.* Volume I–IV, mimeograph. Wilmington, NC: Thalian Hall Commission, 1974.

Wilmington Daily Journal, 1851–1878.

Wilmington Gazette, 1799–1816.

Wilmington Messenger, 1890–1897.

Wilmington Morning Star, 1867–2014.

Consistent with our mission to preserve history on a local level, this book was printed in South Carolina on American-made paper and manufactured entirely in the United States. Products carrying the accredited Forest Stewardship Council (FSC) label are printed on 100 percent FSC-certified paper.

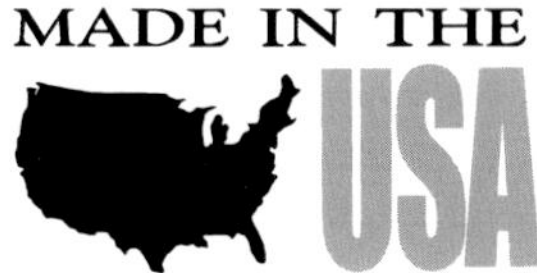